The Portable MLIS

THE PORTABLE MLIS

Insights from the Experts

Edited by Ken Haycock and Brooke E. Sheldon

LIBRARIES
UNLIMITED
A Member of the Greenwood Publishing Group
Westport, Connecticut • London

Library of Congress Cataloging-in-Publication Data

The portable MLIS : insights from the experts / edited by Ken Haycock and
Brooke E. Sheldon.
    p. cm.
  Includes bibliographical references and index.
  ISBN 978–1–59158–547–3 (alk. paper)
  1. Library science. 2. Information science. 3. Libraries. 4. Librarians.
5. Library science—United States. 6. Information science—United States.
7. Libraries—United States. 8. Librarians—United States. I. Haycock, Ken.
II. Sheldon, Brooke E. III. Title: Portable master of library and information
science.
  Z665.P83 2008
  020—dc22   2008010351

British Library Cataloguing in Publication Data is available.

Library of Congress Catalog Card Number: 2008010351
ISBN: 978–1–59158–547–3

First published in 2008

Libraries Unlimited, 88 Post Road West, Westport, CT 06881
A Member of the Greenwood Publishing Group, Inc.
www.lu.com

Printed in the United States of America

∞™

The paper used in this book complies with the
Permanent Paper Standard issued by the National
Information Standards Organization (Z39.48–1984).

10 9 8 7 6 5 4 3 2

Contents

14, 15, C

v

Preface

Typically, interested laypeople and students are introduced to the knowledge, skills, and abilities of professional librarians piecemeal or through introductory or core courses. Unlike other fields (e.g., business administration, management), there is no published broad overview of the profession. Almost peculiarly, the basic foundation course in Library and Information Science (LIS) education is typically about information in its social context, or libraries and their mission, but not about the competencies of professional librarians as a foundation for future courses. This work fills that gap. Whether as an introduction to the profession or as a response to an educated family member or relative ("what does a librarian actually do?") this work is designed to be accessible, comprehensive, and useful as an introduction to the work of the professional librarian.

The core competencies of professional librarians have been defined by several professional associations. The editors have synthesized these competencies into core areas and supplemented them with foundational principles and context. As the subtitle suggests, we sought out the leading thinkers in each area for contributions, providing in each chapter an introduction to the knowledge, skills, and abilities connected with the area, as well as current and emerging applications and trends and issues. A limited number of key resources are listed for further reading.

In approaching the individuals invited to contribute to this book, we looked for authentic practitioners and educators whose work has had and is having a profound effect on the values and practices of librarianship. We have been successful in capturing the current thoughts of eighteen leaders in the profession whose combined experience (including the editors!) totals almost 1,000 years.

We begin with a seemingly simple yet surprisingly complex task of outlining how one thinks like a librarian. After several approaches, we offer a brief role statement for a professional librarian and the characteristics of a library and then settle on Ranganathan's five laws of library science as appropriate filters used by professional librarians to make judgments and decisions: library resources are for use; library resources are for all; every resource has its user; save the time of the user (and the staff); the library is a growing organism. Essentially, the user or potential user is at the center of a service profession and its decision-making processes.

FOUNDATIONS, VALUES, AND CONTEXT

In "Stepping Back and Looking Forward: Reflections on the Foundations of Libraries and Librarianship," Richard Rubin provides an eminently readable and subtly humorous picture of how libraries and their missions evolved. We learn that the motivations of early librarians/book collectors rarely reflected today's values of access to all and the right of free expression guaranteed by the First Amendment. Rubin's optimism for the future of librarianship comes through in his discussion of values.

Michael Gorman, in his essay "Professional Ethics and Values in a Changing World," makes the compelling point that librarians should not only be familiar with all of the policies and techniques concerned with the interaction between humans and the human record but that the application of these techniques must be informed by the ethics and values of the profession. Having defined ethics, he goes on to explain why we must also have professional values, and why each value on the Gorman list has its place in the professional librarian's value system. He presents these values not in the abstract, but in context with current historic and political events.

In "Human Rights, Democracy, and Librarians," Kathleen de la Peña McCook and Katharine Phenix give an amazing preview into a larger forthcoming work on the Universal Declaration of Human Rights (UDHR) and libraries. They go well beyond reviewing the importance of the library in a democratic society and discuss the larger challenges librarians face. "How does a human rights perspective inform the daily actions of a librarian?" the authors ask. To begin with, they say "Librarians cannot be neutral in their practice of librarianship." The chapter is rich with well-documented examples of librarians who have been lonely heroes but powerful human advocates for people's right to know.

Donald Case, in his essay on "Information Seeking" explains with great lucidity how "scholars have moved away from a preoccupation with library use and user studies and their emphasis on institutional sources and searches, to a focus on how individuals encounter and make sense of their environment." He discusses research showing our natural tendency to rely on the most easily available sources of information rather than the "best" source. Compounding this is the profusion of information available from too many sources and the problem of interpreting and understanding it. The librarian's dual role, says Case, is to "teach students and other users the skills to enable them to become effective seekers of information and to filter and guide users to the answers to their questions."

In her engaging paper, "Careers and Environments," Laura Kane reveals all: where librarians work (literally hundreds of different types of libraries and environments) and what librarians do (an amazing range of jobs in libraries, in every other discipline, in the private and not for profit sectors, and government agencies). Kane makes a very strong and appealing case for librarianship as a profession that can accommodate the most esoteric of interests.

FUNCTIONS AND COMPETENCIES

Moving into functions and competencies, Brooke Sheldon's essay "Another Look at Leadership" highlights five principles that if practised should help new librarians who are interested in moving up in the organization. A major point is that management is not leadership, and every new professional needs to understand the differences. The overall message of the chapter? We all have leadership potential and strengths, and there are specific ways to utilize, refine, and expand them in one's career.

Leadership is important at all levels of the organization but as Barbara Moran points out in her chapter "Management: An Essential Skill for Today's Librarians," what many people entering the library profession don't realize is the amount of time that nearly all professional librarians spend in managing— managing resources, facilities, and people. Moran, who literally "writes the books" on library management, gives an overview of the most important elements of library management, discusses the specific skills needed, and concludes with very practical suggestions on how librarians can acquire managerial expertise.

A major aspect of management is the ability to market one's library, as vividly described by Christie Koontz in her chapter "Marketing—The Driving Force of Your Library." Koontz outlines a systems approach that relies on "designing a product or service in terms of the consumer's needs and desires, with consumer satisfaction as its goal." From market research to feedback-evaluation, all of the steps are here, and the reader gains a clear understanding that library marketing is *not* library promotion!

Consummate practitioner, researcher, and writer G. Edward Evans in his essay "Reflections on Creating Information Service Collections" has chosen not to delve into the nitty-gritty of collection development. Instead, he offers seven suggestions for those interested in collection development, which he believes are critical to success in any environment. This is vintage Evans reflecting on a highly productive career but using examples that are extremely pertinent to the complexities and controversies of managing collections of resources today.

In Arlene Taylor's chapter "Organization and Representation of Information/Knowledge" we move to what many believe to be the heart of library science. Taylor, a master teacher and writer, discusses the major activities involved in the organization of recorded information from identifying the existence of a resource to providing the means to locate each resource or a copy of it. She describes the functions of cataloging and of classification systems, of processing and locating materials. Thoroughly up to date, the chapter includes difficulties inherent in organizing the Internet, the organization of digital libraries, and information architecture in an excellent overview of a rapidly developing field.

Judith Weedman presents a most understandable and interesting introduction in her chapter "Information Retrieval: Designing, Querying, and Evaluating Information Systems" to the complexities of designing an information retrieval system and the need for training searchers to ask the "right" questions. Librarians and other information professionals play a key role, not only in designing systems, but also as intermediaries in helping clients translate their questions so that search engines can retrieve the relevant documents.

Since there are many openings, and changes, in reference and information services, David Tyckoson's chapter "Reference Service: The Personal Side of Librarianship" will be very helpful to those interested in direct interaction with library users. This well-written essay has it all: the history and importance of reference service and how its role has shifted over the years from answering specific questions to research counselor. He notes that while reference librarians still consult reference books, the primary tool of today's reference specialist is a computer with an Internet connection. From the reference interview (a critical part of the process) to the difficulties of measuring and evaluating reference transactions, and a look at the future of reference services, this is indeed a comprehensive overview.

Linda Main's "Librarians: The Best Googlers in the World" is a snappy and exciting introduction to the ways new professionals librarians are performing in the age of blogs, wikis, and RSS feeds. She makes the point that "the role of the librarian has not changed. It has merely expanded into a virtual space where the Web is no longer a static and mainly one way medium where visitors to sites merely read the content fed to them and play no active role." Main describes the communication tools of Web 2.0 and gives examples of how librarians are using the tools to empower and involve clients. The essay describes the need for librarians to understand the concept of fair use, copyright, common licensing, and other issues that permeate the digital environment. The virtual world (e.g., Second Life) is here to stay, and Main makes a strong case for the need for librarians who are "agile, imaginative, can learn constantly, and foster change."

Mary K. Chelton's personal and delightful writing style has never been more apparent than in "Readers Advisory Services: How to Help Users Find a 'Good Book.'" Chelton pulls no punches when she discusses the misconceptions many librarians have about their ability to advise readers, and the mistakes libraries make in attempting to attract readers to books. This well-documented essay on the current state of RA services tells us what Readers Advisory Services ought to be, how to work with readers, and discusses a wide range of options to promote reading in the community in traditional ways and using new technology. This is essential reading for librarians who are interested in promoting the joys of reading.

It is important for professional librarians to understand the difference between "library research" and true research, and Ron Powell, a prolific writer in all aspects of research, carefully makes that distinction in his chapter "Research." He goes on to describe various types of research and research methods and the research report, and stresses the importance of librarians not just keeping up with research in the field, but being able to critically evaluate the methodology used, "even if they are not inclined to conduct their own research." An understanding of research methods is vital to professionals who serve researchers, and in academic and certain special libraries where librarians are often expected to conduct and publish their own research as part of the tenure and promotion process. Powell obviously feels and documents that not enough attention has been paid to teaching research in LIS programs, but he cites encouraging signs for the future in the profession at large.

Charles McClure's essay on evaluation, "Learning and Using Evaluation: A Practical Introduction," logically follows Powell's overview of research. McClure, a major architect of library planning and evaluation, takes us through a range of ongoing evaluation and assessment activities. He stresses the importance of accountability in allocating resources, indicates criteria that can be used to measure outcomes and impact, and takes the reader through the steps of an entire evaluation process. Finally, he provides detailed guidelines for writing the evaluation report.

MOVING BEYOND BOUNDARIES

Moving to broader issues in the final section of the book, Barbara Ford directs our attention to the important role of "LIS Professionals in a Global Society." Informed by her current international work and career long convictions on the importance of "Local Touch . . . Global Reach," Ford argues forcefully for the importance of "ubiquitous open, free access to information as the key perquisite for a peaceful, equitable world." She also sees public libraries as key players in helping societies address health and social issues, and her essay includes many examples of libraries fulfilling these roles. Ford is optimistic about the changes information technology is bringing to developing countries, but worried about the politics of how to use the new technologies in positive ways for the benefit of all. She concludes with a list of ideas that library professionals can use in their libraries and individually to have "global impact and focus."

As each chapter provides insight to trends and issues in specific areas, Ken Haycock focuses on broader "Issues and Trends." Haycock is concerned about professional librarians' social disdain about all matters related to a business-orientation when the library is in fact a business, receiving and allocating resources for the greatest possible impact. He notes that the library's business is community development, however one might define "community." There is a growing importance in the library as physical space and as a virtual space. As libraries incorporate more Web 2.0 technologies, however, client needs and professional values tend to clash. Perhaps inevitably, roles and relationships of professional librarians are being redefined with many results, not the least of which is the continuing tension between professionals in the field and the educators who prepare them.

THE PORTABLE MLIS

Our goal is to provide a broad overview of the profession, its foundations, current practice, and future trends. It is designed to be accessible, relatively free of jargon, providing insights to the beginner and layperson about the continually evolving, changing, and exciting world of the professional librarian.

Librarianship truly is the twenty-first-century profession.

Ken Haycock
San Jose, California

Brooke Sheldon
Santa Fe, New Mexico

How to Think Like a Librarian: An Introduction

Ken Haycock and Brooke E. Sheldon

Let's start with the basics.

What is a library?

What is a librarian?

What does it mean to think like a librarian?

The word library means many different things to different people. Sometimes it is simply a collection of books (your home library) or a meeting room (the company board room might be called the library) or even a bar (throw a few books on the wall as wallpaper and voila you have the "library bar").

We propose here some characteristics of what we mean by a library.

Typically there is a collection of resources (variously called books and other media, or electronic resources or data objects or even "stuff") that address the unique informational and/or literary needs of a defined clientele or population; these resources are organized for use through an accessible catalog or other search system and effectively exploited through appropriate programs and services; these activities and processes are managed, evaluated, and improved by trained personnel.

Overall, librarians enable society, and each individual, to access and make effective use of society's recorded information and ideas. But what does that mean? Typically, librarians plan, implement, and promote the preservation, organization, and effective use in their own organization. Professional librarians hold a graduate degree in Library and Information Studies accredited by the American Library Association (ALA); outside North America a graduate degree recognized by the national accrediting agency or association is considered equivalent. For teacher-librarians in elementary and secondary schools, a graduate degree in school library media accredited by the ALA and the National Council for the Accreditation of Teacher Education is considered equivalent.

We have all heard the stories about the "bunheads" obsessed with quiet and order, but profiles of negative images simply reflect ignorance as professional librarians assume leadership positions in their communities, whether municipal or corporate. The jokes about getting a degree to stamp out books means only that the speaker hasn't been in a library in a few decades. The comments about the Internet replacing libraries simply suggests ignorance of the increased use of libraries and the role librarians play at the major search firms in quality assurance. Rather than declining in use and support, libraries are being refurbished and rebuilt as communities revitalize the downtown core to contribute to economic development and enhance libraries as neighborhood centers to contribute to social development. Indeed, the profession of librarianship is often listed a one of the "hot" careers of the twenty-first century.

Professional librarians are smart and savvy, contributing to the cultural, economic, educational, social, and technological well-being of their communities. Public librarians change lives; the stories are innumerable. Teacher-librarians contribute to student achievement when they collaborate with teachers. Law librarians save their firms time and money as they support communities of practice. Medical librarians save lives when consulted by physicians. Academic librarians advance scholarship and teaching and learning. Study after study documents the contributions of professional librarians.

THINKING LIKE A LIBRARIAN

What then does it mean to "think like a librarian?"

There are many lens or filters through which librarians determine how best to serve their particular community. Some of these are based on the values of the profession; some based in the profession's code of ethics. These remain constant over time.

Similarly, in spite of the incredible technological advances transforming libraries and librarianship, there are basic principles that influence the decision-making process of every professional librarian.

These principles begin with the basic five laws of librarianship. Shiyali Ramamrita Ranganathan, a well-respected Indian leader in library science, first promulgated these five laws in 1931. They form the foundation for professional education and thinking like a librarian, even when they are not articulated.

Simply stated these laws are:

1. Books are for use.
2. Books are for all.
3. Every book its reader.
4. Save the time of the reader.
5. The library is a growing organism.

These might be restated as:

1. Library resources are for use.
2. Library resources are for all.
3. Every resource its user.

4. Save the time of the user.

5. The library is a growing organism.

Regardless of the language used, the five laws are the bedrock of librarianship as a service profession.

The First Law: Books Are for Use

Restated: Library Resources Are for Use

The first imperative for a professional librarian is access and service.

From the location of the facility (or ease of access to the resources of an e-branch), librarians begin with the "end user" in mind. How can the resources acquired for this particular clientele or community be made as accessible as possible? What hours of service are most appropriate? How can the physical or virtual space be made attractive and easy to use?

What training is necessary for staff to be able to deliver high-quality and effective service? What understandings do we need of our communities to ensure that we are meeting their needs? How can we offer personal service? These are issues that professional librarians face as they work to improve use.

Books are obviously still important. It is interesting in a highly technological "information age" to note the return of importance of reading and readers and thus of readers' advisory services by librarians. In some public libraries, clients (or users or patrons or customers if you prefer) can make an appointment with a readers' advisory librarian to develop a reading plan.

The Second Law: Books Are for All

Restated: Library Resources Are for All

Librarians have a strong sense of service, of social justice, and of defense of human rights, which manifests itself in a variety of ways, including the public's right to know, equitable access to information, freedom of expression, and intellectual freedom. From the notion of the people's university to community development, librarians have worked to ensure access to information and ideas regardless of socioeconomic class, gender, orientation, ability, religion, ethnic background, or immigrant status. The work of librarians has always included opening doors and developing programs for the disadvantaged, whether literacy classes for new immigrants of encouraging reading by reluctant boys. The library is the marketplace of ideas, the living room of the community.

Reference and information services have similarly been developed and delivered to ensure that services are available at point of need. With more users finding information on their own, librarians have moved themselves and reference stations or kiosks to academic departments and student union buildings on campus at high traffic times to be readily available, and have developed medical information programs in public libraries. Services are delivered face-to-face, by telephone, by e-mail, by virtual chat, by instant messaging. Of course, instruction has always been available to users and focuses more now on enabling customers to find, evaluate, and use current, reliable, and accurate sources on the Web.

Librarians have also moved to embedding their collections and organizing tools into Web search engines to make their resources accessible to everyone. Much attention is paid to the "digital divide," such that libraries provide the necessary equipment for all users to access electronic resources and the instruction to enable effective use.

Marketing, public relations, publicity, promotion—these focus on ensuring that the resources are meeting the needs and interests of particular segments of the community and that individuals and groups are aware of the resources and assistance available.

Not surprisingly, librarians feel strong obligations to advocate for legislation and funding that assures this access, whether support for the first amendment rights of young people, copyright rules for fair use, or open source software. Indeed the American Library Association supports a Washington office of professional lobbyists and alerts members to federal issues affecting not only support for libraries but the ancillary issues around all facets of equitable and unfettered access for all. State associations typically do the same.

The Third Law: Every Book Its Reader

Restated: Every Resource Its User

Librarians have moved beyond a disdain for marketing to recognize the need to identify the needs, desires, and interests of target market segments, whether teenagers or small business, and to adjust resources and services to meet those needs.

Resources are carefully selected and organized for ease of access. They then promote use though displays, reading lists, newsletters, research guides, or pathfinders as well as outreach and extension services. Resources not available locally are obtained through interlibrary loans. It is all about connections—between the user and the necessary resource, no matter where it might be.

Librarians are less constrained by "containers" than concerned about making content available. They work both to encourage book clubs in the library and community and to integrate Web resources in their catalogues. Their catalogues are also becoming more and more user friendly and integrated with other services. Cross-references and connections make searching and finding easier.

When seeing a new format, a librarian will first determine how to provide effective and efficient access and how to preserve it.

The Fourth Law: Save the Time of the Reader

Restated: Save the Time of the User

In Ranganathan's day, this was accomplished much more easily through well-situated branch libraries, appropriate hours of service, open shelves, shelf labels and arrangements, and efficient systems. Policies and procedures were designed to save time and support users.

Today, this law is even more critical as convenience often trumps quality in information-searching. Librarians provide computer terminals with printers, self-check out and self-check in of resources. They work to save the time of the staff to free them to work more directly with clients in the stacks and at the terminals.

Meta-searching capabilities through multiple channels and electronic advising of related resources is becoming more common.

The Fifth Law: The Library Is a Growing Organism

Restated? Not necessary

Some might argue that terminology should be changed, such as the "information agency," but regardless of our change in terms, our clients still typically return to the term "library."

Although Ranganathan focused on physical growth and planning for an increased collection and physical plant, he also spoke to the spirit of the library as an instrument of universal education and to the variety of environments in which librarians practise (academic, public, school, special/corporate library environments).

For the twenty-first century, there is no question about the necessity of more "public spaces" in especially academic and public libraries. In the college and university setting, space for study, for group work, for instruction are all necessitating more space even as more resources are acquired electronically. In public libraries, as public space generally diminishes, gathering spaces for community programs and events, as well as a coffee with neighbors, is becoming more important.

There is also no question that the library is growing and evolving as a conceptual organism. Librarians recognize that physical space is important but so too are resources and services in virtual space, whether simply database access or services in immersive environments like Second Life, which meet more needs of more users.

Librarians are becoming critical partners with the larger community as they are freed to work more closely with community groups on community issues. Library Web sites are moving from simple electronic resources to electronic or virtual branches and provide a full range of services "24/7" to those unable or unwilling to come to the physical space.

Thinking like a librarian? Always remember library resources are for use, they are for all segments of the community, especially the underserved, each resource should have a user, save the time of users and of staff, and recognize that the library is an evolving organism.

Professional librarians are members of an affinity group. They are connected through a common endeavor, organized around a whole process involving multiple but integrated functions, with both extensive knowledge as generalists and intensive knowledge in one or more areas. They are bound by their service ethic and these foundational laws.

Change is the constant while the principles for decision-making remain unchanged.

Part **1**

Foundations, Values and Context

1

Stepping Back and Looking Forward: Reflections on the Foundations of Libraries and Librarianship

Richard E. Rubin

Libraries are not important; they are essential. Libraries are about what we think and do. They are about who we were, who we are, and who we want to be. In a world as complex as ours, in a society as various and intricate, libraries are conduits and reflections of our intellectual energy, creativity, productivity, and humanity. Yet, although we might think that libraries are indispensable, this might not be what others think. Libraries might be perceived by some as expensive, inconvenient, unresponsive, and, with the ubiquity of the World Wide Web, unnecessary.

Without advocates who understand their significance, libraries might well fall into disuse and obsolescence, marginalized by those who neither understand their contributions nor their potential. That is why it is important to be familiar with the foundations of our profession and of libraries in general. It is hard to be passionate advocates of libraries and librarians if we are not familiar with our roots. We need to understand and communicate not only what we do and how we do it, but *why* we do what we do. Although one of the exciting aspects of our field is that it is constantly changing, this dynamism rests on firm foundations—these foundations sometimes quake and shift a bit, but they also serve to keep us secure and upright. Understanding our foundations helps us maintain our equilibrium in a changing world.

SOME HISTORICAL REFLECTIONS ON THE MISSIONS OF LIBRARIES

Libraries are reflections of the societies in which they are embedded. There is no one correct mission for a library and history has seen the library perform many functions. What distinguishes libraries as libraries is that, historically, they store physical records—some type of knowledge that is valued by society and that requires organization so that the knowledge can be preserved and used. The types of knowledge libraries have contained have varied widely depending on the purposes they were intended to serve.

The various missions of libraries highlight their adaptability and their capacity to serve different and multiple purposes. Historically, there is an ebb and flow of the mission of libraries: missions begin, disappear for a while, only to return in another time and place. Libraries are invented and reinvented. There is no smooth evolution that describes the development of libraries because they emerge and change as a function of the particular societies that produced them. To some extent, libraries represent a cultural exclamation point: evidence that the society has matured beyond subsistence and social simplicity. They establish a standard signifying a society's development.

The following are "thumbnail" sketches of some of the missions libraries have undertaken in the Western world in the past and how those missions have changed and adapted. This is not intended as a complete history, but a highly selective overview of some of the important missions that libraries have assumed. Following a look at these missions, we will explore the values expressed by libraries and librarianship today.

"Taking Care of Business": The Practical Archive

Consider some of the earliest of libraries—those that appear in Sumeria around 3000 B.C.E. Sumerian civilization was an early center of trade and commerce. As such, there was a need to collect and maintain commercial records. Sumerian libraries reflected this purpose by serving as an archive of commercial records that included land contracts and agreements. The challenge of maintaining such records must have been considerable because there was no paper to record such transactions. Rather, the Sumerians incised the records on clay tablets using a stylus. The language used was known as cuneiform. The process of recording information must have been very cumbersome but the sophistication of Sumerian society had generated a need to store, organize, and preserve records—hence, the library as archive.

"Keeping the Faith": The Religious Collection

In addition to commercial activity, religion is another basic and stabilizing aspect of society. This was certainly true of the Egyptian world around 2500 B.C.E. Religious traditions and practice were deeply integrated into Egyptian society and Egyptian temples played a central role in this world. Libraries were housed within these temples and the temple priests served as the librarians. Not surprisingly, the libraries contained primarily religious writings including the iconic "Book of the Dead" and works on healing. The contents were recorded in hieroglyphs on papyrus (an early form of paper made from reeds). The paper was then rolled into a scroll. (It is a curiosity that today we still use a twenty-first-century version of the scroll—rolls of microfilm!)

"It's All about Me": The Self-Aggrandizing Library

Sometimes, libraries, even great ones, were created by an individual primarily for his or her own glorification. Around the seventh century B.C.E., Ashurbanipal, the leader of Assyria, created such a library in the city of Nineveh. It is said that Ashurbanipal sent messengers throughout the known world to retrieve items in the Assyrian language for his library. The number of items might well have exceeded 30,000 clay tablets. Although the primary purpose was the glorification of Ashurbanipal, the library nonetheless allowed for study and learning. That fine libraries could signify social status might have begun with Ashurbanipal, but it certainly did not end there as evidenced by the individual names that grace the facades of some of the finest libraries in America.

"It's the Thought that Counts": The Scholarly Library

A few centuries later, around 300 B.C.E., libraries assumed yet another purpose. With the rise of Greek culture and the growth of its philosophical schools, scholarship became an important function. The most notable library during the Greek period was the Alexandrian Library in Alexandria, Egypt. Although named for the great military genius, Alexander the Great, the actual construction of the library occurred under the subsequent leaderships of Ptolemy I and Ptolemy II. The Alexandrian established the standard as the first major research library whereby a vast collection of works in the Greek language or works translated into Greek (perhaps a half-million items total) were brought together for consultation by scholars from throughout the known world. The collection was systematically arranged with a library catalog called the *Pinakes*. Scholars received assistance from librarians who were themselves scholars. The Alexandrian was the first great scholarly research collection and its subsequent deterioration and demise, although shrouded in mystery, probably began around 50 B.C.E. and was a great loss.

"Me Again": The Return of the Private Library for Self-Aggrandizement

Although the Roman Empire borrowed much from Greek culture (including its books), when it came to libraries, the Romans produced no libraries that rivaled the Alexandrian. Rather, Roman libraries were small and tended to be private—often held by prominent Roman military or political figures. The libraries were more reflections of personal taste and status than scholarship per se. Yet, learned individuals such as Cicero had them and used them. Interestingly, the Roman culture tended to emphasize orality rather than silent reading. The seemingly natural act of silent reading, so common to us, was uncommon to them at the time. Roman libraries were often places where people read aloud. There were a small number of "public" libraries during this period, promoted by Julius Caesar and others. One should not, however, equate these libraries with the modern public library. The Roman public libraries served a very small and privileged group as only a small percentage of Romans were literate.

"For Heaven's Sake": The Return of the Religious Collection

Preoccupation with religious matters followed the fall of the Roman Empire as political and economic dislocations were coupled with a rise of ecclesiastical authority. By the fifth century A.C.E., the small religious communities that subsequently arose in Western Europe produced a variety of monasteries of considerable prominence. Some of the monastic traditions were "bookish" in orientation—the most notable being the Benedictine Order. These monasteries included rooms known as "scriptoria" where the copying of books occurred. The reasons why monks copied texts were various, some more noble than others. On the one hand, the copying of ecclesiastical texts was a sacred task that preserved the works of the early church fathers. Making copies allowed these texts to be shared with other monasteries—literally spreading the Word. The execution of this important responsibility often resulted in beautifully embellished "illuminated" manuscripts. On the other hand, the often tedious nature of copying was intended to help focus a monk's concentration on religious, rather than worldly, matters. Copying a dry, boring text could also serve as a punishment. Under such circumstances, it is not surprising that copying was an imperfect activity at best, and monks were known to alter texts when they did not agree with them. Nonetheless, the monasteries of Western Europe conserved many of the great texts, the religious as well as the secular (profane?) works of the Greeks and Romans. When the Renaissance of Western Europe finally arrived, many of the books from these monasteries formed a substantive part of future library collections.

"Think Again": The Return of the Scholarly Library

While the intellectual lights of Western Europe were dimmed by political, religious, and economic upheaval, the Byzantine and Arab world experienced a social, economic, scientific, and religious Renaissance. By the seventh century A.C.E. in cities such as Constantinople, Baghdad, Damascus, Cairo, and Cordoba, universities with great libraries in the spirit of the Alexandrian were blossoming. Some of these libraries had vast collections sometimes approaching a half-million items. Scholars could consult a multitude of resources, many of them from the Greeks and Romans, in history, mathematics, literature, medicine, and science. It is in fact to the Moslem Empire that we owe the greatest debt for the Renaissance in Western Europe for it would not have been possible without the works maintained and conserved in the libraries of the Arab and Byzantine world during this period.

"Me Again, Again . . . ": The Return of the Private Library for Self-Aggrandizement

As Western Europe emerged from the medieval period, ecclesiastical domination waned and secular governments arose along with increased interest in politics, philosophy, and science. Italy in the fourteenth century was the home of wealthy, powerful leaders who were not only strong militarily but who also promoted secular learning and the arts. These princes became patrons of the great artists and thinkers of the time. They were interested in the writings of the classical Greeks and Romans and wished to possess their writings, sending book collectors throughout Europe to gather (in many cases rescuing) many of the texts that had been stored, sometimes quite badly, within monasteries. These substantial, princely libraries gave testimony to the learning and importance of their owners.

"Start the Presses": A New Beginning for Libraries

Before we turn to the developments in the nineteenth century that produced a new and unique mission for libraries, it is important to note a significant factor that established the foundation for these events—the invention of the printing press around 1450 in Germany. One cannot speak of books and libraries without recognizing the incredible changes that the printing press produced. As a result of this new technology, more individual book titles could be produced, more books of the same title could be produced, and the text itself, so susceptible to error when prepared by a copyist, was now much more consistent. The result was that more people could be exposed to books and more places could hold book collections.[1] As we examine the last of the library missions, it is important to recognize that such a mission would not be possible without the printing press.

"AND NOW FOR SOMETHING COMPLETELY DIFFERENT": THE MODERN MISSION OF THE AMERICAN PUBLIC LIBRARY

Archives, religion, scholarship, and ego: each in their own way reflected a fundamental mission that libraries continued to play from the Renaissance until the nineteenth century. Over this period, these various purposes were reflected in the growth of university libraries, cathedral libraries, and national libraries. In the nineteenth century a new mission arose—*the mission of serving the common person*. Although a few such libraries might have existed as early as ancient Rome, it took the Anglo-American traditions of the nineteenth century to bring to fruition institutions whose primary purpose was to serve the average citizen as a vehicle for both education and pleasure.

The rise of the public library in America in the middle of the nineteenth century has both a romantic and a less popular explanation. On the romantic side, some have characterized the growth of the public library as an outgrowth of the recognition that an informed citizenry was critical for the success of a democratic society. As the country matured politically, socially, economically, industrially, and educationally, and increasing wealth produced cities and towns with municipal services, a civic institution was needed to ensure that all citizens could be well-informed and occupationally skilled. When the first major public library was founded in Boston in the early 1850s, it was seen as a logical product of these forces. Although other types of libraries predated the Boston Public Library, such as the "social libraries" and the "circulating libraries," they were only for small groups of fee-paying members or those who could afford to pay a rental fee per item. These collections were intended either for educational purposes (social libraries) or for pure entertainment (circulating libraries). In neither case were the collections intended to provide broad-based service to the entire public. The Boston Public library, on the other hand, possessed the distinguishing features that characterize the modern public library. It was open to all members of the public, used voluntarily, managed by a publicly appointed or elected board, financed by public dollars, and was free to the public.

A less idealistic interpretation of the founding of the Boston Public Library is more controversial. Some argue that the Boston Public Library and other public libraries arose less as a result of high-minded individuals seeking a healthy democracy through a well-informed citizenry and more from a need to indoctrinate the mass of immigrants entering America in the nineteenth century to American values, customs, and expectations. From this perspective, the public library was seen as a form of social control whose purpose was to socialize new citizens to a particular (capitalistic?) value system.[2] This interpretation is not without merit and certainly worthy of discussion. For example, one can apply both motives to the philanthropy of Andrew Carnegie. Carnegie, the greatest benefactor of public libraries in America, helped build more than 2,000 libraries in a 40-year period. Carnegie believed that public libraries could be a grand source of knowledge and center for self-improvement. At the same time, as a major industrialist, he needed a workforce that had strong work values, and he viewed libraries as a great place to inculcate those values.

It is true that the clientele of the Boston Public Library was white and middle class, and that the collection, no doubt, reflected the prevailing middle-class values of the mid-nineteenth-century society in which it was embedded. These facts however are not sufficient to resolve the debate. From a broad historical perspective, the Boston Public Library (and similar institutions arising in Britain at about the same time) was a significant social breakthrough. The Boston Public Library was a library created for the many, not for a particular religious community or the wealthiest individuals. Although there might be some aspects of self-aggrandizement (civic pride) on the part of Boston, and the debate over motivations notwithstanding, this new purpose—to serve the average citizen—must now be added to functions served by a library and takes a special place.

The growth and development of the modern *librarian* paralleled the growth and development of the modern public library. The librarians of the past were a very small group. Depending on the mission of the library, they were priests, monks, scholars, or merely tenders of the books. They were also almost exclusively male. With the growth of the American public library and the dramatic expansion of library buildings through the philanthropy of Andrew Carnegie, there was a need for a much different and much larger labor force. The library workforce that emerged at the end of the century in America was largely female, and largely educated in the technical aspects of the profession, e.g., classification. There were several reasons why late nineteenth century librarianship possessed these characteristics. Among them were (1) the need for a significant low-paid workforce to fill jobs in a large number of newly constructed public libraries; (2) the perceived educational and socialization function of libraries that were conducive to female employment; and (3) the rise of the technical education movement that became prominent as the industrial revolution matured in the United States.

Many of the cities, towns, and rural areas that acquired initial funding for their public libraries had little fiscal means to maintain them. Similarly, public libraries were perceived as educational and social institutions with strong service orientations. These two factors created an opportunity for women who could be paid low wages (please, don't shoot the messenger!) and whose work roles were consonant with creating an appropriate nurturing atmosphere in the library setting.[3] In addition, these factors must be coupled with an industrial age that promoted more generalized technical education, in contrast to apprenticeship, so that individuals could move from place to place performing jobs with similar characteristics.[4] The systematization of work was a common practice as the industrial revolution infused American society including librarianship. It is no coincidence that the Dewey Decimal Classification System (an important intellectual technology for librarianship) was developed during this period and could be applied from library to library.

As the role of the librarian evolved from its late nineteenth-century roots, the emphasis on service to the common citizen has remained a constant. Certainly, nineteenth-century librarians were more likely to serve the better educated and those with higher incomes, but as libraries have grown in sophistication and social acumen, many broad-based services have emerged including special services to children and young adults, mobile services, reference services, services to individuals with disabilities, and services to ethnic communities. Librarians' commitments to the development, maintenance, and growth of such services have been manifest for decades.

THE ROLE AND VALUES OF LIBRARIES AND LIBRARIANS TODAY

To some extent, modern libraries serve all the previous historical missions that libraries have played: a source for education and learning, a center for personal pleasure and entertainment, an archive of societal, religious values, and materials, and an exemplar of social development. But in a broad, integrative sense, it is fair to ask "What do today's libraries stand for, what are their values, and what are the values of the librarians who serve within them?"

It is important to remember, of course, that there are many types and subdivisions of libraries; "academic" libraries, for example, can be subdivided into university, college, community college, and technical libraries. Each of these has both shared and unique functions. The ensuing discussion highlights the values of libraries and librarians generally with some special emphasis on the public library because of the great breadth of its mission and its ubiquity in American society. In fact, there are many examples of the intersection of values among different types of libraries and much of this discussion pertains on a more universal level.

There are many ways that one might approach a discussion of the professional values of libraries and librarians. Thankfully, the American Library Association (ALA), the oldest and largest professional library association, has promulgated important documents that express these values succinctly: the ALA Core Values, ALA Code of Ethics, and the ALA Library Bill of Rights (see Appendix A, B, and C, respectively). Since it began in 1876 under the leadership of Melvil Dewey, the ALA has steadfastly maintained a position of leadership in developing and guiding professional practice and policy for librarianship in the United States. While encouraging open discussion and debate among its leaders and members, the Association has established consensus on many important values and expressed this consensus through its stated policies. Although somewhat overlapping, each conveys revealing perspectives on the special purposes that libraries serve. Below is a brief discussion of four of these key values.

Belief in Intellectual Freedom

It is sometimes said that the First Amendment to the U.S. Constitution is first among equals in regard to the other Amendments in that it expresses a primary belief, a belief so fundamental that, except in very special cases, it trumps other considerations. So it is with librarians' belief in Intellectual Freedom that takes as its underpinning the First Amendment. For librarians, Intellectual Freedom embodies the strong conviction that a democratic society functions best when ideas can be openly expressed. Inherent in this conviction is that (1) an effective democratic society relies on the ability of all individuals to gain access to the ideas of others without barriers; and (2) although truth is highly valued, it must be acknowledged that in many cases, there are differences of opinions about what is true and what is false, and therefore active exploration and discussion of different points-of-views are the best ways to deal with issues of truth in a democratic society.

From the librarian's perspective, the right of free expression guaranteed by the First Amendment must be accompanied by the complementary right to have unimpeded access to those expressions. Thus, American libraries are foremost places where people can obtain the expressions of others: authors, musicians, poets, politicians, scientists, etc. The library is in many ways a critical public forum where people voluntarily select the ideas they wish to explore. Because peoples' values, interests, and beliefs can differ substantially, the librarian must accommodate this heterogeneity.

Intellectual Freedom requires librarians to be open-minded (tolerant) concerning the subjects and the points-of-view that they make available through the library collection. It is arrogant to assume that one can know the "truth" about many matters of importance in this world; it is an act of humility to accept that there are many perspectives on these matters. Librarians express this humility by assuring a wide range of expressions in the library collection. So it is that the ALA Library Bill of Rights exhorts librarians to build collections representing the widest range of points-of-view.

A commitment to Intellectual Freedom also requires that librarians respect the individuality and diversity of patrons, and eradicate real or perceived barriers to their inquiries. It requires that librarians address each inquiry with equal energy and provide information objectively and nonjudgmentally. It requires that librarians protect confidentiality and the individual's right to know, sometimes in the face of considerable pressure.

Adhering to these principles can be challenging. Consider, for example, the rights of young people in a digital age. Librarians are frequently asked to restrict young people's access to certain books, periodicals, videos, DVDs, and the Internet on the grounds that barriers are needed to protect young people from harmful or objectionable materials. On the surface such restrictions seem reasonable and proper. However, problems arise when one probes a little deeper and asks such questions as: "Who is to decide what can be seen or not seen?"; "Does everyone agree on which material should be prohibited?"; "To what extent are we inadvertently restricting appropriate materials, e.g., through computer filtering, while trying to restrict inappropriate materials?"; and "Who is ultimately responsible for what a young person is reading or seeing—the librarian or the parent?" The struggles to protect Intellectual Freedom are considerable and the role of the librarian is sometimes difficult, often requiring great courage, patience, and understanding. But as we look back, throughout history there are few occasions when we laud the censorious and berate those who fought for freedom of expression. The odds are that those who fight for the Intellectual Freedom of others will find that, in the long run, a salutary judgment awaits them.

Belief in Service and the Public Good

As the new professions of social work, public education, nursing, and librarianship emerged at the end of the nineteenth century, they served as important counterbalances to self-interested, commercial motivations, and unhealthy social byproducts of the industrial revolution.[5] Service rather than selfishness was the hallmark of these professions. As librarians, it is gratifying to work in a profession that benefits so many and has so few detractors. Modern American libraries are quintessentially noble establishments; their primary role is to serve the public. The public is each and every individual. Librarians serve each person who enters or contacts us by phone, fax, or e-mail. The ALA Code of Ethics reminds us that the level of service must be of the "highest" for all our users and that we must never consider our own interests above those of the library user. It also requires us to improve ourselves constantly through continuing education.

The Library Bill of Rights reminds us that library service is provided to all, regardless of origin, age, background, or views. Each person benefits individually by our library service, but the aggregation of these individual interactions creates a collective good as well. Fundamental to our beliefs is that libraries change society for the better; that our world is a better place because of what librarians do; that collectively, people enjoy life and prosper more where libraries exist. This broad notion of the public good should not be lost in our focus on the rights of individual patrons and our duty to serve them. There is a forest (the society as whole), as well as the trees (each individual library user). The beauty of libraries is that in serving the latter, the former is also served.

Belief in Education

Among the ALA "core values" for libraries and librarians is "Education and Lifelong Learning." A belief in education is inextricably bound to the conception of libraries as repositories of books and its necessary complement—reading. When people consider why their local libraries are important, one often hears about the importance of libraries in education and reading. Historically, this association has been particularly beneficial for libraries because education provides a strong rationale for political and fiscal support in the community. Publicly supported libraries in the United States have always been associated with education whether it was self-education for the purpose of social or economic advancement, education for children, or as handmaiden to formal higher education.

There is no doubt that the role of the library is evolving and in today's digital environment, it is common today to characterize the purpose of libraries as "information access," but "information access" is only one current manifestation of the age-old function of education. The educational function in all its forms remains an important responsibility of librarians. In addition to responding to requests for information, librarians instruct users in how to obtain and evaluate information and assist patrons in their process of inquiry, including helping them clarify and define their needs. They also organize knowledge so that patrons' learning processes are facilitated. Although for today's young people the link between the book and education is more tenuous, the library continues to support education by providing access to knowledge through computers, databases, and the Internet as well as books. The educational function continues to provide a strong case for continued public support for libraries.

Belief in the Value of the Past: Preservation

It is sometimes considered passé to conceive of a library as a repository, but in fact, that remains one of its essential functions. If we are to have access to the intellectual content of our civilization, then we must be committed to preserving the ideas and expressions of the past. Not merely to store contents, but to represent, organize, and maintain those contents in such a way that people have access to the materials of the past, both the intellectual content and the material itself as artifact. It is, however, passé to think of repositories as *only* physical places. Librarians are on the forefront of maintaining physical repositories, but also creating digital repositories that make information and artifacts available to those who would never be able to consult them in the past. Respect for (albeit not necessarily agreement with) the artists, writers, philosophers, political figures, theologians, and scientists of the past helps ensure a continuity to our civilization—the possibility of understanding ourselves and others. The librarian knows that the failure to maintain the evidence of the past sets the present adrift, without context. In some sense, the desire to preserve the past is yet another expression of tolerance and humility. Preservation activities recognize that many ideas of the past are of value today; perhaps some are of even greater value than those of the present. Librarians are committed to the belief that the ideas of the past must be available as part of the repertoire of knowledge to which everyone should have access.

CONCLUSION

Suddenly, we find ourselves wondering if libraries will disappear: an outdated artifact of a book publishing industry under stress, a diminished interest in reading, and a rapidly growing Internet generation. At the beginning of this chapter, it was noted that libraries are characterized by the maintenance of physical records. As these records are transmuted into bits and bytes, will the digitized world supplant libraries or will libraries simply accommodate to the changing nature of records themselves? Are libraries riding into the sunset? Certainly, there are some clouds on the horizon: young people, for example, are relying more and more on Web searching for getting information; they trust the Web almost as much as they trust librarians. They value the Net's speed and convenience.[6] Will our libraries be able to compete?

Libraries, however, are not merely important; they are essential. As archives served the Sumerians, religious collections served the Egyptians and monks, and research collections served the Greeks and Arabs, will our libraries without respond to the need to organize and make accessible the prodigious amount of knowledge our society has created and continues to generate? The challenges are great; but there is a certain constancy to modern American libraries and librarianship that is unlikely to change—the dedication to serving each and every individual. The values expressed by the ALA Core Values, the ALA Code of Ethics, and the ALA Library Bill of Rights are testimony to this constancy. But change will come as well: the next horizon is not far away.

SUGGESTIONS FOR FURTHER READING

American Library Association. *Intellectual Freedom Manual*, 7th ed. Chicago: ALA, 2006.

Gorman, Michael. "Five New Laws of Librarianship." *American Libraries* 26 (September 1995), 784–785.

Harris, Michael and Elmer D. Johnson. *History of Libraries in the Western World.* Metuchen, NJ: Scarecrow, 1984.

Harris, Roma M. *Librarianship: The Erosion of a Woman's Profession.* Norwood, NJ: Ablex, 1992.

Rubin, Richard. *Foundations of Library and Information Science*, 2nd ed. New York: Neal-Schuman, 2004.

Chapter 2

Professional Ethics and Values in a Changing World

Michael Gorman

Even today, most people with MLIS degrees work in libraries of one kind or another. There are, however, increasing numbers of people holding the degree who work in other fields in which the policies and practices of librarianship have application and value. Such people are generally described as "information professionals" (a vague term made vaguer by the lack of an agreed definition of "information"). It is generally accepted that many of the techniques developed and refined in libraries (organization of information, reference work, information competence, library information technology, etc.) are relevant to other areas—this is after all, why nonlibrary employers hire people with MLIS degrees—but the question of the ethics and values of librarianship is seldom discussed in this context. I would contend that those ethics and values are the bedrock upon which the work of librarians/"information professionals" should be based, irrespective of the area in which MLIS skills are practiced.

Librarianship is concerned with the interaction of humans and the human record—the texts, images, and symbolic representations in all formats that we have inherited from our ancestors over several millennia. Librarians assist in that interaction by organizing and preserving subsets of the human record, by providing access to those subsets, and by providing assistance and guidance to those wishing to explore the human record. The human record comes to us in many formats—manuscripts, printed pages, digital documents and resources, etc.—but the format is secondary to the transcendent importance of the texts, images, and symbolic representations themselves. The possessor of an MLIS should be familiar with all the policies and techniques connected with the interaction between humans and the human record, no matter where those policies and techniques are applied, but that knowledge and those applications must be informed by the agreed ethics and values of our profession.

ETHICS

Webster's *New collegiate dictionary* defines "ethics" as "The science of moral duty; broadly, the science of ideal human character. Moral principles, quality, or practice." Our professional statement on the moral duties of our profession, the way of life of an ideal professional, and our moral principles and practice is contained in the ALA *Code of Ethics* (see Appendix B) last revised in 1995 (and in the process of revision as I write), which "states the values to which we are committed, and embodies the ethical responsibilities of the profession in this changing information environment" in the following eight categories:

I. We provide the highest level of service to all library users through appropriate and usefully organized resources; equitable service policies; equitable access; and accurate, unbiased, and courteous responses to all requests.

II. We uphold the principles of intellectual freedom and resist all efforts to censor library resources.

III. We protect each library user's right to privacy and confidentiality with respect to information sought or received and resources consulted, borrowed, acquired or transmitted.

IV. We recognize and respect intellectual property rights.

V. We treat co-workers and other colleagues with respect, fairness and good faith, and advocate conditions of employment that safeguard the rights and welfare of all employees of our institutions.

VI. We do not advance private interests at the expense of library users, colleagues, or our employing institutions.

VII. We distinguish between our personal convictions and professional duties and do not allow our personal beliefs to interfere with fair representation of the aims of our institutions or the provision of access to their information resources.

VIII. We strive for excellence in the profession by maintaining and enhancing our own knowledge and skills, by encouraging the professional development of co-workers, and by fostering the aspirations of potential members of the profession.

It is easy to see that despite the library-centric language, these ethical prescriptions are applicable to professional work in all arenas and not just to the work of those of us who work in libraries. Here is my (unofficial) rewording intended to make that clear (rewordings in italics).

I. We provide the highest level of service to all *we serve* through appropriate and usefully organized resources; equitable service policies; equitable access; and accurate, unbiased, and courteous responses to all requests.

II. We uphold the principles of intellectual freedom and resist all efforts to censor *any part of the human record.*

III. We protect *the right of all we serve* to privacy and confidentiality with respect to information sought or received and resources consulted, borrowed, acquired or transmitted.

IV. We recognize and respect intellectual property rights.

V. We treat co-workers and other colleagues with respect, fairness, and good faith, and advocate conditions of employment that safeguard the rights and welfare of all employees of our institutions.

VI. We do not advance private interests at the expense of *those we serve*, colleagues, or our *employers*.

VII. We distinguish between our personal convictions and professional duties and do not allow our personal beliefs to interfere with fair representation of the aims of our institutions or the provision of access to their information resources.

VIII. We strive for excellence in the profession by maintaining and enhancing our own knowledge and skills, by encouraging the professional development of co-workers, and by fostering the aspirations of potential members of the profession.

Anyone who follows these guidelines conscientiously would be an exemplary, as well as productive, professional in any environment.

VALUES

"Values" is a more slippery concept than ethics to many people. They understand that there is a need for ethical statements for members of a profession but often do not understand the usefulness or applicability of a statement of values. This confusion is quite understandable, after all, you only have to think of phrases such as "family values" (used extensively by politicians for shady purposes) to realize what a problem the word "values" can be. In such cases, the usage is cosmetic. It means "the things I purport to believe in and that you should be made to conform to." We are asked to accept such beliefs on faith and custom, not on the basis of rational analysis. The plain fact is that values *are* beliefs, albeit beliefs that are shared by members of a group may or may not be based on faith (otherwise known as lack of verifiable evidence), and have been held for a period of time. Given that definition, the next question we have to answer is: Is there a cluster of such beliefs (otherwise known as a value system) that is shared by all members of our profession? This is a knotty enough question if it is asked of those of us in the twenty-first century, it becomes even knottier when we reach into the past and try to discern a golden thread that links us to Callimachus, the great library of Alexandria, the monks of medieval England and their chained libraries, the librarians of the Enlightenment, the great reformist public librarians of the nineteenth century, the long and diverse history of libraries and related institutions in the twentieth century, and the changing face of our profession today.

Perhaps there is another question we should ask first—why bother? Since discussion of values can and does revolve around hair-splitting and dispute, why not leave it up to every member of our profession to sort out her or his own beliefs and destiny? I think there are a number of reasons why any group should seek to create a statement of its values and why we, in particular, should attempt to do so now.

The first reason is the crisis of confidence that we see in some areas of our profession—that existential dread that perhaps our professional knowledge and practices will not survive or will be so transformed by digital technology as to be unrecognizable. This lack of confidence leads to the acceptance of the idea that there is no such thing as our profession—there is no golden thread that links professionals working in a variety of different library and nonlibrary environments and that links those professionals to the past. If that were true, then obviously there could be no set of professional "core values." On the other hand, if we can formulate and define our values, we can state what we as a profession believe in and what is the essential basis of all our work.

The second reason for formulating a set of values is to provide all of us with yardsticks with which we can judge all our services and plans.

The third reason is that values provide a basis for discussion and some basic premises that we need if we are to work fruitfully with others.

The fourth and last reason is that explicit values are important psychologically to individuals and groups. If individuals and groups share values and act on them, then even failure is bearable because those individuals and groups know that what was tried was honorable and the effort itself was worthwhile. We live and work in a time in which many of us are insecure about our work and our future. Belief in a strong statement of values can be a great thing in dealing with existential anxiety!

In the course of writing my book *Our enduring values*, I listed eight values derived from previous writings that I will discuss and show how they refer to our work today. (See also Appendix A for ALA's statement of core values.)

A. Stewardship

There are only three ways in which human beings learn. They learn from experience and have been doing so for as long as there have been human beings. They learn from interaction with people who know more than they, and have been doing so since the first wise woman passed on the oral traditions of her long ago band of early humans. Lastly, they learn from interacting with the human record—the texts, writings, images, sounds, and symbolic representations that document the knowledge of the ages. Humans have been learning in that way since writing and drawing were invented and the age of miracles began. We have a unique role in preserving and transmitting that human record on behalf of future generations. I do not use the word "unique" lightly. Many of our values and missions are shared with other groups and interests, but we alone are dedicated to the preservation of recorded knowledge and information. If a substantial amount of the human record were to be available in, and *only* in, digital form, we would be facing a crisis in the preservation of the human record that will dwarf anything that we have seen hitherto. It is imperative that we work together to produce a grand plan for future stewardship that contains practical and cost-effective means of ensuring that future generations know what we know. We should also be stewards of our profession, reinvigorating the LIS education system to ensure the onward transmission of our values and practices.

B. Service

Ours is a profession defined by service. We serve both individuals and humanity as a whole in what we do. Every aspect of our professional work, every action that we take can and should be measured in terms of service. Our service can be as large as the creation of a complex computerized information retrieval system or as small as a single brief act of helpfulness—but it can and should pervade our professional lives so that it becomes the yardstick by which we measure all our plans and projects and the means by which we assess success or failure of all our programs.

C. Intellectual Freedom

Intellectual freedom can be defined quite simply. Individuals are entitled to think and believe whatever they wish and that freedom to think and believe is vitiated if access to words and images conveying the thoughts and beliefs of others is restricted. Allowing others to have access to writings and images of which you approve is easy; the difficult part is allowing that access to writings and images of which you disapprove. The book banners, film burners, Internet censors, and record smashers are always with us. People who do not believe that you should be allowed to read and see things of which they disapprove are found in every society. The classic reasons for that denial are sedition, blasphemy, and obscenity, and though the latter has been the focus of censors for the last few decades (*to the impure all things are impure*, Oscar Wilde), but sedition is making a comeback in contemporary America (see the obnoxious "USA PATRIOT Act") and blasphemy cannot be far behind given the current tide of socio-religious fundamentalism.

We believe in intellectual freedom because it is as natural to us, and as necessary to us, as the air that we breathe. Censorship is anathema to us because it inhibits our role in life—to make the recorded knowledge and information of humankind freely available to everyone, regardless of faith or the lack of it, ethnicity, gender, age, or any other of the categories that divide us one from the other. I strongly believe we should be absolutists when it comes to intellectual freedom and carry out our tasks without reference to our own opinions or the opinions of those who want to restrict free access to knowledge. All the more reason to support our professional associations' offices of intellectual freedom in the great work they do on our behalf to protect this most important professional value.

D. Equity of Access

Intellectual freedom is inextricably linked to equity of access to the human record. Much is made of the "digital divide"—the idea that the poor and other disadvantaged have less access to technology than others. I believe that divide is a part, and not the most significant part, of a societal divide in the United States, one of the features of which is the lack of equal access to the human record and to the services provided by libraries and other related institutions. It is too often taken for granted that if you live in the United States and are poor, handicapped, a member of a minority, very young, very old, and/or live in a rural area, you will not have access to the full range of social services (including library and information services) and the other goods of a civilized society. It is important to beat the censors and make the human record accessible to everybody without fear or favor, but it is equally important to ensure that such access is practically possible and not biased in favor of the better off or the more powerful. Such unfettered access is brought into question by some aspects of technology and by the tide of privatization. The idea of charging for access to library and information services is much more popular today than it was before and the tendency is to write off sections of society as doomed to be information poor. I am not saying that libraries and other related services that use technology intensively as an enhancement to their services are inevitably going to betray the value of equity of access, but I am saying that there are some inherent contradictions in society and in our use of technology that should make us very sensitive to the idea that access to the human record should be freely available to all—irrespective of social standing and economic circumstances.

E. Privacy

A major affliction of American public life today is the wholesale and largely successful attack on the right to privacy. Letters are read, traps are laid, e-mails are reconstructed, bookstore records are happy hunting grounds for inquisitors, the most private aspects of lives are laid bare, and the right to your own thoughts, your own relationships, and your own beliefs is trampled on by zealots and bigots. This is the world of *1984*, the world of mind control, the world of mental totalitarianism. The confidentiality of library and information records is not the most sensational weapon in the fight for privacy, but it is important, both on practical and moral grounds. In practical terms, a lot of the relationship between those in our profession and society at large is based on trust. On moral grounds, we must start with the premise that everyone is entitled to freedom of access, freedom to read texts and view images, and freedom of thought and expression. None of those freedoms can survive in an atmosphere in which access is monitored and individual use patterns are made known to anyone without permission.

F. Literacy and Learning

Our profession is an essential part of the culture of learning because of the importance of our contribution to making the human record accessible. The flight from books and reading that can be seen in the writings of the more fervid technophiles among us is a flat betrayal of the history and culture of libraries. The importance of the interaction between the scholar or student and the text transcends the medium used to convey that text. An illiterate with a computer is, essentially, no better off than an illiterate with a book. Literacy is much misunderstood today—it is not a simple question of being able to read or being unable to read. True literacy is a process by which, once able to read, an individual becomes more and more literate throughout life, more and more able to interact with complex texts and, thereby, to acquire knowledge and understanding. It is a key element in the enterprise—learning—to which all our work is dedicated. Instead of seeing the world as divided between the illiterate, a-literate, and literate, we should see literacy as an open-ended range of possibilities in which we work with educators and students to learn and become more learned using sustained reading of texts as a central part of the life of the mind.

G. Rationalism

I am sure that I am not alone in being distressed by the great tide of fundamentalism, superstition, and plain craziness in the world today. From religious bigots to faith healers to militants of all stripes, the world seems to be full of people who are convinced that they know the One True Way and are aggressively intolerant of those who do not share their beliefs and prejudices. I think that our profession is, above all, a child of the Enlightenment and of rationalism. We stand, above all, for the notion that human beings are improved by the acquisition of knowledge and information and that no bar should be placed in their way. We stand for the individual human being pursuing whichever avenues of enquiry she or he wishes. We also stand for rationalism as the basis for all of our policies and procedures. Ours is a supremely rational profession and should resist the forces of irrationalism both external and internal.

H. Democracy

Democracy, in name if not always fully in practice, is now the dominant global political idea. It is an idea that depends on knowledge and education. It is a sad irony that as American democracy has reached its theoretical ideal—the enfranchisement of all adults, irrespective of gender and race—it is in danger because of an increasingly ill-informed, easily manipulated, and apathetic electorate. The rights for which, at different times, revolutionaries, women, and ethnic minorities fought are being vitiated by a culture of sound bites, political ignorance, and unreasoning dislike of government. Our profession is part of the solution to this modern ill. As an integral part of the educational process and as custodians and explainers of the records of humankind, we stand for the means to achieve a better democracy. The best antidote to being conned by TV is a well-reasoned book, article, or other text. All our other values and ideas are democratic values and ideas—intellectual freedom, the common good, service to all, the transmission of the human record to future generations, free access to knowledge and information, nondiscrimination, etc. Our profession has grown and flourished in the soil of democracy and our fate is inextricably bound up with the fate of democracy.

THE GENERAL GOOD

I did not include "the common good" or any synonymous term in my list of values but I do believe it goes to the heart of our discussion of ethics and values. Social conservatives in the United States are fond of talking about "culture wars"—a term that posits a divide between those who have a paternalistic, militarist, repressive, and reactionary view of the world and those who do not. If you worship the flag, are antifeminist, deny the value of public service (other than the kind in which people get killed), and believe in censoring books and art work you are in one army and, if you are a feminist, procivil rights and equal treatment under the law, and believe in intellectual freedom, you are in the other. You are beyond the pale if, even worse, you are a pacifist and tired of wars on this and that and the metaphorical use of war images. To my mind there is a conflict that is wider than these cultural and societal hot button matters. It is the gulf in thinking and social policy that exists between those who believe in unfettered individualism and those who believe in the greater good. The late great Mike Royko said that the motto of the city of Chicago should be *Ubi est meum?* (Where is mine?). I would suggest that attitude is not restricted to that great city and that a tax phobic, selfish, government-hating tendency is a major force in American society. Such people do not believe in the greater good—that impulse that sees investment in social institutions as good because societies are improved when its citizens are healthy, educated, and literate. Perhaps, when it comes down to it, *this* is the overarching belief that underlies all our ethics and values—a belief that is selfless, optimistic, idealistic, and progressive and that reconciles the rights of the individual with the greater good of society—and provides the answer to the question "Why is our profession important?" That answer being "Because we contribute to all that we value about society—the greater good."

SUGGESTION FOR FURTHER READING

Gorman, Michael. *Our Enduring Values: Librarianship in the 21st Century*. Chicago: ALA, 2000.

Human Rights, Democracy, and Librarians

Kathleen de la Peña McCook and Katharine Phenix

"ALA recognizes its broad social responsibilities. The broad social responsibilities of the American Library Association are defined in terms of [1] the contributions that librarianship can make in ameliorating or solving the critical problems of society; [2] support for efforts to help inform and educate the people of the United States on these problems and to encourage them to examine the many views on and the facts regarding each problem; and [3] the willingness of ALA to take a position on current critical issues with the relationship to libraries and library service set forth in the position statement."
—American Library Association Policy Manual (Section 1.1)

THE CONNECTION OF LIBRARIANSHIP TO DEMOCRACY

What is the ethical foundation of librarianship? To what extent should librarians work to solve the critical problems of society? We assert that a human rights perspective is the way that twenty-first-century librarians must look at the world and practice our craft. Libraries have long been the willing tools of democracy. In this chapter we review the traditional wisdom and canon of the importance of the library in a democratic society but wish to take the reader further in an understanding of the larger issues we face in our chosen field of work.

The foundational ideas of the public library recognize that a democratic society relies on an informed citizenry and that educated citizens would in turn elect enlightened legislators or representatives and participate intelligently in decision-making in local and national issues of common interest. Without regard to income, race, sexual orientation, religion, or physical ability, our good

voters attend school by virtue of a free and/or affordable education and beyond school, they have access to lifelong learning, enjoyment, and entertainment through cultural institutions such as museums, history centers, national
parks, and the public library.

The Trustees of the Boston Public Library epitomized the sentiment in their
report of 1852. The report noted that "the largest possible number of persons
should be induced to read and understand questions . . . going down to the very
foundations of social order . . . which we as a people are constantly required
to decide and do decide, either ignorantly or wisely."[1] The librarian fulfills
the essential role of helping these persons to "decide" wisely on matters of
representative government and all aspects of life in a democracy.

How is democracy served in a public library on a typical day in 2008? The
public librarian provides the price and place for the nearest GED test to a
high-school drop out. The public library provides cookbooks for a diabetic so
she will stay healthy in spite of a serious condition. The public librarian provides authors, titles, and read-alikes for a Federal Air Marshall, who spends
his working days reading on the plane. The public library provides child cus-
tody forms from the Internet, *Lord of the Flies* for a school assignment, and a
personal or printed lesson on how to obtain a free e-mail account.

These tasks are daily and routine but they are not small and/or incon-
sequential. Each one is a step toward personal agency, independence, self-
actualization for otherwise marginalized people or those bowling alone. Maybe
some, most, or all of these tasks can theoretically be accomplished at home,
the office or with a best friend, however what other public institution is prepared with the resources and the staff to help people of all ages and abilities in
these diverse endeavors? This public librarian has performed these services in
one day, and thus coped with literacy, education, health, reading needs, and
life and death. How does a human rights perspective inform the daily actions
of a librarian?

We try here in the sixtieth anniversary year of the Universal Declaration of
Human Rights[2] to provide a context that will help new librarians see how their
work is part of a different way of looking at human capabilities and promise.
We honor the 2008 theme of "dignity and justice for all of us" that reinforces
the vision of the Universal Declaration of Human Rights as a commitment to
universal dignity and justice.

CONNECTING THE HOPE FOR HUMAN RIGHTS TO LIBRARIANSHIP AND DEMOCRACY

"Where, after all, do universal human rights begin? In small places, close to
home—so close and so small that they cannot be seen on any maps of the
world. Yet they are the world of the individual person; the neighborhood he
lives in; the school or college he attends; the factory, farm, or office where
he works. Such are the places where every man, woman, and child seeks
equal justice, equal opportunity, equal dignity without discrimination. Unless
these rights have meaning there, they have little meaning anywhere. Without
concerted citizen action to uphold them close to home, we shall look in vain
for progress in the larger world."

—Eleanor Roosevelt

For many years the role of librarians in advancing "deliberative democracy" has been a central feature of the way librarians have characterized our work life as we have noted above and has been discussed at length in the recent American Library Association monograph, *Libraries and Democracy: The Cornerstones of Liberty.*[3]

But this is a time that global issues such as climate change and ocean death demand that people look beyond borders. This is a time to step back and see that serving democracy, while an important component in the way librarians deliver service, is only part of a larger world view that is informed by human rights and that enlarges and expands the scope of our practice. By adopting a human rights perspective librarians also adopt a mode of practice that rejects the idea of professional neutrality. As Eleanor Roosevelt observed in the quote at the start of this section, human rights start in small places, close to home.

Librarians cannot be neutral in their practice of librarianship. The stance of neutrality is a myth, a code word, as Myles Horton of Highlander once noted, "for the existing system."[4] For example, the American Library Association states its commitment to the Freedom to Read:

> The freedom to read is essential to our democracy. It is continuously under attack. Private groups and public authorities in various parts of the country are working to remove or limit access to reading materials, to censor content in schools, to label "controversial" views, to distribute lists of "objectionable" books or authors, and to purge libraries.[5]

In this statement, librarians profess to be advocates for the minority, the opposition, and the unpopular and difficult voices. Performing this duty may well place us as adversaries in an arena with our own "democratic" government.

Those aspects of librarianship that commit librarians to serve democracy and human rights are what make the discipline essential to the survival of the human spirit. We assert that this commitment does not permit the librarian to be neutral. On this point Jensen, speaking at the Texas Library Association, was clear: "A claim to neutrality means simply that one isn't taking a position on that distribution of power and its consequences, which is a passive acceptance of the existing distribution. That is a political choice."[6] The political part comes in when librarians take our role seriously, and when we support democratic principles that may not be those of the democratic state. For example, African Americans were denied the right to read in public libraries in the segregated South. A librarian truly committed to the Freedom to Read would have ignored Jim Crow Laws in 1953. This is an example of when the rule within the democracy (Jim Crow Laws) should have been defied.

Writing now in a time of endless war, we are prompted to think back on how the ideal of democracy has been used to promote repressive government goals in the United States. Woodrow Wilson, in asserting that those who opposed World War I would have to sacrifice civil liberties, made much the same arguments as those that were used by George W. Bush to put forth the Uniting and Strengthening America by Providing Appropriate Tools Required to Intercept and Obstruct Terrorism Act of 2001 (USAPATRIOT Act). Wilson supported passage of the Espionage Act of 1917 that aimed to quell antiwar sentiment and actions. He also oversaw the Palmer Raids (1918–1921) on suspected communists carried out by Attorney General Palmer and the Justice Department in response to the Red Scare. Many librarians in U.S. libraries acted as "good citizens," and collaborated in the censorship of German materials during World War I.[7]

By contrast in the post-9/11 United States, the American Library Association passed the "Resolution Reaffirming the Principles of Intellectual Freedom in the Aftermath of Terrorist Attacks (2002)." Why did U.S. librarians move from a stance of accepting governmental speech suppression in 1918 to their opposition to aspects of the USAPATRIOT Act in 2002?

When we review the many government-initiated attacks on free speech in the twentieth century, we realize that the ideals of democracy librarians embrace today are often different than the "democracy" promoted by the government at the local, state, or federal levels. Joyce Latham's dissertation on the American public library and the left-led CIO, a case study of the Chicago Public Library (1929–1952), examines the involvement of librarians who challenged the cultural hegemony dominant within the library profession that lead to the profession's commitment to intellectual freedom and a stronger identification with diverse service populations.[8] The Chicago Public Library was the first public institution to issue an intellectual freedom policy (1936) and Latham demonstrates how connections among the staff of the Chicago Public Library, Des Moines Public Library, and John Chancellor of ALA's Adult Education committee were probable influences.[9]

The banning of the *Grapes of Wrath* in 1938–1939 was a defining moment for the profession. The fire was lit by poet Stanley Kunitz, who went on to become the poet laureate of the United States. Kunitz, at the time editor of *Wilson Library Bulletin*, pointed out that the Kern County (CA) County Commissioners who ordered the *Grapes of Wrath* removed from the county libraries likely had the fruit growers' interests in mind (over the migrant workers' labor organizing interests) rather than outrage over the purported "obscenity." We like to imagine the librarians of the late 1930s recognized the literary and social importance of Steinbeck's work (he won the Nobel Prize for Literature in 1962) when they protested the banning of this title. Taken together—the power of Steinbeck's book, the Library Bill of Rights (LBR) drafted by Forrest Spaulding in Des Moines, Iowa (1938), and the LBR's adoption by ALA in 1939—we have the moment defining modern librarianship as a profession committed to intellectual freedom and the right to read over governmental dictates.[10]

The ideal of democracy was used to justify political goals during and after the Second World War. A series of government actions put security issues, as perceived by politicians and bureaucrats, ahead of civil rights. Investigations by the House Un-American Activities/Dies Committee (1938–1944), the Smith Act (Alien Registration Act 1940), propaganda distributed by the Office of War Information, Executive Order 9066 (detention of Japanese citizens, 1942), and Executive Order 9835 (Truman's loyalty program 1947)—all placed security issues above democratic principles, as discussed in Stone's *Perilous Times: Free Speech in Wartime*.[11] As director of the U.S. Office of Facts and Figures, Archibald MacLeish, also Librarian of Congress, both prevented foreign propaganda from reaching the public and propagated on behalf of America and the allied cause. While librarians have been good at supporting the idealized democracy that responded to government directives, it has been more of a challenge for librarians when those directives actually fly in the face of democratic principles. Adult educator, John M. Chancellor resigned from the American Library Association Headquarters staff in 1942 partly because he was unhappy at the direction of ALA in wartime.[12] He wrote of democracy:

> Is democracy something we have really achieved in America, or is it a developing infant that must now either begin to grow or remain anaemic or die? Do we realize that a major part of this "defense" of democracy is in the last analysis a defense against ourselves and our own selfish shortsightedness?[13]

Chancellor saw the inherent conflict between support of democratic ideals and librarianship's service to wartime action. Two decades later the profession caught up to Chancellor's recognition of this dissonance and designated him an ALA Honorary Member in 1962. What happened in the next 20 years that moved librarians from supporting government policies to actively working toward the realization of broader and more ethical ideals?

As World War II was in its final months, the blueprint for the United Nations was developed and finalized in San Francisco in 1945. Strong support for human rights was expressed in the UN Charter Preamble that stated, "We the peoples of the United Nations [are] determined—to reaffirm faith in fundamental human rights, in the dignity and worth of the human person, in the equal rights of men and women and of nations large and small." Article 68 of the Charter required: "The Economic and Social Council shall set up commissions in economic and social fields and for the promotion of human rights, . . . " The Commission on Human Rights, chaired by Eleanor Roosevelt, drafted an international bill of human rights and based its work on a UNESCO philosophers committee.

The Universal Declaration of Human Rights (UDHR)[14] was endorsed on December 10, 1948 by the General Assembly of the United Nations without amendment. Johannes Morsink, who has written the history of the drafting and intent of the UDHR, calls it the moral anchor of a worldwide human rights movement.[15] And in a recent assessment of the impact of the UDHR, Glendon has noted, "what is most encouraging, however, is the proof that men and women of goodwill can make a difference. The imaginations, actions, decisions, sacrifices, and personal examples of countless individuals have helped to bolster the chances of reason and conscience against power and interest."[16]

Did life in the United States change after the UN adopted the UDHR in 1948? Ahead were the House Un-American Activities Committee (Hollywood hearings, blacklisting, 1947–1960); Dennis v. United States on teaching communism as a "clear and present danger" (1951); McCarthyism (1950–1954); Brown versus the Board of Education of Topeka, Kansas (1954); "the Silent Generation" of the 1950s; the Montgomery Bus Boycott (1955); COINTELPRO (secret FBI actions against civil rights, antiwar and communist threats (1956–1971); Operation CHAOS, Lyndon Johnson's CIA internal espionage (1969–1974); and the Nixon "enemies list" (1970). Those beginning to work as librarians should review histories of how the profession confronted these challenges to democracy and human rights.

The revised Library Bill of Rights (1948), the "Statement on Labeling" (1951), the "Freedom to Read Statement," and the "Overseas Library Statement" (1953) are clear indications of the stands made by the American Library Association against threats to collection development and intellectual freedom during the onset of the Cold War.[17]

These actions by librarians were taken because many members of the profession recognized that some politicians such as Joseph McCarthy subverted the ideal of democratic government in ways that threatened the civic and human rights of citizens. And in this recognition, because it is the nature of librarianship to be intimately connected with the flow of information, access to it, and the politics within, some librarians recognized they had to give up neutrality. They became lonely heroes. Librarians among those we call heroes have lost their jobs, their reputations, and their lives by promoting access to all materials by banned people, and access to banned materials for all people.[18] Some like Lucy Randolph Mason and Hilda Hulbert, librarians at the Highlander Folk School in Monteagle, Tennessee, could not help seeing the connections between libraries, information, and social justice. In 1935 Hulbert, who was shot in the ankle while walking with striking textile workers, wrote these words to the Southern Field Director of ALA: "Crying for education and information and contact with the great army of workers in the same situation, the southern worker needs books as never before, and this is a great challenge to me."[19] We also point out that sometimes 10, sometimes 20, and sometimes 50 years later the deeds of many of these brave librarians have been recognized and honored.

We librarians have opportunities like no other profession also to be powerful human rights advocates by performing our work mindful of the information barriers we break down with every open library door. Michael Gorman, a past president of the American Library Association, has written: "The ethical quandary that faces each librarian devoted to equity of library service is the degree to which he or she should work in the wider societal and political context to bring about changes that will narrow the library divide."[20] We believe that as we librarians grow in understanding of the importance of a human rights perspective in our work, we will lead the world to end information inequities.

ACCEPTANCE OF A HUMAN RIGHTS PARADIGM IN LIBRARIANSHIP

After viewing the constraints of trying to be democratic without being illegal given the pressures placed on the profession by the politics of state and national government, we begin to see where "neutrality" is not an option, and oppositional action is required. As the world becomes flat and flatter, we can look to an international recognition of the essential human rights of all peoples, and fold our work as librarians into this modern world and embrace the UDHR as an overarching set of principles, a new paradigm, within which democracy falls.

The UDHR is made up of a Preamble and thirty Articles. It is beyond the scope of this introductory chapter on librarianship and democracy to discuss the connections that exist between *each* Article and library practice (these connections do exist and are being developed by the authors for a larger project), but by way of illustration we touch on Articles 7, 12, and 19 to demonstrate the expansive world view that librarians embrace when moving to a human rights paradigm as a foundation for library service. How have librarians in the United States incorporated human rights precepts into library canon and practice? The policies of librarianship as adopted by the Association and codified in the American Library Association policy manual were developed as a result of profession-wide discussion and debate. After 1948 human rights has become a broadly accepted world view and we see a gradual internalization of human rights principles in many venues of human action.

Article 7

All are equal before the law and are entitled without any discrimination to equal protection of the law. All are entitled to equal protection against any discrimination in violation of this Declaration and against any incitement to such discrimination.

Libraries in the south provided little or no service to African-Americans and were segregated until the Civil Rights movement of the 1950s–1960s. The American Library Association did not take a stand against segregation among state chapters until 1963. Our national association met in cities where some of its members could not walk in the front door. Much was made of the prudent policy of not alienating state chapters who were militantly segregated, as Jim Crow was not a "library issue."

Yet equality of all people was declared a human right in 1948 in the Universal Declaration of Human Rights and some brave librarians in the south also stood up for civil rights.[21] Juliette Hampton Morgan left her position at the Montgomery, Alabama Carnegie library after months of suffering angry taunts and a cross burning on her lawn by those who were enraged by her letters and actions in favor of civil rights before and during the Montgomery bus boycott. While her director and the library board did not yield to pressure from the mayor and other segregationists to fire her, she was asked not to profess any more public support for the civil rights movement, and the mayor threatened to withhold municipal funding for the library. Morgan died soon after and may have taken her own life after struggling with hatred and ostracism from friends and family because she pointed out the injustices of segregation in letters and street action. The White Citizen's Council burned a cross on her lawn in Montgomery because she stood up to the injustices of segregation. Is it not fitting that half a century later the main city library has recently been renamed in her honor?

In 1959 another Alabama librarian, Emily Wheelock Reed, was pressured to remove *A Rabbit's Wedding*, by Garth Williams, from the state library collection. State Senator E.O. "Big Ed" Eddins believed the children's' book to be pro-integrationist brainwashing because one bunny was black and the other white. The press made light of the controversy but Reed's job and the library budget went under attack and she left the state for another job shortly afterwards.

In 1950, Ruth Brown, of the Bartlesville, Oklahoma Public Library, was fired after 30 years, ostensibly because the library owned *The Nation, The New Republic,* and *Soviet Russia Today,* but actually because of her work with the Congress of Racial Equality (CORE).[22] Brown and her friends established the

Committee on the Practice of Democracy in Bartlesville in 1946. This was the first CORE affiliate group south of the Mason-Dixon Line. In March 2007, the library hosted a celebration of Ruth Brown's life and unveiled a bronze bust.

Librarianship caught up to the human rights examples of librarians like Morgan, Reed, and Brown who defied the laws of their states to speak out for the right of all people to read. Though lawbreakers in their time, we have seen that their commitment to human rights transcended unfair and outdated state laws.

Today *Equitable Access to Information and Library Services* and *Diversity* are two of the seven Key Action Areas of the American Library Association. New librarians will find the efforts made during the second half of the twentieth century to emphasize service to diverse communities very much in accord with the world focus on human rights as outlined in Article 7.[23]

Article 12

No one shall be subjected to arbitrary interference with his privacy, family, home or correspondence, nor to attacks upon his honour and reputation. Everyone has the right to the protection of the law against such interference or attacks.

In matters of privacy librarians have taken principled stands. Zoia Horn, a reference librarian at Bucknell University, was held at the Dauphine County Jail for 20 days in 1971. She refused to testify at the trial of antiwar activists known as the Harrisburg Seven about their library use. She prepared a statement to the judge on freedom of thought, freedom of association, and freedom of speech although was never able to utter it. Horn's unwillingness to compromise her commitment to privacy as a library principle in deference to government pressure and without any support from ALA at the time has been recognized by her designation as the Robert B. Downs Intellectual Freedom Award winner and having a California Intellectual Freedom Award named after her.

Librarians' actions to protect privacy reverberate in the latest librarian defense of democracy and human rights. In one instance, an FBI agent visited the library and wanted the names of all library patrons who borrowed *Bin Laden: The Man Who Declared War on America*. The librarian, Joan Airoldi, challenged the "fishing expedition" and demanded a subpoena. She said, "Libraries are a haven where people should be able to seek whatever information they want to pursue without any threat of government intervention."[24]

It happened again—when the FBI served the Library Connection in Connecticut a national security letter to gain access to patron records without a court order, demanding silence and secrecy.[25] In *Doe v. Gonzales* librarians' protection of patron privacy was upheld. The American Library Association Council passed a resolution honoring their courage with these words:

RESOLVED, that the American Library Association strongly commend the stand of the Connecticut John Does—George Christian, Barbara Bailey,

Peter Chase, and Janet Nocek—in their successful legal battle to defend the privacy of library user records; and be it further

RESOLVED, that the American Library Association condemn the use of National Security Letters to demand any library records; and be it further

RESOLVED, that the American Library Association reaffirm its opposition to sections of the USA PATRIOT Act that infringe on library patrons' ability to access library services without privacy safeguards.

Adopted by the ALA Council, unanimously, on Wednesday, June 28, 2006.

The American Library Association has a strong history of defending privacy. Key actions include the first ALA Code of Ethics (1939); the Policy on the Confidentiality of Library Records (1971, 1986); revisions and updates relating to Privacy: An Interpretation of the Library Bill of Rights (2002), and the *Privacy Toolkit* (2005). The *Privacy Toolkit* assists libraries and librarians in understanding privacy and its relationship to information access in libraries, and provides action tools that apply to their local circumstances. The justification for privacy is based on the First and Fourth Amendments but also references the UDHR.[26]

Article 19

Everyone has the right to freedom of opinion and expression; this right includes freedom to hold opinions without interference and to seek, receive, and impart information and ideas through any media and regardless of frontiers.

Essential to a democracy that operates in an environment of free choice is a free press, freedom of speech, and a place to collect, organize, and store all this discourse. The American Library Association's "Free Expression: An Interpretation of the Library Bill of Rights" cites Article 19 of the Universal Declaration of Human Rights and states:

Freedom of expression is an inalienable human right and the foundation for self-government. Freedom of expression encompasses the freedoms of speech, press, religion, assembly, and association, and the corollary right to receive information.

Activism in the 1960s puts librarians in the position of defending open access to information and democratic values in opposition to another war. Abbot-Hoduski[27] describes the situation when Joan Bodger resigned her position at the Missouri State Library Commission in 1969 after writing a letter to the Columbia (MO) *Daily Tribune*, saying she would include the *Free Press* in a display of student newspapers in the State Library. The newspaper included a cartoon that, in opposition to the war in Vietnam, depicted the rape of the Statue of Liberty by a policeman.

In 1996 Louisiana high school librarian Deloris Wilson at West Monroe High School was ordered to remove *Heartbreak and Roses: Real Life Stories of Troubled Love; Gays In or Out of the Military; Everything You Need to*

Know About Incest; and *Everything You Need to Know About Abstinence* from her library shelves. After protesting she was then told to remove all books with sexual content. Her response was to pull 200 books, including several Bibles. Wilson was eventually named plaintiff in a suit by ACLU against the Ouachita Parish School Board. In 2001 she received the Robert B. Downs Intellectual Freedom Award and the PEN/Newman's Own First Amendment Award.

Perhaps the most widely publicized case of a librarian defending the people's right to know in this century has been librarian Ann Sparanese's defense of Michael Moore's book, *Stupid White Men and Other Excuses for the State of the Nation*. A *Salon* writer observed: "When Michael Moore's publisher insisted he rewrite his new book to be less critical of President Bush, it took an outraged librarian to get it back in the stores."[28] In 2003 the American Library Association honored Ann Sparanese with the Futas Catalyst for Change Award.

These are but three examples of librarians standing up and risking jobs and livelihood for the right of their patrons to read freely. The PEN American Center and the Newman's Own Foundation has presented its PEN/Newman's Own award to Wilson and other librarians who fought to safeguard freedom of expression through the written word. The ALA Office of Intellectual Freedom sponsors banned books week, provides programming to support intellectual freedom defense, honors defenders of intellectual freedom and develops, recommends, and maintains a total intellectual freedom program for the American Library Association.

By reviewing our history we see librarians' defense of intellectual freedom can be viewed within the framework of the UDHR. In 1990–1991 Article 19 of the UDHR was added to the ALA Policy Manual as Policy 58.4. In 1996–1997 the Association added Policy 58.4.1, "Human Rights and Freedom of Expression" stating "The ALA shall work with other associations and institutions that belong to IFLA to develop positions and programmatic plans of action in support of human rights and freedom of expression."

A HUMAN RIGHTS PERSPECTIVE FOR LIBRARIANS IN THE TWENTY-FIRST CENTURY

We believe that librarians in the twenty-first century will gradually adopt a comprehensive human rights perspective as the framework for characterizing our values.[29] Toni Samek, honored with the first annual *Library Journal* teaching award[30] is an advocate for the importance of human rights to the work of librarians. Samek notes in her monograph, *Librarianship and Human Rights: A Twenty-First Century Guide*:

> Historically, the profession's claim to library neutrality has drawn a line between professional issues such as literacy and so-called non-library issues such as war. A similar line has categorically divided library advocacy and library activism. This book strongly supports the international library movement known in the 21st century as critical librarianship,

which aims to blur these lines and to expose them as both counter-intuitive and counter-productive to the development of more humanistic (and less techno-managerial) library and information work.[31]

In this essay we have asserted that as librarians we operate under great truths, bills of rights, ethics statements, mission statements, and promises of quality service for pure democracy, but we fall short much of the time. Because, like real estate developers who will always want the open space until it isn't open space anymore, the pressure to ignore or slight or skimp or forget and/or avoid our responsibilities as agents of information rights, human rights, is inexorable. It is so much easier to stretch the budget by closing the doors early, thus cutting off the full-time working people. It is so much cheaper to avoid worrying about bilingual services or collections for that minority who don't come in to use our services anyway. It is sometimes worrisome to buy the materials your GLBT (gay, lesbian, bisexual, and transgender) patrons might find necessary, because you know you have other patron populations who will be vocal and unhappy with such use of their tax money.

If librarians don't keep touching base, looking back, remembering the big picture of our main purpose, which is to keep information freely flowing, take tax dollars and give our communities (in the broadest sense) what they want and what they need, we will lose it all. We will overdue fine our public until they don't dare come in, buy the books our loudest patrons clamor for until we have created a library just for the few and the loudest. We will purchase the titles vendors tell us to (who are in turn told what to publish by their corporate HQs), accept only the Web sites our corporate controlled filters filter, and hire the library staff that gets along with us.

We have written this essay from the vantage that a world view with a human rights perspective will move librarians from a stance of neutrality to work passionately on behalf of human capabilities. The coming global information society will extend the range of our practice as defined at the World Summit on the Information Society.[32]

Encounters are just beginning between human rights activists and the global information society agenda and it will be up to librarians to activate service with a human rights perspective for all people.[33] By summarizing the path of librarianship from support of democracy to support of human rights, we hope we have helped to suggest new directions for library workers. We are in agreement with Toni Samek and Mark Rosenzweig looking to a more humanistic librarianship grounded in an unfettered cultural record, with respect for cultural diversity and opposition to the commodification of information.[34]

SUGGESTIONS FOR FURTHER READING

Buschman, John E. *Dismantling the Public Sphere: Situating and Sustaining Librarianship in the Age of the New Public Philosophy*. Westport, CT: Libraries Unlimited, 2003.

Information for Social Change 25 (Summer, 2007), entire issue.

Kranich, Nancy. *Libraries and Democracy: The Cornerstones of Liberty*. Chicago: ALA, 2001.

Knuth, Rebecca. *Burning Books and Leveling Libraries: Extremist Violence and Cultural Destruction.* Westport, CT: Greenwood, 2006.

Robbins, Louise S. *Censorship and the American Public Library: The American Library Association's Response to Threats to Intellectual freedom: 1939–1969.* Westport, CT: Greenwood, 1996.

Chapter 4

Information Seeking

Donald O. Case

INTRODUCTION AND SOME DEFINITIONS

The library field has more than its share of jargon. Visitors to libraries do not always know what we are talking about when we speak of "serials," "periodicals," "ILL," and "subject headings." Similarly, when librarians and information scientists study what goes on in libraries, they have their own special terms for the activities and results they study. "Evaluation," for example, is a term that libraries share with many other institutions (schools, governments, businesses) to refer to the systematic study of a service or program. Research may be conducted in order to judge how an activity of the library (e.g., a summer reading program for teens or an electronic catalog) is serving the needs of library users, how satisfied those users are with the service or program, how much it costs, and so forth. Evaluative research is used to guide funding decisions and shares commonalities with what I will discuss in this chapter—which is something called "information seeking," or "information behavior."[1]

You are probably thinking (and rightly so) "Aha! More jargon!" "Information seeking" is a term that became popular several decades ago to describe the common human cycle of needing, looking for, choosing, and using information of some kind. Such behavior is essential to human existence. Anticipating your upcoming vacation, you may decide to visit another country, and therefore look for information about airline schedules, ticket prices, hotel and tour options. Or, you might have an assignment from school or work to investigate some topic and write a report about it—leading you to visit the library and to search the Internet.

Information seeking is a behavior so commonplace that it is generally not an object of concern until time pressure makes it so. If we are making a major decision (e.g., buying a house) or completing a task with a strict deadline (e.g., writing a report for work or school), we will be in information seeking mode: talking to others, searching the Web, reading magazines, watching the news, and so on. We may do everything we can to satisfy our desire for input, until either our need is satisfied or we run out of time. More commonly, it is the latter, as the demand for "information" is usually elastic—there is always more that one could know. After our need is met (or we give up) we return to a more passive state of information seeking, at least as regards the object of our earlier curiosity.

Consider also cases in which getting the information does not concern an immediate task like buying or writing something. Our daily life is full of instances in which we become interested in learning more about a topic after accidentally encountering some bit of information about it. This sort of curiosity, unmotivated by an immediate goal, is a common aspect of human life.

Librarians have been primarily concerned with searches that involve library collections and services, yet examples of information seeking are infinite and extend well beyond the library into workplace settings and all aspects of everyday life. One would think that the term "information seeking," as broad and vague as it is, would be "enough," yet in recent years scholars have added an even broader term—"information behavior"—that takes in an even wider range of human phenomena, such as cases in which we accidentally encounter information that we were not seeking or investigations of cases in which people are actually trying to avoid information. Such subtleties are not always relevant to everyday practice in libraries, yet they are clearly related. The term "information behavior" arose because scholars have moved away from a preoccupation with "library use and user studies" and its emphasis on institutional sources and searches, and toward a focus on how individuals encounter and make sense of their environment. For the purposes of this chapter, I will avoid the more esoteric topics (like avoidance and sense-making), and stick to those that are usually considered in the use of libraries and other, formal, information sources like the World Wide Web.

Before we go on to consider what information seeking is and what research on information behavior can tell us, I will summarize what I have said thus far by giving you some brief definitions:

- An *information need* is a recognition that your knowledge is inadequate to satisfy a goal that you have.
- *Information seeking* is a conscious effort to acquire information in response to a need or gap in your knowledge.
- *Information behavior* encompasses information seeking as well as the totality of other unintentional or passive behaviors (such as glimpsing or encountering information), as well as purposive behaviors that do not involve seeking, such as actively avoiding information.

THE IMPLICATIONS OF THE WEB

There is no doubt that the emergence of the World Wide Web has altered both the way that people seek information and the way that libraries (and other institutions) operate. In fact, the Internet, of which the Web is one part, could serve as a metaphor for information behavior and the way our view of it has changed. Just think back to a time before the World Wide Web was available in our homes, offices, and libraries. The kinds of information available (at least in terms of its meaning) were pretty much the same as today; however, much of it was found only in a physical format—in individual minds, paper documents, filing cabinets, etc. Because it was divided by source, by location, by person, and/or by channel, it was not always easily located or examined. Getting ready for a trip, we might listen to the weather forecast on the radio, read about a destination in a travel guide, call hotels to make reservations, telephone an airline to learn departure times and fares, visit a travel agent to pick up a ticket, and so on. Yet now it is possible to find all that travel-related information on a single Web site. In some cases many different channels of communication have collapsed into just one.

One implication of the flowering of the Web is that more of us "browse" for information rather than doing formal searches, as we used to do in libraries and files. This is because information is more abundant, less "segregated," and—in many cases—not as carefully indexed or cataloged. With the power to search for words and phrases in documents and on Web sites, information seekers tend to simply type some keywords into a search engine (e.g., Google) and see what comes up—then browse through the results until they find something that satisfies them. Such changes in the way that people look for information have spawned much new research and development.

Another implication of the Web is that it has led to a misguided notion that most documents (e.g., books and magazines) and certain institutions (e.g., publishers and libraries) are going to disappear. Librarians strongly disagree with this notion, and not out of self interest: it is because they have been hearing these predictions (e.g., "the paperless office") since the 1950s, because they see the problems people have in finding information in this new environment, and because the reality is that people still prefer physical documents. For many of us, the first thing we do with an electronic document is to print it and, despite years of marketing, reading a book of any length on a screen has failed to become popular. The ways in which computers and networks have changed the way people find information has contributed to a new appreciation for investigation of information seeking—which have documented the kinds of behaviors and trends that librarians see on the job everyday.

A BIT OF THEORY

I have said that librarians observe information seeking everyday, and that they often conduct formal evaluations of their services in order to make decisions about improving them. All that is on the practical level, but why do people seek information in the ways that they do? That calls for a theory.[2]

One commonly used theory is the so-called "Principle of Least Effort"[3] (hereafter, "PLE"), sometimes referred to as "The Law of Least Effort" or "Zipf's Law." It originally appeared in a book by George Zipf[4] of Harvard University, whose area of expertise was what we would now call Linguistics. Indeed, the inspiration for the theory came to Zipf through patterns he saw in language usage, such as that in novels. He initially conducted statistical analysis of word usage in documents and later analyzed other artifacts of human activity, such as the census and other government records. Zipf intended to develop a broad explanation for human activity that used "resources" of any kind: tools, words, time, money, etc.

The PLE's premise is that in performing tasks (e.g., writing or speaking) individuals adopt a course of action that will expend the probable least average of their work—the least effort. An example would be how we behave when we sit down to fill out annual tax forms. If the taxes are complex enough and the work takes long enough, what we would observe at the end is a pattern among the documents used: nearest the seated taxpayer would be the completed forms and most important records (e.g., a statement of taxes withheld from wages); a little further away might be other important records (e.g., check registers) and further away still other records (e.g., credit card bills); further away yet might be instruction sheets, tax tables, unused tax forms, etc. All of these documents would form an arc around the taxpayer, with the most-used documents closest at hand, and the least-used further away. We *could* have kept them in some other order (alphabetical, or by category) but instead, we tend put the most-used items close at hand as we use them, while the less-used items get pushed off to the periphery. So we end up with an arrangement that is governed by ease of use, not by some logical scheme of organization. It is simply "easier" that way.

Another example might be your personal files. Are they neatly alphabet-ized by topic (". . . car insurance, car repair, cell phone contract, credit card bills . . . ")? Or, like many people, do you have a file drawer in which the files you use most frequently are in the front of the drawer, and the ones you hardly ever use toward the back? In fact, the PLE is sometimes called the "80/20 Rule" because in so many situations about 20 percent of files account for 80 percent of the total usage of all files. Similarly, about 20 percent of a library's collec-tion accounts for 80 percent of its circulated items, just as about 20 percent of English words account for 80 percent of all words used in most documents. In this way it is similar to other "power laws," like Pareto's Law regarding income distributions (i.e., most societies have a just few high earners, and a whole lot of others who make much less money).

The implications of the PLE for information seeking are many. For instance, we tend to be very habitual about our sources of information. A number of empirical studies have found that as knowledge of a source and its potential contents and capabilities increases, the use of that source tends to increase. That is, we tend to return to the sources that we have used in the past in strong preference to trying out new sources of information. For example, a common challenge for academic librarians these days is to try to persuade undergradu-ates to try using something other than Google for all their academic research.

Zipf's theory has been used in many fields, yet it is particularly applicable to libraries and information work, and especially relevant to studying the *lack* of use of libraries and library materials; the reality is that some library resources are judged to require too much effort, especially when compared to a simple (but often suboptimal) use of an Internet search engine. As many librarians believe an important aspect of their job is to teach users to be more thorough about their searches for information, the tendency for students and others to do "quick and dirty" research is frustrating. However, consider the likely viewpoint of a teen-aged student: if I can "get by" with doing less, why not? In fact we are all guilty of "getting by," and that is the reality that Zipf noted in his work; when we believe that it really matters, we can behave in highly organized ways and spend scads of time accomplishing a task to perfection but to behave that way all the time would exhaust us; therefore, over the long haul, we tend to minimize the amount of resources required to reach a satisfactory (and typically *not* optimal) goal. Thus, the PLE predicts that seekers will often minimize the effort required to obtain information, even if it means accepting a lower quality or quantity of information.

In this sense PLE is rather different than the "cost-benefit" viewpoint often taken in economics, in which humans are viewed as rational calculators of "trade-offs" in allocating resources; yes people may behave that way in special situations (playing competitive games, making professional decisions, or in buying expensive items like houses), but we do not normally have the time or inclination to calculate every aspect of our behavior. Rather, we simply have a tendency to expend less effort whenever possible.

Of course, there are many other theories that might apply to information-seeking situations. However, the Principle of Least Effort is a general, well-established, and pragmatic one that seems especially applicable to information seeking.

WHAT HAVE WE LEARNED ABOUT INFORMATION SEEKING?

You will see in the next few paragraphs that the Principle of Least Effort also characterizes some aspects of information seeking. After about 30 years of investigations that assumed that people were mostly rational and optimal about their search for, and use of, information, librarians and researchers began to take a different view. During the 1970s and 1980s commentaries by Dr. Brenda Dervin[5] (now at Ohio State University) pointed out that formal systems for disseminating information often failed—especially for the average person. Around this time several studies documented that even highly trained scientists, engineers, and managers were often unsystematic about their information seeking. Dervin, along with Professor Tom Wilson[6] (of the University of Sheffield), were foremost among many who advocated new ways of thinking about and studying information seeking. Following are a few generalizations about what we have learned regarding information behavior.

For many tasks and decisions in life, people tend to settle for the first satisfactory solution to a problem, rather than the best solution. For input, we tend to rely on easily available sources of information, such as that provided by nearby people. We often fail to seek out more "objective" information and do not always use it when it is available.

Correspondingly, we use formal sources rarely, instead gathering and applying information from informal sources, chiefly friends and family, throughout our lives. We do not rely on institutions like schools and libraries for most of our information, partly because what they teach us is generic and outside of a context in which it can be useful. Facts that are disseminated out of context tend to be ignored, as people cannot form a complete picture of their meaning and implications.

"Having information" is not the same as "being informed." Most formal systems of information distribution (such as schools, libraries, and the news media) are predicated on the idea that "more information is always better," yet increasing the flow of information does not always result in an informed person, partly because too much information leads to overload and thence to deliberate ignoring of additional data. For most of the situations we face there is not a problem getting enough information but rather with interpreting and understanding what information we already have.

Information seeking is a dynamic process. That is, our perception of what information we need often shifts in the course of a search. Satisfying one information need may also give rise to other needs. Information seeking is rarely a simple, linear process that comes to complete fruition.

Information cannot substitute for many human needs, nor even facilitate all of them. People may want information in order to learn or understand, yet they are much more likely to need physical and psychological necessities of daily life, such as food, shelter, clothing, money, and love. While we would like to believe that "teaching someone to fish" will make someone forever self-sufficient, the reality is that sometimes you still need to give them a fish.

Institutions like medical clinics, libraries, and government agencies are prone to giving "canned" responses that are not always useful to the people who visit them. This is because institutions focus on finding solutions to problems and favor providing an answer of some type to every request they receive. Yet the answers provided will always be limited by the resources and language of the given agency. Information systems such as libraries or broadcasters define themselves in terms of the units they disseminate: in the case of libraries, this is books, journals, or Web sites; in the case of broadcasters, it is programs, ads, or public service announcements. But what individuals need are not always these things; rather, they may need responses, solutions, instructions, ideas, friendships, and so forth. If the user wants something more than a book or a fact—e.g., reassurance or a deeper understanding—this is unlikely to be forthcoming, and the user may go away dissatisfied.

Formal information systems are always somewhat behind the curve, as the needs of the public are constantly changing—and may always be vague and ambiguous, as well. So we continue to come up with our own answers to our own unique, unpredictable questions, without resorting to formal information systems. At times those answers might even come from aspects of popular culture, rather than books, newspapers, or experts: TV programs, songs on the radio, Internet mailing list discussions, and so forth, sometimes address our information needs or provide inspiration for solving our problems.

Finally—as I just mentioned "problems"—I should add that not all information seeking is driven by the perception of a problem or of uncertainty. Some information behavior is truly creative or serendipitous, sparked by some internal or external event that piques our interest, perhaps for unconscious reasons.

CONCLUSION

I have made the case that information seeking is an ubiquitous human activity. It continues to be an object of both professional concern and scholarly investigation, as the information landscape shifts in wake of the phenomenal success of the World Wide Web. Librarians are on the forefront of efforts to provide users of libraries (particularly students[7]), with the kind of skills and knowledge that will allow them to become effective seekers of information. In a world in which a major problem is *too much* information from *too many* sources, libraries play an important role in filtering and guiding users to the answers to their questions.

SUGGESTIONS FOR FURTHER READING

Case, Donald O. *Looking for Information: A Survey of Research on Information Seeking, Needs, and Behavior*, 2nd ed. New York: Academic Press/Elsevier, 2006.

Chelton, Mary K. and Colleen Cool (eds.). *Youth Information-seeking Behavior: Theories, Models and Issues*. Lanham, MD: Scarecrow Press, 2004.

Fisher, Karen E., Sandra Erdelez, and Lynne E. F. McKechnie (eds.). *Theories of Information Behavior*. Medford, NJ: Information Today, 2005.

Chapter 5

Careers and Environments

Laura Kane

Everyone has a secret image in his or her head of what librarians look like. They are simply afraid to admit it for fear of being pummeled by one. This is not to say, however, that the image is the same for everyone. There are so many varieties of the "stereotypical librarian" now that the phrase is almost contradictory. There really *is* no stereotype anymore. There was a time when librarians routinely donned stalwart armor and took up their weapons in the crusade against hair buns, wire-rimmed glasses, and the command "shush." As a result, librarians in the media morphed from shy to bold, from dowdy to chic, from androgynous to sexy. Now there is a crusade against librarians in tight skirts, lacy bras, and 4-inch heels. You just can't win.

Visual image, though, is not a big issue here. Like professionals in any career, librarianship is open to anyone regardless of personality, body type, gender, religion, political affiliation, or undergarment preference. The bigger issue becomes evident when you hear someone say, "I've always wanted to work in a library because I love to read!" Let me give you some career advice for free: if you're interested in becoming a librarian because you love books, you might consider simply getting a job in a bookstore. Librarianship is not all about books, and librarians don't sit around and read all day.

So what *do* librarians do all day? What types of jobs are available? What is the work environment like? Will this career fit well with my other interests? I hope you will find the answers in the text that follows. Most importantly, you will be pleased to discover that, no matter your particular interests, the library profession holds a place for *you.*

THE ENVIRONMENTS

Before you can understand the types of library jobs available, you must first have some sense of the diverse environments in which librarians work. A library is a library, you say? In some ways, you are correct. Most libraries have similar overarching missions: to provide information to patrons. What differs drastically among the assorted library environments are the answers to these three questions:

What are the demographics of the library's primary clientele?

What is the nature of the information most commonly sought?

Given the answer to these two questions, how does one best orchestrate resources to add value to the organization's mission and advance its agenda?

From there one can determine the best mix of collections, organization, programs, and services to fit the needs of the organization.

Traditional Libraries

In the beginning . . . there were libraries. And those ancient libraries probably weren't a whole heck of a lot different in appearance or purpose from some of the libraries still in existence today. Had there been a library in the Garden of Eden—and who's to say there hadn't been?—it would have had walls surrounding knowledge in some format or other. The walls may have been made of twisting ropes of ivy and the knowledge within may have been in the form of tempting red apples or manuals on the rapid production of fig-leaf clothing; regardless, there would have been some kind of visible structure encasing bits of wisdom within. This is the tradition of the word "library" as we have known it throughout history. Libraries fitting this tradition are still common today. Most have structural units (i.e., walls) built to house and protect the world's knowledge manifested in various formats. The "walls" of today's traditional libraries may be plain, they may be decorated with murals or graffiti, or they may be made of glass or artistic sculptures. The collections within vary from shelves of books to racks of DVDs to computerized databases. But they are still recognizable as "libraries" as we have known them since time began. We will begin with these.

Public Libraries

Who doesn't remember the childhood excitement of getting a first library card, of making careful selections from row upon row of imagined worlds bound between two hard covers, of walking in spaces smelling of dust and fantasy? Who doesn't remember with fondness this almost indescribable draw of the public library? Okay, maybe I'm projecting my warm memories onto your own experiences, but nearly everyone has set foot at one time or another in a public library. This is the type of library environment most people can readily associate with.

Of all library types, public libraries serve the information needs of the widest variety of population groups, including children, students, professionals, the elderly, and all groups in-between. These institutions are normally supported by local, state, or federal monies and have "open door" policies with very few user restrictions. Public libraries strive to provide an eclectic mix of materials for reading, listening, and viewing. Collections may include books, journals, newspapers, magazines, audio recordings, and video recordings. There are also collections for special populations, such as "Talking Books" for the visually impaired or resources in Spanish for Latinos. Materials may be used in-house or checked out free of charge for set periods of time.

Public libraries are known for their success in enriching communities through various programs designed to meet specific needs within the local populations. Did you ever join a summer reading program when you were a kid—reading as many books as you could to get that gilded certificate or that shiny medal? You were desperate to see your name in bold black marker on the "Top Summer Readers" wall. This is an example of a public library program aimed to promote literacy and to teach lifelong learning skills. Other common public library programs include story hours for children, reading clubs, homework help for teens, adult literacy programs, and technology training. Exhibits and lectures on various historical, social, and educational topics are also commonplace in public libraries. Through inventive programming and clever marketing, public libraries are able to make a real difference in community life.

Academic Libraries

A strange semantic phenomenon takes place in the lives of college students—the word "home" is replaced by the word "library." This is because many students spend so much of their time studying at their university or college library that it may as well be called their second home. This is the tradition of the academic library. Commonly referred to as research libraries, they are used by university and college students and faculty as a place for study and research.

The mission of an academic library is to support the curricula of the various educational tracks offered by the college or university and to meet the information and research needs of the students and faculty. These libraries may be large or small, and may serve the needs of a single academic program or of an entire university system. Regardless of size or scope, they typically offer resources in a wide range of formats. There will be materials in the traditional printed format, but there will also be electronic collections of books, journals, and databases accessible through computers on or off campus. Convenience, accessibility, and currency are important issues in an academic library, and if information needs cannot be met locally, the library generally ensures that the needed information will be obtained from another academic institution.

Academic libraries are supported by their parent institutions and use of library materials is generally restricted to those enrolled in academic programs and to those who teach those programs. Collections are closely tied to the teaching curriculum. You will likely find dog-eared copies of *War and Peace* or *Gone With the Wind* in a liberal arts college library, but not so likely in an engineering library. A library supporting an entire university system will naturally offer collections covering a wide scope of subjects.

The acquisition of knowledge through formal channels has been a pursuit of humankind throughout history. Hence, there has always been a need for academic libraries to support this scholarly pursuit. This is not likely to change anytime soon.

Special Libraries

"All libraries are special." Well, of course they are! There are, however, certain libraries that have traditionally been dubbed "Special Libraries" because of the fact that they cover specific disciplines or serve particular groups of people. Included in this category are medical libraries, law libraries, and corporate libraries.

Medical Libraries. Where do you suppose a person goes when he or she leaves a doctor's office with a disease diagnosis but is still plagued with unanswered questions? You may be surprised to learn that people often visit medical libraries to find more information about their conditions. Traditionally, medical libraries serve the information needs of students or professionals in medical schools, hospitals, or clinics. In recent years, the clientele of medical libraries has extended to include consumers. The mission of today's medical libraries, then, depends on the institution it serves. In academic medical centers (a fancy phrase for "medical schools"), libraries provide medical information services to students, faculty, researchers, and physicians in affiliated hospitals. Usually such libraries are open to the public, with some restrictions on the use and circulation of materials. Materials may include any combination of books, journals (in print and electronic formats), and online databases. Hospital libraries, usually much smaller in scale, may offer services and resources only to professional staff (doctors and nurses) or to patients as well. Consumer health libraries typically carry medical literature written specifically for the general lay public. Medical libraries can also be found in various industries such as the biotechnology, insurance, and pharmaceutical industries.

Law Libraries. If you've ever watched *Law & Order* or some similar crime drama, you've heard the actor attorneys spout statements like, "In Kane vs. Townsend, chewing gum while wearing dentures was declared unconstitutional in Kentucky." (I made this up.) In real life, an attorney's career hinges upon his or her ability to locate relevant laws and rulings and to apply them to current cases. Collecting, organizing, and making accessible these vast amounts of legal information is the purpose of law libraries. Law libraries are usually affiliated with law firms, law schools, or courts, and are designed to assist law students, attorneys, judges, and law clerks in finding legal resources. They typically house large collections of federal or state court decisions (in print or electronic format), government agency publications, and other resources related to the legal system.

Corporate Libraries. Corporate libraries exist to support the very specific information needs of companies and businesses. When a CEO yells at a staff meeting, "Find out how Company X is marketing their dandruff shampoo ASAP!!" you can bet the staff will make a beeline to the corporate library. These libraries collect, organize, and disseminate resources that apply directly to a business's ability to remain competitive with other similar businesses. They might offer competitive intelligence research, information analysis, market research, and information retrieval. Today's corporate libraries leverage information to increase their companies' competitive edge in the marketplace.

Most are fairly small in size simply because they have such a narrow subject focus.

School Libraries

Libraries in elementary, middle, and high schools, sometimes called school library media centers or resource centers, are similar to academic libraries in purpose: they exist to support educational programs. The age of the primary patrons, though, drops 10 or 20 years, and the collections reflect the reading levels of the student bodies. They are also similar in purpose to special libraries as they are comparatively small with a narrowly defined purpose. Obviously, literacy is a primary focus of school libraries, and "information literacy" (the ability to derive, make, and share meaning from information) is often an integral part of each school's curriculum. If you ask my 7-year-old son what his favorite subject is, he will respond in one of two ways: "Recess!" (big surprise, right?) or, on better days, "Library." He considers "Library" to be a regular part of his school subjects. I am tickled pink by this, not just because I am a librarian and a Geek with a capital "G," but also because it shows me what a wonderful job the school is doing to integrate the library into daily learning activities.

School libraries are commonly the hub of activity within a school. In addition to housing collections of fiction and nonfiction books, they often function as media centers outfitted with computers and audio-visual equipment and production services. Hence, not only do they promote information literacy, they help to strengthen technology proficiency as well.

"Library 2.0" (Nontraditional) Environments

In order to compete in the information industry and to keep up with changing technologies, libraries have had to "think outside the box." They have done a fantastic job, too. In fact, in some cases the "box" is completely gone. There are libraries today with no walls, no books, no journals, and no print materials of any kind. Adam and Eve would not recognize them as libraries because they bear no resemblance to those "traditional" warehouses of information (not to mention, there are no apples).

There is no agreed-upon name for these nontraditional libraries. They can be called Digital Libraries or Electronic Libraries or Virtual Libraries. I've even heard the term Invisible Libraries. "Library 2.0" is the newest iteration, and doubtless there is another catchy appellation around the corner. Their commonality lies in the format of the information offered to patrons: it is generally all electronic and therefore not restricted by the limitations and boundaries of walls and buildings. Whether the information comes from a database, an electronic journal, or the Web, it's usually in a digital format. Radical, right? Not really. These libraries may *look* new and radical (if you can see them at all), but their purpose is still the same as it has been for centuries: to get the patron or consumer exactly what information he or she wants.

THE JOBS

Now that we have reviewed the various library settings, we can take a peek into the professional lives of the librarians who work in these settings. You will discover that librarians certainly experience their fair share of excitement and adventure in the workplace. Are you surprised? I'm not surprised that you're surprised. Sometimes, when I tell a new acquaintance that I am a librarian, a strangely glazed look appears on the person's face and heavy silence ensues. As if the person were thinking, "Umm . . . how do I respond to that? *Now* what do we talk about?" I watch them squirm for a moment, but most times I decide to "rescue" them by offering little tidbits of information regarding what I actually do all day. They are usually amazed that a librarian's job can actually be exciting and rewarding. In my interactions with colleagues I have discovered that this is quite common. Many people perceive librarianship to be sedate, calm, and even dull. The stereotype roars its head again! In most cases, this perception is inaccurate. "Prove it!" you say. Okay.

In what follows you first find an overview of traditional positions in two areas—public and technical services. Keep in mind that many library positions combine two or more of these functions, and that, depending on the size of the library, you may not be tied town to one specific job type. In fact, in a small library you may find yourself handling a little bit of everything! Following those sections will be a portion about administrative positions for those interested in becoming library leaders. Finally, we will take a look at some "cutting edge" positions.

Public Services Positions

About half of all library positions fall under the broad category of "public services." The word "public" here simply means the primary clientele of the particular library—it could mean the general population of a community, physicians in a hospital system, law students, elementary school students, or corporate executives. The focal word here is "service." Librarianship is a service profession. Librarians become librarians to serve people in specific ways. We are not out to make money or to further our political gain. We hear a calling to utilize our skills and interests to contribute to society in unique ways.

If you are considering a public services position, mull over the following question carefully: do you like people? The answer will tell you whether or not this is right for you. Interaction with people is essential to these types of positions. You have to like it. You have to be able to interact well with all types of characters and personalities, and you have to be able to adapt to unpredictable situations. At first glance, these criteria might seem to be drawbacks. For many, though, they are benefits. This is where the excitement comes into play. In public services positions, no day is ever exactly the same as the next, and you can "expect the unexpected." This is because people are unpredictable. It is precisely this unpredictability that draws so many to these positions.

Reference

Do you enjoy puzzles? Does hunting for treasure appeal to you? Do you like to help people solve problems? If so, you might look into becoming a reference librarian. The basic duty of the reference librarian is to work with patrons to help them find the information they need. The job involves analyzing users' needs to determine what information is appropriate. Using a structured reference interview, the librarian works with library users to clarify their information needs and determine what information sources will fill them. The help provided may consist of reading material in the form of a book or journal article, or factual information drawn from the library's reference collection. Reference librarians also offer in-depth research assistance and consultation, such as helping a researcher locate journal articles on a specific topic.

The job also includes an instructional role, such as showing users how to access information. Most libraries today offer access to searchable databases such as online catalogs and subscription-based databases. Reference librarians must develop their own searching skills and then help train users to search for the information they need within these databases. In addition, reference librarians often help users navigate the Internet so they can search for relevant information efficiently. We all know how much junk there is "out there." It is up to the reference librarian to develop the skills necessary to sift through the trash to find reliable, authoritative information. A good reference librarian can outwit Google any day!

Many reference librarians specialize in certain subject areas, particularly in large academic libraries or in special libraries. At a university library, for example, there may be a Science Librarian, a Humanities Librarian, or an Engineering Librarian. In hospital settings, Clinical Reference Librarians go on rotations with hospital staff to better determine the medical reference needs of the physicians and their patients. Reference work is the backbone of librarianship. If you think you'd like to be faced with the challenge of answering questions such as "Is Cascara Sagrada a laxative?" or "How many enzymes are associated with magnesium?" on a daily basis, you might just be cut out to be a reference librarian!

Circulation

Circulation librarians are responsible for handling check-out services within libraries. Usually these folks are also responsible for making sure the library is open and staffed at the appropriate times. Mainly managerial in nature, this type of position requires a high "people tolerance factor" because not only does it involve the supervision of staff members, it also requires close interaction with library users. This is the place where the public often confuses support staff and other workers with professional librarians. The circulation desk in most libraries is staffed by clerks and serves as a kind of filter or central access point—users must clear the "circ desk" before they can make use of the library's services. Hence, circulation librarians must be flexible, people-oriented, and well-prepared for any eventuality.

Document Delivery and Interlibrary Loan

Interlibrary loan is a service whereby a user of one library can borrow materials that are owned by another library. Materials may be in the form of books, videos, DVDs, microfilm, or sound recordings. Document delivery usually refers to the supply of journal articles. The librarians who supervise these services are in the business of acquiring information for library patrons when that information is not readily available within their own library. They have the satisfaction of matching people with information that is available beyond the boundaries of their particular library. Very few organizations, other than libraries, can say, "If we don't have that information here, we will get it for you as quickly as possible." Now that's service!

Education and Outreach

Perhaps you feel called to the teaching profession but would rather not deal with the politics of the public or private school systems. As an education librarian, you can teach under the umbrella of librarianship and avoid the daily grind of whiny children or obnoxious teenagers. Librarians in this arena provide educational services to the library's clientele. For example, they may routinely give library tours to various groups, or they may offer formal instruction in the use of library resources. It may surprise you that many librarians use their personal interests to develop educational programs at work. To give you an example, I work in an academic medical library. My undergraduate degree is in Spanish. I am now teaching Medical Spanish to students in our medical school! I also teach a monthly PowerPoint class to faculty, students, and staff, mainly because I enjoy using that software and want to help others master it.

Outreach usually focuses on extending library services to special population groups. Medical librarians might develop consumer health outreach programs to ensure that underserved populations in rural areas have equal access to health information. Public librarians might offer special programs to teach computer skills to the elderly. They might also offer library programs targeted to Hispanic or other ethnic populations. Librarians involved in educational outreach have altruistic natures and find deep satisfaction in enriching the lives of community groups.

Children/Young Adult Services

I know that I made a disparaging remark about whiny children earlier, but I was really kidding. What better satisfaction could there be than to watch a child's eyes sparkle with excitement over finding just the right title in the *Magic Treehouse* series? Or to see a child swell with pride at being able to select his or her own books and check them out with his or her very own library card? Children's librarians, most often employed in public libraries, coordinate library services geared toward one of society's most cherished population groups: children. Not only do they acquire and organize fiction and nonfiction materials for children, they also read to children (remember "Story Hour" at your local library?), assist them in selecting books, and help with schoolwork.

They are also responsible for developing programs that promote reading and literacy (such as summer reading programs) and may teach library literacy as part of a school's curriculum. These days, children's librarians also spend time developing and maintaining child-oriented Web sites that offer online educational games and programs.

The young adult librarian, also called a teen librarian, works primarily with young adults between the ages of 12 and 18. Duties may include: reviewing and ordering teen books, magazines, and media; planning library programs for teens, providing reference services for teens; visiting middle or high schools to promote reading materials; conducting tours for schools or community groups; teaching young adults to use the library's online catalog and databases; and doing outreach to teens in the community.

More often today, youth services librarians are also managing these services and training and supervising other staff to deliver programs.

Teacher-librarians

Most states require that school librarians in public schools be certified teachers. School librarians, called teacher-librarians, are often experienced classroom teachers who have become librarians as well. Teacher-librarians typically plan programs with classroom teachers so that students can access and make effective use of information for classroom assignments. They will coplan, coteach, and coevaluate library-based or resource-based projects. They also promote voluntary reading with teachers and students. Through this collaboration and team teaching, teacher-librarians have been shown to contribute to student achievement.

Technical Services Positions

So you've looked closely at the public services positions, and maybe you've concluded that you don't quite fit that particular mold. You like helping people, but you're not necessarily a "people person" and would rather not have interaction with the public as part of your daily routine. Hey, there's nothing wrong with that! Half of all librarians out there feel the exact same way. Or maybe you have a hidden love for computers and all things technical. Never fear! There are plenty of cool librarian jobs with your name all over them! These jobs fall under the traditional heading of "technical services" because, well, they handle the technical stuff necessary to keep a library running. Technical services librarians work "behind the scenes" to make sure the library and all of its many services continue to operate properly and effectively. They are often invisible to the library's public and they like it that way.

Cataloging and Acquisitions

Acquisitions librarians supervise the ordering of materials, deal with publishers and vendors, and manage the receipt of items purchased. At the beginning of this chapter I advised you not to become a librarian simply because you love books. I maintain my position on that. However, I have to admit that acquisition librarians are certainly in a position to fuel their love of books! They have the privilege of ordering books, pulling them from boxes, removing shrinkwrap to reveal pristine covers, and smelling that fresh ink! Aaaahhh. Oh, sorry—that is actually the support staff they supervise. Back to business. Of course, acquisitions librarians handle the ordering and receiving of many other kinds of materials as well, including journals or magazines, DVDs, videos, audio recordings, kits, etc. They are also responsible for maintaining accounting systems and for allocating budgets for materials.

Catalogers are in a class all their own. Or should I say "classification?" I can say this without being lynched because I used to be a cataloger and I'm very proud of that. Catalogers create and maintain a systematic structure to help library users locate information. This includes analyzing and describing resources according to established standards. This sounds simple, but it can actually be quite challenging. Take, for instance, the *Harry Potter* series of books. Where would you find them in a public library? In the children's section, young adult section, or the adult section? The readership extends to all. Under what subjects would they fall in the online catalog? Fantasy? Magic? Wizards? Boarding schools? All of the above? The cataloger must constantly ask these types of questions in order to ensure that materials can be found easily. They may work in many languages and subjects, handling materials such as books, journals, electronic databases, maps, Web sites, manuscripts and archives, and audio-visual materials. If you are detail-oriented but creative, enjoy challenges, and are capable of following intricate rules, look into this field. You may decide you want to join in on the fun!

Collection Development and Management

Collection services librarians are also called bibliographers, selectors, subject specialists, or curators. They build collections of books, journals, audio-visual materials, or electronic resources that fit within the scope (or profile) of the particular library. They maintain the collections by reviewing titles for preservation, replacement, off-site storage, or removal (also called "weeding" that you might soon discover as being a *bad word* in Library Land—as in gardening, removing the weeds so you can see the flowers. . . .) Collection development librarians also compile lists of books, periodicals, articles, and other resources on particular subjects for use by library patrons. Collection development is fun because you get to analyze a library's collections to determine what materials will make those collections stronger and more valuable to the library's clientele. With proper statistical justification, you can say, "Our client base requires the purchase of more Marvel comic books," or "It is absolutely necessary that we purchase the *Encyclopedia of Noses*."

Journals/Special Collections

Some librarians are responsible for maintaining very specific collections of materials. For example, serials librarians manage all aspects of subscription-based journals, from the activation of subscriptions to maintaining off-site access for users. Government document librarians handle all documents sent to government depository libraries. Conservators maintain collections of rare (and usually expensive) books and materials and have special skill sets for the preservation of such materials.

Information Technology and Systems

If you grew up glued to computers or video games, and your friends called you a "nerd," you might consider becoming a systems librarian. You could consider it even if you were *never* called a nerd, but have always shown proficiency in computer and information systems skills. Systems librarians develop and maintain the technical side of a library's electronic products and services, from the online catalog to subscription-based databases to innovative services such as live chat reference or blogs. They are responsible for planning, installing, operating, and maintaining computer-based systems within libraries. They may also be involved in designing information storage and retrieval systems and developing procedures for collecting, organizing, interpreting, and classifying information. Systems librarians analyze and plan for future information needs, which is a definite challenge in this age of technology.

Administrative Positions

Some people are just cut out to be leaders. Thank goodness for this! Without leaders, society would be fairly chaotic. The same holds true for the library world. (In that Garden of Eden library, I'll bet Eve was the Director; *somebody* had to take charge of them apples!) Librarians in administrative services oversee the management and planning of libraries. Some of their duties include negotiating contracts for services, materials, and equipment; supervising library employees; performing public relations and fundraising duties; preparing budgets; and directing activities to ensure that everything functions properly.

Some administrators and managers work as department heads (for example, Head of Cataloging or Head of Reference). They may be division heads (Head of Technical Services or Head of Public Services). At the highest levels of leadership, they are Deans, Directors, or Head Librarians.

The library world is in need of great leaders. If you feel you have the skills to meet the challenge, go for it! All hail our Library Leaders!

NextGen Librarianship

Did you know that Web-based companies are regularly hiring librarians to organize and disseminate their online data more effectively? Did you know that you could use your library degree to open your own information business? More and more, librarians are applying their information management and research skills to arenas outside of libraries.

There was a time, not long ago, that people were discussing the "demise" of librarianship due to the advent of the Internet and other advanced technologies. There was a fear that people would no longer need librarians since all information was becoming accessible online. Boy, was that ever wrong! Society is coming around to the fact that now, more than ever, the skills and expertise of librarians are necessary in order to mine and manipulate information so that it is usable. These librarians, now sometimes called "NextGen" librarians, are putting their skills to use on the "cutting edge" and are becoming involved with database development, reference tool development, information systems management, publishing, Internet coordination, marketing, advertising, Web content management and design, and training of database users.

Librarians with entrepreneurial interests have started their own consulting practices, acting as freelance reference librarians or information brokers and providing services to other libraries, businesses, government agencies, or the general consumer. Information architects design various systems to help people access information with as little hassle as possible. Knowledge managers identify, accumulate, and apply knowledge to further an organization's goals.

The possibilities of applying the skills you learn as a librarian to revolutionary jobs are endless. The job choice is yours—make the best of it!

THE STEREOTYPE DEBUNKED

I hope I have done a fair job in erasing whatever stereotype of librarianship you housed in your brain before we began. I hope you are excited about this field you have chosen to investigate, and that you continue to be amazed at the possibilities librarianship offers. Most of all, I hope that you now realize that it doesn't matter what your background is or what your skills are or where your interests lie, because you or anyone can find a cozy niche in the awesome field of librarianship!

SUGGESTIONS FOR FURTHER READING ON CAREERS

Dority, Kim G. *Rethinking Information Work: A Career Guide for Librarians and Other Information Professionals.* Westport, CT: Libraries Unlimited, 2006.

Kane, Laura Townsend. *Straight from the Stacks: A Firsthand Guide to Careers in Library and Information Science.* Chicago: ALA, 2003.

Shontz, Priscilla K. (ed.). *The Librarian's Career Guidebook.* Lanham, MD: Scarecrow Press, 2004.

Shontz, Priscilla K. and Richard A. Murray (eds.). *A Day in the Life: Career Options in Library & Information Science.* Westport, CT: Libraries Unlimited, 2007.

SUGGESTIONS FOR FURTHER READING ON ENVIRONMENTS

Bell, Steven J. and John D. Shank. *Academic Librarianship by Design: A Blended Librarian's Guide to the Tools and Techniques.* Chicago: ALA, 2007.

Brophy, Peter. *The Academic Library*, 2nd ed. New York: Neal-Schuman, 2005.

Haycock, Ken. (ed.). *Foundations for Effective School Library Media Programs.* Westport, CT: Libraries Unlimited, 1999.

Hughes-Hassell, Sandra and Violet H. Harada. *School Reform and the School Library Media Specialist*. Westport, CT: Libraries Unlimited, 2007.

McCook, Kathleen. *Introduction to Public Librarianship*. New York: Neal-Schuman, 2004.

Siess, Judith A. *The New OPL Sourcebook: A Guide for Solo and Small Libraries*. Medford, NJ: Information Today, 2006.

Part II

Functions and Competencies

Chapter 6

Another Look at Leadership

Brooke E. Sheldon

Since that first September morning in 1954 at the Campbell Branch Library in Detroit when I failed my first task as a newly credentialed librarian, I have had a healthy respect for new challenges that are always just around the corner. I learned from flunking the production of a passable pot of coffee for the Campbell staff break that Library School (in this case Simmons) doesn't cover everything and that I had better start measuring up (no pun intended) in a variety of ways, not all directly related to professional duties.

Over the years I have become very interested in why some library professionals "succeed" (are offered the top positions, and/or become leaders in the field) and others remain at lower or mid-management levels. Many of course prefer it that way, and would rather remain in their specialty, or avoid the all-consuming and often bureaucratic nature of many high-level positions, or gain deepest satisfaction from serving clients directly. So be it, but this chapter is not for those who are uninterested in leadership roles; for those who are, I will discuss a few leadership principles that I have found most workable. No! Not merely workable, essential to moving up in the LIS profession, or any other profession for that matter.

The principles are:

1. Know yourself: Recognize your leadership strengths
2. Understand the differences between leadership and management
3. Set priorities
4. Develop your emotional intelligence
5. Practise consistency

KNOW YOURSELF: RECOGNIZE YOUR LEADERSHIP STRENGTHS

The path to leadership begins with self reflection and leadership can be learned. Warren Bennis said it best: "Leadership is the marshaling of skills possessed by a majority but used by a minority. But it's something that can be learned by anyone, taught to everyone, denied to no one."[1]

In other words, there is a giant continuum and all of us in our personal and professional lives exhibit leadership qualities every day. These leadership skills are needed in every department and at every level of the organization. The question is: how do we exploit our natural propensity for leadership so that we magnify and grow these qualities and learn to use them as needed?

A good definition of leadership (one of thousands) is:

Leadership is a process whereby an individual motivates a group of people or an entire organization to achieve shared goals.

The earliest research on leadership centered around the study of traits or qualities of leaders in power. Stogdill[2] identified traits that separated the average individual in a group from the leader. These included such qualities as intelligence, alertness, insight, responsibility, initiative, persistence, self-confidence, and sociability. Later he identified more important leadership traits including drive for responsibility, task completion, willingness to accept consequences of decision and action, ability to influence other's behavior, willingness to tolerate frustration and delay, etc.

Other researchers have produced their own lists, but among the main criticisms of trait theory is that hundreds of studies have failed to come up with the list of definitive traits.

Nevertheless, using the trait approach is a useful way to assess yourself. By taking standardized assessments such as the Meyers-Briggs Type Indicator (MBTI) or Buckingham and Clifton's StrengthsFinder Profile[3] or other leadership instruments you can gain awareness and understanding of your qualities and preferences and how these affect your interactions with others. Some instruments are designed so that you can hand them out to coworkers, friends, etc. and have them assess your leadership qualities. Involving others in this process will help eliminate any erroneous self-assumptions about your strengths.

But the key is to focus on your positive attributes. The book *Now, Discover Your Strengths*[4] describes research conducted by the Gallup organization that shows that "[i]t is a flawed assumption that each person's greatest room for growth is in his or her areas of weakness." Rather they say that each person's greatest room for growth is in the areas of his or her greatest strengths, "and this is what organizations should capitalize on." The StrengthsFinder provides a way for you to measure yourself in thirty-four strength areas and begin to utilize and expand them in your personal life and career. The Meyers-Briggs Type Indicator (MBTI) focuses on understanding people's personality preferences and facilitates adopting a leadership style that allows you to express your own preferences.

No one is perfect; the intelligent leader gravitates to coworkers and picks a team that has the qualities needed to reach the goals. Understanding what your personal preferences are, and your strengths, takes a good deal of self-analysis and reflection, but is the all important first step, and is well worth the time. You can learn much from a mentor, or someone you admire, but you never want to be a carbon copy.

A MANAGER IS NOT A LEADER

While every great leader must have some management skills and every successful manager has some qualities of leadership, the perspective of each is quite different.

So often in libraries (and elsewhere) people are promoted because they are efficient, loyal, trustworthy, etc. Great frustration follows when the qualities that worked well on the middle management level simply don't meet the expectations of those who expect to "follow a leader." I have seen newly promoted librarians walk into a situation where they seem to give the impression: "Now, me boss, you worker. From now on we will do it this way." There may be some who will welcome this very authoritative approach, especially if leadership has been lacking for some time, but when assuming a new position it is best to take Peter Drucker's advice: "Treat your workers like volunteers."[5]

Just what is it that people look for, even yearn for, in a leader? As I look around our profession I see many leaders, none of them perfect, but nevertheless possessing extraordinary qualities. Probably most important is the ability to work with staff in developing a vision, be clear about what he or she wishes to accomplish, with the self-confidence to focus on that vision, and proceed with it, no matter what obstacles intervene.

I think of Carla Stoffle and her talented staff at the University of Arizona. She is determined to, and has established, a team-centered administration at the University of Arizona Libraries.

Some might argue that this is hardly a vision, but think about what this "vision" does for the profession. Project teams have been a normal part of operating procedures in business for some time, but very little experimentation that involves hierarchical change is taking place in libraries. Arizona has been the notable exception. In Tucson there is a living laboratory, a library staff undergoing the trials and tribulations, and successes, of inserting a team structure into a hitherto hierarchical system. There are many other innovations at Arizona but the productive use of teams is, in my view, the most significant.

If your goal is to move into a leadership position, even when you are the newest hire at the library, it is important not to compartmentalize your job from the overall issues and goals of the organization. It is all too easy to become obsessed with the needs and problems of your own department. Your ideas, expressed in staff meetings and other appropriate venues, can have an enormous effect on the direction of the library, provided they are presented in a positive way that fits the culture of the organization and your expectations of being heard, and influencing decisions, are realistic. It may not surprise you to know that a new employee with creative ideas is not always welcomed with open arms in a well-established organizational culture. By all means, put your ideas forward, but be sensitive to how they are received and modify your approach as needed. It really doesn't matter how creative you are if no one is listening. And speaking of listening, it is well to remember that listening skills are much more highly valued than oral fluency when you are new in an organization, or as my old friend, the late Tom Galvin, ineloquently expressed it, "When I am new in the group, I try to keep my mouth shut, and my ears flapping." At the same time we should not forget the words of A.J.P. Taylor who said, "All change in history, all advances come from the non-conformists. If there had been no troublemakers, no dissenters, we should still be living in caves."[6]

So, the leader is shaping the future; the manager is maintaining the status quo. The leader is an innovator; the manager is . . . well, a manager, more likely to be focusing on the bottom line and the efficiency of systems, and less likely to be able to inspire the staff to achieve a long range goal. That ability, to not only see the big picture but also to demonstrate the ability to reconstruct the future, is how library directors are selected.

PRIORITIZE YOUR PRIORITIES

In any job there is always too much to do. Leadership demands a combination of relentless focus on the three or four (at the most) important goals or priorities and an ability to subordinate or delegate the details. As Robert Kaplan noted "having fifteen priorities is the same as having none at all."[7]

It sounds only logical to say that one should never have too many priorities, but in fact it is not always so simple. For example, many a director who thought they understood their role in the eighties were not all that happy in the nineties to find that they were expected to spend large percentages of their time in fundraising. Fundraising is one activity that does not lend itself to delegation as well as some other functions. At least this is true in the later phases of the "ask." In most cases, individual donors want the time and attention of the director, not her deputy. This is not necessarily how a director or dean wants to spend his or her time, but it is a necessity for successful fundraising.

Another difficulty in pursuing relentlessly just three or four priorities relates to the one above, but is more closely centered on the nature of library professionals. Whether we entered the field because of a love of research and scholarship, or we have a passion for service, or an avidity for organizing materials and systems, when we move to leadership positions we are not always willing or even able to give up those activities that lured us to the profession in the first place. Thus I vividly recall a dean and colleague who was ten times smarter than I, but in my view, was less successful as a dean because he seemingly spent a majority of the time organizing the files and developing statistical analyses of how the school compared to other schools in the United States. This is interesting stuff but not conducive to moving the school into the twenty-first century.

How to learn to focus on what is critical and delegate or leave (yes, leave!) the rest? That is the situation that all who lead must face, and it is a complex problem that perhaps an examination of Path-Goal theory will help to clarify. This theory, originally developed by Evans[8] and House[9] goes far beyond the trait approach and describes how goal-oriented leaders can adapt their styles either to the situation or to the motivating factors for their staff. Depending on the situation, the leader can be directive (when the leader knows more about the task than the staff member), participative, that is, having staff totally involved in the decision making, or achievement-oriented, that is, challenging staff to perform at the highest possible level. To achieve the goal, leaders may exhibit any or all of these styles with individual subordinates, and in different situations. The latest edition of Peter Northouse's *Leadership Theory and Practice*[10] discusses this as well as the contingency and situational approaches. In fact, this is a very useful book for a broad overview of leadership theory.

LIFELONG LEARNING AND EMOTIONAL INTELLIGENCE

For a person who is interested in librarianship as a career, it is probably gratuitous to stress the need for lifelong learning. Most of the librarians I have known have a natural interest in not only upgrading their skills but also satisfying curiosity and broadening perspectives. Reading, studying, attending, and participating in professional meetings and associations all are very important in helping us gain social awareness, see the big picture, and yes, to use a well worn phrase, to think "out of the box."

These continuing education activities are very important for the growth of the aspiring leader; moreover, recent research provides proof that intelligence (IQ) is but one factor, and in fact a minor factor, in achieving leadership status. Of course, a certain level of intelligence is needed to obtain professional credentials but once you are in the profession, factors other than cognitive intelligence appear to be the chief determinants of success. An example of this research on the limits of IQ as a predictor is the Sommerville study[11] of 450 boys. Two-thirds were from welfare families and one-third had IQs below 90. The study found that IQ had little relation to how well they did at work. What made the biggest difference were childhood abilities such as being able to handle frustration, control emotions, and get along with other people. Another longitudinal study[12] describes eighty Ph.D.s in science who underwent a battery of personality tests, IQ tests, and interviews in the 1950s when they were graduate students at Berkeley. Forty years later, now in their early seventies, their success was evaluated in terms of resumes, peer evaluations, and sources like *American Men and Women of Science*. Results were that social and emotional abilities were four times more important than IQ in determining professional success and prestige.

Obviously, cognitive ability is the basis for success in science and of course in library and information science. But the current research and interest in emotional intelligence make a strong case for what I have long believed: "It's not always what you know but who you know" and those who say "I would rather be respected than liked" should probably reconsider. It is possible to be both without being a wimp.

Then what are some of the skills or qualities associated with emotional intelligence (EI)?

To name a few: relationship management; ability to attune ourselves to/or influence the emotions of another person; accurate self-assessment; adaptability; empathy; and communication. There are many qualities that fall under the rubric of EI, but in my view the most important is that general area of communication that concerns itself with empathy. And how does one become more empathic? I think it is much more than a series of techniques for understanding what a person is saying. It centers around developing one's listening skills. The art of listening is the most powerful yet underrated quality of professionals and leaders.

In my book *Leaders in Libraries*[13] I talked about the power in being a good listener and quoted Tom Phelps, Head of Library Programs for the National Endowment for the Humanities, who said: "... the frustration in the listening. Did you hear it right? Did you hear enough of it? Listening and then trying in a skillful way to put these ideas together in a coherent whole; getting support for those ideas (not just financial) and then giving it back ... in some regard I think I have been successful in not having to internalize it and be in control of everything, letting it go at the time it needs to be let go ... then moving on to other things ... "

To paraphrase John Gardner in *On Leadership*,[14] an e-mail message is not enough. Nothing can substitute for the leader listening attentively and responding informally. The wise leader is always looking for ways to say "I hear you."

One lesson I have learned (alas, too late!) is that it is not a good idea to be selective about those peers or staff members from whom you accept advice. In my various administrative roles, I had a theory that in any move to implement change there would always be an individual, or a group, that would be negative and that the thing to do was "work with the leadership" and eventually everybody, one way or the other, kicking and screaming, would climb aboard. On some levels, I still believe this, but in retrospect I recognize that I ignored some very creative but "difficult" thinkers and had I listened and reflected more, and encouraged constructive dissent, the overall results might have been much better. Some examples are the distance education programs initiated at the University of Texas at Austin that now no longer exist; and my modest attempt to improve funding capabilities for libraries when I was President of the ALA, and I moved ahead without the support of the ALA Committee on Legislation. Years later, by the time I failed retirement and went out to Arizona to help with re-accreditation, and the threatened closure of the school, my listening skills had improved. So had my ability to brew coffee!

PRACTICE CONSISTENCY

What do we mean by consistency? And why is it an essential quality for a leader? Bennis says "we trust people who are predictable, who make their positions clear."[15]

My own goal for consistency has always been that staff and faculty when they come into my office to discuss a problem will, if they stop to think about it, never be surprised by my response because it will be grounded in the values and ethics of our profession. Certainly I have never fully reached this goal, but it has provided a way to step back and discuss a dilemma, large or small, with a certain amount of objectivity. To be able to do this takes what John W.

Berry has referred to as "a strong ideological commitment—a point of view that undergirds your work."[16]

It is not about refusing to change your mind on various issues, but it is about taking a stand based on your personal values and beliefs. You can do this whether or not you hold a leadership position, whether or not you become active and speak up in professional organizations, and whether or not you write for professional journals and other media. But if you want to influence the future of librarianship, you should consider doing all three.

DEVELOPING LEADERS: SUMMARY AND CONCLUSION

Back in 1991, in discussing the need for library schools to focus more on educating students for leadership positions and in fact put leadership in the mainstream of library education, I suggested that we should hope to develop the following qualities and competencies[17]:

- The ability to develop and share with others a vision that extends beyond immediate concerns; an understanding of the difference between strategic planning and visionary leadership.
- An understanding of how change occurs and affects the immediate environment; an understanding of how to create and initiate change.
- An understanding of risk taking as it relates to leadership vs. management (i.e., the ability to make decisions in the absence of full information).
- An understanding of the positive uses of power.
- Skills in conflict management.
- Skills in communicating, negotiating, clarifying, and recommending policy options.
- Sensitivity and perspective toward the complex problems library organizations face in the context of their political environments.
- The development of a strong ideological commitment and sense of professional ethics. Social responsibility; the capacity to take a global view and move away from short term bottom line thinking; becoming actively engaged in long term planning for the betterment of society.
- The ability to follow as well as lead and to engender broad support for the causes that affect our profession.

In examining this somewhat unwieldy and verbose 16-year-old list, I would change little except to be more explicit. That is, I would emphasize self-assessment, goal and priority setting, emotional intelligence, and practising consistency. At least this week. And I would tell the LIS school deans again: listen up! The practitioners are deploring the lack of people who want (or are able) to assume leadership positions in a rapidly graying profession. The schools should be paying attention. As of this writing I am waiting for that flagship school to initiate a systematic leadership program (not necessarily for credit) for all students—not just a special course or institute—and to seriously look at leadership potential in enrollment decisions.

Ever the optimist, I believe that the schools will respond, and the leaders will come!

SUGGESTIONS FOR FURTHER READING

Bennis, Warren. *On Becoming a Leader.* Reading, MA: Addison Wesley, 1989.

Bennis, Warren and Joan Goldsmith. *Learning to Lead.* Reading, MA: Addison Wesley, 1997.

Buckingham, Marcus and Curt Coffman. *First, Break All the Rules.* New York: Simon & Schuster, 1999.

Goleman, Daniel, Richard Boyatzis, and Annie McKee. *Primal Leadership.* Boston: Harvard Business School Press, 2002.

Hesselbein, Frances and Paul M. Cohen. *Leader to Leader: Enduring Insights on Leadership from the Drucker Foundation's Award Winning Journal.* San Francisco: Jossey Bass, 1999.

Useem, Michael. *The Leadership Moment.* New York: Three Rivers Press, 1998.

Chapter 7

Management: An Essential Skill for Today's Librarians

Barbara B. Moran

So you think you might like to become a librarian? Perhaps you think you would enjoy working with books or archives. Maybe you are attracted to the new technologies that are part of librarianship and want to build digital libraries or provide better online access to resources. Possibly you are looking forward to working with patrons and helping to link individuals to the information they need. Or it may be that you see yourself as a readers' advisor or a children's librarian performing during a story hour. Have you thought about yourself as a manager? What many people entering the library profession overlook is the amount of time that nearly all professional librarians spend in managing—managing resources, facilities, and people. In fact management is a key element in the work of almost all professional librarians today. It is almost certain that if you become a librarian, you will also be a manager.

Librarianship, like many other service professions, often attracts individuals who do not have a strong desire to manage. Some individuals enter the profession with no intention of becoming a manager; instead they want to work with information and people. Almost all librarians enjoy the traditional tasks associated with the profession, collecting, organizing, preserving, and disseminating information, but most librarians have to combine work on these tasks with managerial responsibilities. In the United States, for example, the proportion of nonprofessional library employees continues to increase, and, as a result, most professional librarians are spending less time performing the traditional tasks of librarians and more time managing the work of the support staff. Since professional librarians customarily supervise the nonprofessionals, it is common for new librarians to begin to manage as soon as they are hired.

So, if you become a librarian, in your first job you will likely find yourself spending at least some time on tasks that will be considered "managerial." Managing is a new role for many people who become librarians. Some individuals when first asked to manage are reluctant to accept the responsibility. They may believe that "managers are born not made," and are convinced they were not born to be one. Although new professionals sometimes assume managerial duties unwillingly, most can learn to be very effective managers. However, knowing how to manage well is rarely an innate skill. It takes time to learn to be a good manager, and people usually improve in their management skills as they continue in management positions.

There will be a tremendous need for managers in all twenty-first-century libraries. Talented people who are willing to become managers will be in great demand, but how can we ensure that there will be an adequate supply of library managers to meet the need? This chapter will provide an overview of the most important elements of library management, will discuss the skills needed by managers, and will conclude with suggestions for ways that librarians can learn to be excellent managers.

THE IMPORTANCE OF MANAGEMENT

The importance of management to librarians has grown over the years as libraries have become larger—larger in terms of budgets, collections, and staff. There is an obvious need for management skills at the level of library director, especially in large libraries. Library directors in major national, public, and academic libraries face enormous challenges in managing organizations that are in many ways the equivalent of large for-profit corporations. In fact, these library directors are necessarily becoming more like chief executive officers (CEOs) of large corporations than the scholars they used to be. These directors are responsible for very large budgets. The Library of Congress has a budget of over US$600 million. The British Library has a budget of almost £130 million or about US$260 million. Of course we would expect these large national libraries to have sizeable budgets, but it is very common for directors in many types of libraries to be dealing with multimillion dollar budgets. Even in libraries with smaller budgets, knowing how to secure and manage funding is critical for the institution's success. Directors are also in charge of many employees and large physical plants, and managing people and physical resources is often more difficult than managing money.

But it is not just library directors who need to have managerial skills. Libraries need good managers at all levels to manage the change as they face the redefined world of information provision. The demands on every librarian's managerial ability have become larger and more complex in recent years. The traditional managerial hierarchy is being affected by many of the changes in today's workplace, including the increasing popularity of team-based organizations, which has led to a flattening of the pyramid and the elimination of some middle-management positions. Librarians in all types of libraries also contribute to management by working on committees or task forces and by supervising support staff. In most of today's organizations, including libraries, management responsibility is being distributed more widely throughout the organization than it was in the past. Today, librarians are facing greater challenges than before resulting from increased competition, growing globalization, ever changing technology, and the pace of change. Although management is sometimes a difficult undertaking, it also presents great opportunities and allows one to make changes in organizations. We are badly in need of people who are both willing and able to serve as managers, in order to ensure the success of libraries in the future.

The need for managers in all types of libraries will grow in the next decade. The Baby Boom generation is beginning to reach retirement age, and most library managers fall in this very large age cohort. The vast majority of people working and managing in libraries now are Baby Boomers born somewhere between 1946 and 1964. The Boomers were followed by a much smaller cohort, often called GenX, born between 1965 and 1978. Individuals belonging to GenY (or the Millennials) were born between 1979 and 2000, and are just beginning to be part of the library workforce. It is the GenX and GenY librarians (often called NextGen librarians) who will be the managers of the libraries of the twenty-first century.

Libraries have over the years adopted many management principles from business, industry, and government. Management in all types of organizations is very similar and library managers have borrowed principles and practices from the nonlibrary world that they think will contribute to the successful operation of their organizations.

There is, of course, a major difference between most libraries and businesses; almost all libraries function as not-for-profit organizations. The biggest difference between these two types of organizations is their "bottom line." Businesses are "for-profit" organizations and must provide their own funding from profits derived from services or products sold. "Not-for-profit" organizations depend on funding from outside sources. In libraries, this funding often comes from public resources given by federal, state, or city government. Although there are some differences in the management between the for-profit and the not-for-profit sectors, there are many more similarities than differences, and managers in both sectors encounter many of the same problems and challenges.

Management in the not-for-profit sector is sometimes viewed as more difficult because the goals of these organizations are often difficult to articulate. The goal of the for-profit organization is fairly straightforward; it exists to make money for its owners. The goal of a not-for-profit is usually not so clear-cut. Not-for-profits exist to "serve society" in some way, and that goal may be interpreted in different fashions. Not only do managers in not-for-profits sometimes have more trouble setting goals, but it can be equally hard to assess whether the organization has achieved these goals. Nevertheless, whatever the nature of the enterprise, it must operate to provide a product to customers or patrons, to give the employees and employers a sense of well-being and self-esteem, to maintain an attractive and healthy environment, and to provide consistent and efficient services. A well-managed library accomplishes all of these objectives better than one that is poorly managed.

WHAT IS MANAGEMENT?

Management has been defined in many ways, but the basic task of management is using organizational resources to achieve objectives through planning, organizing, staffing (human resources), leading, and controlling. Managers are those individuals within an organization who are in a position to make the decisions that allow an organization to reach its objectives. They work to ensure that these objectives are reached both effectively and efficiently. Early in the twentieth century, Mary Follett defined management as "the art of getting things done through people."[1] This definition is still relevant because it is impossible for anyone to manage alone. Managers have to use the skills and labor of others to succeed.

Henry Mintzberg, in a seminal study entitled *The nature of managerial work*,[2] examined what managers actually do. To gather his data, he observed managers during the course of their workdays. He found that managers work at demanding activities characterized by their variety, fragmentation, and brevity. Managers rarely have long stretches of uninterrupted time to spend on any one task. They simultaneously work at a variety of tasks, each for a short period of time. Their days are fragmented and there are many demands on their time. A manager accomplishes a great deal of work at a very fast pace and for most managers, there is usually more to be done than there is time in which to do it. Managers are required to assume a great deal of responsibility. They are responsible for other people, their actions, and the success or failure of the enterprise. Managers are held accountable at various levels for the operation of a team, a unit, a division, or a whole organization. Managers, especially at upper levels, typically have heavy workloads and often feel stress because of their managerial duties.

Under such circumstances, why would anyone want to be a manager? Although there are many challenges and difficulties associated with management, most competent managers enjoy their jobs. They like the sense of autonomy and the ability to set their own agendas and are proud of being able to make a difference and of performing well. They are challenged by the diversity of the work they do and the diversity of the people— staff, customers, and other stakeholders—with whom they work. Most managers appreciate the higher salaries that accompany managerial positions. Managers are monetarily rewarded because they are accountable for the actions of others and for the achievement of organizational objectives.

Because today's libraries are complex organizations located in rapidly changing environments, being a manager requires both managerial skills and hard work but it can be extremely rewarding. Individuals who become managers have an opportunity to make an impact on their organizations. Top managers set the tone for the entire organization and make the difference between one that is mediocre and one that is outstanding. Lower level managers allow the people they supervise to accomplish their work more efficiently. Managers who are accomplishing their jobs well experience a great sense of self-satisfaction and fulfillment.

LEVELS OF MANAGEMENT

Managers can be categorized in a number of ways. One of the most common is to think about managers within a vertical hierarchy. Managers can be found at all levels of the organization, but the ones nearer the top have broader responsibilities and authority than those at lower levels. In most typical organizations, including libraries, management can be divided into three levels.

- *Top management,* which in libraries usually refers to the director and the assistant and associate directors, is responsible for the overall functioning of the entire organization. In most organizations, managers at the highest levels have the power to establish organization-wide policy and are influential in setting the leadership style throughout the organization. In modern librarians, most directors no longer make important decisions without consulting with others who will be affected by the decisions. The older autocratic style of management has been replaced by a more participative one. Nonetheless, all decisions made about an organization are the ultimate responsibility of the top manager. An example of a decision that would be made by a top manager would be a decision to close branch libraries in a city where funding to the public library system has been slashed because of declining tax revenue.

- *Middle management* is in charge of specific subunits or functions of the organization. In libraries, department heads are middle managers whose management responsibilities are focused on the successful functioning of individual areas of the library. Middle managers, in addition to leading their specific subunits or functions, also serve as liaisons between top management and supervisors. The head of a collection development department in an academic library who has to decide how to allocate funding between print and electronic formats provides an example of the type of responsibility held by middle managers.

- *Supervisors,* sometimes called first-line managers, are the managers in the lowest position of the management hierarchy. Supervisors lead the day-to-day activities of individual employees as they work to accomplish the desired organizational objectives, and they are responsible for the production of goods or services. These managers implement procedures and processes that allow their units to work effectively and efficiently. A supervisor would make decisions about employee work schedules and would be responsible for training new employees in that unit.

Management takes place throughout the organization, but the management differs depending on the level and scope of responsibility associated with the position.

THE FUNCTIONS OF MANAGEMENT

It is likely that you have a fairly good idea of some of the things that managers do, but perhaps you want to get a more specific idea of how managers spend their time. As stated before, managers are typically very busy people with a number of responsibilities. Many managers seem to be juggling a number of responsibilities, almost at the same time. Some managerial functions are engaged in almost daily, while others are performed on a more irregular basis. For these reasons, it is sometimes difficult to tease out the actual strands of the fabric of managerial life. One very common way to view management is as a set of common processes or functions that, when properly carried out, lead to organizational efficiency and effectiveness. The managerial functions are those tasks that managers perform as part of their managerial positions. These functions can be classified in various ways, but, regardless of the terminology used, it is generally agreed that managers in all types of organizations perform five main functions: planning, organizing, staffing (human resources), leading, and controlling.

Planning is the first function carried out by all managers. Planning allows managers to think ahead to the things that need to be done and to the methods for getting them done to accomplish the organization's goals. Planning defines where the organization wants to be in the future, and facilitates the transition from today until tomorrow. All levels of library managers engage in planning. A director might be heavily involved in planning for a new building while a supervisor might be planning how to handle the arrival of a large shipment of materials from a vendor.

Organizing is the second function of management. Managers must establish the formal structure of authority through which work subdivisions are arranged. They must first decide how to match individuals and their talents with the kinds of functions and structures that are needed to get the job done, and then how to structure the organization so that there is easy communication among the subunits. The subunits of any organization are similar to building blocks that can be arranged in many ways. For example, many university libraries have recently had to decide where to put the increasingly important function of user education. Should that function be made part of the reference department or should a new department be formed?

Staffing (Human Resources) is the third managerial function. This human resources function is sometimes called staffing or personnel and involves hiring, training, compensating, and retaining the people necessary to achieve the organizational objectives. Libraries and other information agencies are becoming more automated, but they are still highly labor-intensive organizations. Most of them still devote between 50 and 60 percent of their budgets to employee costs. In such labor-intensive organizations, the human resources are especially critical to success, because almost everything else in the organization depends on them. An HR management challenge that most libraries are facing relates to staff development. With all of the changes occurring in the world of librarianship, how can the skills of long-time employees be kept up to date? In response to this challenge, many librarians have planned extensive staff development efforts and are encouraging employees to take courses and to attend conferences and workshops where they can learn and update skills.

Leading involves creating a shared culture and values, communicating goals to and motivating employees at all levels of the organization. All of the subfunctions encompassed under the category of "leading" focus on the human element in the organization. This human element is very important, since employees' attitudes, personality attributes, and perceptions affect the way they work. A director who is able to persuade employees to accept major changes in the organizational structure or a supervisor who is able to motivate employees to accomplish at a higher level than they had previously attained are both contributing to the organization by their skill in the managerial function of leading.

Controlling means monitoring the activities of an organization to be sure it is on the right path to meet its goals. Controlling involves first analyzing the way in which the organization is operating, and then feeding information back into the planning process so that the organization has a way of continually examining and correcting its goals in light of current information. Controlling is the mirror image of planning. In planning, managers establish where the organization is going, and in controlling, they decide whether they are on target to reach these goals. If planning allows an organization to decide where it is going, controlling allows it to know if it has gotten there. An example of a manager who is engaged in controlling is a department head looking at best practices and trying to establish "benchmarks" to measure whether his or her employees are accomplishing as much as they could be.

So planning, organizing, human resources, leading, and controlling are the primary functions of management. All managers engage in performing these five functions, although managers at different levels and in different parts of an organization differ in the time they devote to them and the depth at which they perform them.

MANAGERIAL SKILLS NEEDED BY LIBRARIANS

A manager's job is complex and multidimensional and managers need to have a number of skills to succeed. What managerial skills do librarians need? The skills necessary to be a successful library manager vary according to the different levels of management. Robert Katz[3] identified three managerial skills essential to successful management: technical, human, and conceptual skills. Technical skills, those skills that relate to specific functions and tasks, are most important at the first-line level. To be an effective supervisor, an individual has to understand the process that is being carried out. It would be very difficult for a library manager to supervise a group of copy catalogers without knowing about cataloging and classification. On the other hand, the library director may have had such technical knowledge at one time, but because the director no longer catalogs, he or she may not still possess such skills, especially in newer competencies such as producing metadata records. Because top-level managers are often in charge of many diverse units, they often have either never known or have lost proficiency in many of the technical skills that are so important for lower level managers.

At the upper level, however, managers need to have more conceptual skills and be able to look at the "big picture" of the organization. These managers need to be able to communicate what is going on in the library to the outside world. They need to be able to articulate a vision of the organization at the present time and the organization's plans for the future.

The human skill, the ability to interact effectively with people is important at all levels. All managers are dealing with other people as a part of their positions. Upper level managers often deal with hundreds of people during the course of the week ranging from government officials to donors to disgruntled patrons or employees. Supervisors deal on a daily basis with employees and interpersonal skills are very important here also. Having good people skills is essential to success in management.

Katz provides us with a framework of three essential skills but there are many others specific skills that are important to success in management. Managers need to possess both "hard" skills, which include the technical and specific business skills, and "soft" skills, which include the interpersonal skills. In the fairy tale, each of Sleeping Beauty's fairy godmothers gave her a gift to make her as nearly perfect as possible. If there were fairy godmothers to endow new managers with gifts, what type of traits would they bestow? Although it is impossible to provide a comprehensive list of management skills most experts would agree that the following are important for all managers.

- *Political Skills.* Libraries are intensely political organizations and awareness of this is vital to survival in today's climate. Managers have to be skilled negotiators and diplomats.

- *Communication Skills.* Managers need to be able to communicate information both within the organizations and to the external world. It is important to be able to transmit information about ideas and services effectively to both employees and constituents—customers, patrons, users, and potential users of information services.

- *Problem-Solving Skills.* Problem-solving is one of the most important day-to-day activities of a manager. Managers need to be able to analyze a situation and come up with a solution.

- *People Skills.* People possess many different dimensions, and a manager has to deal with all of these dimensions. The skills most needed in this area are those that typically fall under the categories of communication, conflict resolution, and interpersonal skills. In more and more organizations, managers are responsible for the coordination of team-based initiatives. Managers need to know the best techniques for managing teams as well as individuals.

- *Financial Skills.* All managers need a sound grounding in financial skills including where funding comes from, where it goes, and how to get it. Managers should understand balance sheets and return on investment. Managers should also have knowledge of marketing since marketing of organizations or services often results in funding for them. Additionally, in more and more libraries, fundraising has become a primary responsibility, especially for top managers.

But the fairy godmothers could not stop there because there are many other skills that help people succeed in management. A sense of humor is always useful. Seeing things through the eyes of others in the organization can facilitate cooperation and reduce conflict among disparate points of view. Good managers know how to collaborate and work well with others. They need flexibility to be able to cope with ambiguity. They need to be able to handle change and maintain a positive attitude toward change management. Being willing to be a risk-taker is often a vital skill. Managers need an ability to make decisions in a timely fashion. They need to be ethical and be able to articulate their values and beliefs. Unfortunately, since managers are not blessed with fairy godmothers, they all have to cultivate and work at these skills and traits. No manager is a complete master of all of the skills that might be useful to him or her. But, good managers know that their success is dependent upon their skills and knowledge, and they never stop learning or developing skills throughout the course of their careers.

DECIDING TO BECOME A MANAGER

Opportunities for good managers are unlimited and many organizations are competing for the services of the talented managers of the twenty-first century. Individuals who have learned to network effectively, to think strategically, and to manage skillfully have numerous opportunities to assume new, more challenging positions.

After reading this far, you probably are convinced that you will do at least some management in any type of professional position you assume in a library. But, perhaps you have decided that you are at least interested in exploring the possibility of becoming an upper level library manager and you think you might aspire to becoming a library director someday. How can you know whether this is the right path for you to pursue?

Before deciding to pursue a managerial career, an individual should be certain that he or she wants to assume the responsibilities of management. Individuals vary greatly in what they hope to achieve from their career. Edgar Schein,[4] a professor at MIT, has developed one of the best validated and most commonly used models for discovering career interests. His "career anchors" are composed of a combination of motivation, attitude, and values. Schein states that these anchors are formed early in life and that they both guide and constrain an individual throughout an entire career. These anchors are what an individual "holds" to—the career values an individual would not give up even in the face of difficulty. One of Schein's career anchors is General Management Competence. People who have that as their anchor want to manage or supervise people. They enjoy authority and responsibility and thrive on analyzing issues, solving problems, and being in charge of something complex. They also enjoy the opportunity to make decisions and like directing, coordinating, and influencing others more than perfecting a particular skill or way of doing things. If you have some or many of these traits it is likely that you will enjoy management and be a success at it.

So if you want to become an upper level manager, what are the steps that you should take? Getting ahead in management frequently seems to be affected by serendipity. Often, someone just seems to be in the right place at the right time, and then moves up the career ladder because of it. Although serendipity and luck sometimes play a role in becoming a manager, it is wise to plan and to prepare for such a move from the start of one's career to be sure to be ready when the opportunity presents itself. Individuals who wish to become library managers should try to acquire skills both before and after they enter librarianship.

ACQUIRING MANAGEMENT SKILLS

The first opportunity to learn to be a manager often comes as part of the educational preparation for entering the profession. Management is taught as a part of the curriculum in all LIS programs, and most schools offer many more than one management course, including such offerings as human resource management, strategic planning, marketing, and financial management. Sometimes students do not see themselves as future managers, so they often do not take the management courses that are offered unless they are required to do so. However, if you think you are interested in management you should take as many management related courses as possible.

When newly minted librarians begin their professional careers, it is then that they see the importance of learning about management. Although a few graduates of LIS schools get jobs as directors of small libraries and thus become top managers right away, most graduates go to work in larger organizations where they have a chance to learn some management skills before they themselves become middle or top-level managers. Observation and on-the-job training are important aspects of development as a manager. One can learn from other managers who are higher in the management structure, as well as from those that are on the same level. All managers learn from doing. Often mistakes are made when a person is learning to manage, but making mistakes is one way of learning. New managers can learn from other managers in the organization and from professional colleagues outside the organization through mentoring and networking. Aspiring managers can learn a great deal from more experienced managers who have already acquired many of the skills and the characteristics that they would like to emulate. They can also observe bad managers and observe ways not to do things.

To succeed at management do the best you can in every position you hold. Even entry level jobs in libraries usually present at least some opportunity to work autonomously and to exercise creativity. But, in addition to working hard, be sure that your manager knows that you are interested in moving up in the organization at some time in the future. Although you may assume that your boss knows this, be explicit about it. Let people know that you would appreciate help in learning what you need to know to be promoted to a higher level.

In every position you hold, begin to think about the skills and the experiences you will need to qualify you for the type of position you desire next. How can they be acquired? Once again you can enlist your manager's help in finding ways to acquire those skills and experiences. You should also be looking for opportunities on your own. Are there opportunities for you to acquire management experience on committees either in the library or in a professional organization? Are there courses or workshops that you could take to increase your capabilities?

Most individuals who attain top positions have worked in a number of organizations throughout the course of their careers. Don't be afraid to look for another job if you are "stuck" in your present organization and are no longer learning and being challenged by your job. It is sometimes a risk to change organizations, but it is a mistake to stay too long in a position where you are not continuing to learn and advance.

Mentoring is extremely helpful if a person wants to become a manager. Mentors help protégés advance in an organization by informally teaching them about the job and the organization. Also, as protégés begin to ascend the organizational ladder, mentors often sponsor them and use their connections to help them advance either in their present organization or in another one.

But on-the-job education is rarely enough. Continuing education is an important part of every professional's career development. Most large libraries provide staff development classes to teach the management skills that are needed by many of the managers within the organization. Library organizations, both state and national, provide other opportunities to learn management skills. These organizations often provide preconference workshops or institutes on specific managerial topics.

So aspiring library managers can improve their knowledge by attending a wide variety of educational offerings. Sometimes managers, having recognized that to manage large and complex organizations requires a great deal of advanced management expertise, want a more systematic immersion in the discipline, and so they decide to get an additional degree in the field of management. Today, many library directors have MBA degrees, while others have master's degrees in public administration.

One important component in every manager's continuing education is keeping up-to-date by reading both LIS management literature and management literature in general. Most librarians have easy access to both types of literature, which can provide a quick way to stay abreast of current trends. In addition, there is a wealth of management information available at one's fingertips through the Internet. Lifelong learning is important for all librarians but it is critical for all managers.

CONCLUSION

Good managers are vital to the existence of libraries of all types. It is clear that librarians of the future will be working in environments that will continue to be turbulent and fast-changing. Many experts have stated that managers need to be prepared to confront a period of chaotic change, or what some of them have called permanent "white water." If the management of organizations used to be like a pleasant boat ride down a calm quiet river, it is a different type of boat ride today. The river is full of rapids, whirlpools, eddies, and endless white water. The library profession will need to have new librarians like yourself ready to assume managerial positions and take the helm as libraries continue their exhilarating journey into the future.

SUGGESTIONS FOR FURTHER READING

Drucker, Peter F. *The Essential Drucker*. New York: HarperCollins, 2003. For over 60 years, the writings of Peter Drucker, the world's best known management guru, have been indispensable to anyone interested in management.

Harvard Business Review is a general-interest management journal published monthly by the Harvard School of Business. Its articles cover a range of managerial issues and this publication is considered essential reading by most upper level managers in all types of organizations.

Library Administration and Management is published by the Library Administration and Management Association, one of the divisions of ALA. The articles in this journal address a wide variety of managerial issues confronting library managers on all levels.

Stueart, Robert D. and Barbara B. Moran. *Library and Information Center Management*, 7th ed. Westport, CT: Libraries Unlimited, 2007. This textbook, which covers all aspects of library management, is often used in management classes in LIS programs.

Chapter 8

Marketing—The Driving Force of Your Library

Christie Koontz

WHAT MARKETING IS *NOT*

Marketing is commonly associated with fast-buck Madison Avenue advertising campaigns designed to sell, influence, and persuade people to buy things they do not want or need. This is not surprising in light of the fact that the average person is hit with thousands of advertising impressions per day. An advertising or "ad" impression is simply an exposure to some type of advertisement such as a matchbook cover, Internet pop-up, or a radio ad. It does seem that someone is always trying to persuade us to buy something.[1]

WHAT MARKETING IS . . .

But marketing is much more than advertising, selling, persuasion, or promotion. Marketing is a tried and true systematic approach that relies heavily on designing a service or product in terms of the consumers' needs and desires, with consumer satisfaction as its goal. The marketing function is the driving force of any successful business. True marketing is also the heart of any advocacy effort that attempts to communicate the library's value to key stakeholders and funders. Advocacy in some ways is "simply" marketing an issue.

When you complete this chapter you will embrace this statement and know how to conduct marketing activities.

In recent years nonprofit agencies also turned to marketing techniques. Libraries, museums, hospitals, zoos, schools, and universities are faced with the need to utilize diminishing public funds more efficiently, to provide materials and programs conveniently and effectively, and to serve diverse and demanding clientele within an ever-changing competitive environment.

Philip Kotler is given credit for broadening the concept of marketing to include nonprofit groups and offers my favorite definition of marketing: "Marketing is the implementation and control of carefully formulated programs designed to bring about voluntary exchanges of values with target markets for the purpose of achieving organizational objectives. It relies heavily on designing the organization's offering in terms of the target markets' needs and desires and on using effective pricing, communication, and distribution to inform, motivate and service the market."[2] He simplifies his statement saying, "Marketing is getting the right goods and services to the right people at the right place at the right time at the right price with the right communication and promotion—marketing is a human activity directed at satisfying needs and wants through exchange processes."[3]

HISTORY OF MARKETING (BRIEF!)

Briefly, and from a historic perspective, the concept of marketing originated within the business sector of society in the 1950s. Prior to that time emphasis was placed on producing products without regard for consumer needs or demands, coupled with the intent to sell that same product to an undefined market for a profit. Demand at this time was far greater than supply and the customer usually sought out the producer. Eventually this trend reversed and consumers realized they could make choices as well as demands of the producers. Hence marketing was born. Slowly government and nonprofit sectors began to adopt marketing practices. Once again marketing currently is perceived two ways: one, selling, influencing, and persuading people to buy things they do not necessarily want; and two, a weaker meaning in the public mind—yet more correct—is the concept of sensitively serving and satisfying human needs. It is this second side of marketing that attracts libraries.

AN INTRODUCTION TO MARKETING ACTIVITIES

To further illustrate marketing and its application to libraries, the elements of a marketing model will be described. A model is simply a step-by-step emulation of a process that illuminates the important components or variables that are imperative to the success of the process. While the model is a simplification, it will provide a vehicle to better understand important concepts and principles that will be covered in the three marketing lessons to follow. The steps include: (1) market research; (2) market segmentation; (3) the marketing mix (the 4 Ps—product, price, place, and promotion); and (4) marketing evaluation and performance measures.

SO WHAT BUSINESS ARE WE IN?

The marketing model represents only marketing-specific activities based upon a mission statement. All organizations that market must have a mission statement. The mission statement answers what business are we in? What are our goals and objectives? How will these be accomplished? Who are our customers? The answers to these questions depend upon a detailed analysis of the characteristics of the population to be served, an analysis of the strengths and weaknesses of your collection, staff, facilities and image, and developing a sense of new opportunities or even threats to the agency. In marketing this is called the "SWOT" list, assessing strengths, weaknesses, opportunities, and threats.

AND NOW, WITHOUT FURTHER ADIEU—THE MARKETING MODEL

Step One: Market Research

Market research is nothing more than finding out all you can about your market. A market or the ideal potential market is all the people who have some stated interest in a particular product or service or could be expected to do so.

Internal Records

You might ask "how do you find out all about your market?" A good first starting place is the internal records of your library. These records might include circulation data that provides as much as your computerized or manual circulation system is set up to tell you. For example, for a school media center, you might know from circulation data the age, grade level, sex, or reading interests of your users. A public library's circulation data might provide the geographic residence of users as well as age, sex, and type of reading material checked out. A university library may know class, field of study, or if the student or faculty member is full- or part time. Other possible hand-kept statistics that find their way into internal records might include in-house use of various types of materials, number of reference questions asked, number of reference questions answered per hour, number of directional queries, number of online searches performed, and the subjects of the searches.

In short, the internal records are a gold mine of market information including user data, product uses and preferences, peak hours of services, etc. If librarians are cognizant of the many uses of this data, they and the staff will be avid gatherers.

External Data or What's Happening Outside the Library's Doors

When the major types of users are identified, another source of market research is secondary data about the external environment of the library. This may include information about groups or potential markets important to the library. For example, for a university library these potential markets might include not only students and faculty, but school officials, funding officials, vendors, parents, campus groups and organizations, or friends of the library. These people are stakeholders in the library's business—in other words they are people with a vested interest in the library. Secondary data about the community within which the library resides include information such as growth trends in the general population, or sociological trends, i.e., number of working mothers, the birth rate, education levels of parents, number and diversity of ethnic groups, expected budget highs and lows. All are of major importance to the well-being of the library. The external environment of the library must be constantly and consciously researched.

Look Way Beyond the Library's Doors

Market research of society as a whole, regarding trends in health, sexual mores, entertainment, and sports, are all important in assessing the information, education, and entertainment needs of the library's population. This information is useful, if not essential, for developing the library's collection of services and materials and programs.

New Concept—Competition! (What? The Library Has Competitors?)

Who are the library's competitors? The concept and nature of the library residing within a competitive market is new to many librarians employed by public and nonprofit agencies. More and more librarians must be aware not only of direct competitors such as television, newspapers, magazine subscriptions, or information brokers, but also of other public agencies that compete for the same public monies such as schools, fire, and police.

Library customers and potential customers are constantly faced with choices. For example, a public library customer might prefer the immediate gratification of buying a best seller at the local bookstore or ordering online, rather than waiting two to four weeks to borrow it from the library. A faculty member of the university may order and buy books separately that he is unable to get within the specified time frame from interlibrary loan. A school-age child may opt for an athletic event over the library's after-school book talk. Parents may purchase children's books if too much time is needed to use the library's services successfully. User's personal time carries a price tag that contributes to the competitive environment. Libraries do reside in a competitive environment, whether library professionals or educators acknowledge it or not. Remember—competition can be healthy and productive!

Use Your Professional Talents for Your Own Library

Finally, we must remember to look for market research information in our own libraries—right under our own noses. As librarians we are used to collecting and doling out information to others; much of that same information we can use for our own purposes and for the library's well-being. And when purchasing or adding to computer systems we can glean as much information as possible about what our users need and want by identifying materials and services used, how often, what is not available that should be, etc.

Step Two: Market Segmentation

Who Are Some of the People Who May Use the Library and How Are They Alike?

The second step of the marketing model, necessarily based upon market research, is market segmentation. A market segment is a group of potential users who share similar wants and needs. Market segmentation is based on the fact that markets are heterogeneous. It is imperative for library managers to define and understand various markets in order to allocate resources efficiently and to provide services effectively.

Libraries Have Been Segmenting Markets for a Hundred Years!

Libraries historically segment their markets in a variety of ways. By materials and services, for example, fiction readers, story hour attendees, genealogy enthusiasts. Or perhaps by age groups—such as young adults, juveniles, adults, the elderly. A university typically segments by field of study, or class level—freshmen, sophomore, junior, senior, graduate student—or by faculty, staff, or community member. Special interest groups such as clubs or civic or campus organizations might constitute a segment in a high school library. An elementary school may have after-school or preschool as well as standard grade levels. A special library may segment by department or division served.

What Are Other Ways to Segment Library Markets?

The private sector learned long ago that treating all customers the same may achieve profit on some levels. But they also learned when the differences of customers within the market are ignored, the result may be that no one is really getting what they want and need from the product or service designed for a mass market.

So some of the other important ways that businesses segment their customers include the following:

1. *Geographic.* For the public library this may be a market defined by what zip code the users reside in, or neighborhood or census tract. The most ideal is actual determination of your geographic market by determining where your users live. Since circulation records are largely digital, a library can have the county planning office run these addresses through their geographic information system software and plot these out to indicate the dispersion of customers around individual branch facilities.

2. *Demographic.* These socioeconomic descriptors may include age, sex, family size, income, education, ethnicity or race, perhaps religion. Because demographics are easy to measure they are popular for marketers to use—yet alone, they may not always yield the greatest insights and results.

3. *Lifestyle.* This segment includes the attitudes, opinions, and interests of people. People in the same demographic groups can exhibit very different attitudes, lifestyles, and opinions. Therefore, for a finer tuning of a user profile, these measures are useful. This kind of information about users may be gained through in-depth interviews, possibly gleaned from national studies of same or available library research.

4. *Behavioristic.* This segmentation is considered the most meaningful, utilizing geographic, demographic, and psychographic information and further descriptors. The following are behavioristic methods of segmenting:

> *Benefit Sought*: This segmentation is an extremely useful way to think. All products and services are capable of being classified as to what benefit they provide to certain market segments. For example, a hypothetical library is seeking to determine the benefits of its best seller collection to users. The following information was extracted from a user questionnaire:

Primary Benefits	%Users	Average Age	Income	Self-Concept
Relaxing Often informative & educational	53	62	$75,000	Pleased with self Informed & up to date
Like to read all best sellers	9	54	$45,000	Open-minded

> As we can see one product may offer different benefits to various markets or members of the same market. In communicating the benefits, a library must be careful not to alienate other segments. Using the scenario above as an example, a promotional campaign that communicated "you read best sellers because you simply like to read every one," might contrast negatively with the self-image of a user who simply finds a best seller every now and then relaxing.

> Another example might be the benefits of an online computerized search. Benefits, remember, may be real or imagined. While researchers may be the library's prime market for this service in the university library, the benefits of the search may be different to different students, e.g., saves your time, you feel more secure about the exhaustive nature of the search, your research is improved, your self-esteem is improved.

> *Actual Customer or Potential Customer*: This is another behavior category that is familiar to libraries. This is not always as helpful to libraries

because often actual customers and potential customers may share common characteristics. Only in-depth research might illuminate why an individual does not utilize library services and materials. While many libraries conduct user studies and surveys, this is often simply describing the "contented" group—the group who uses the library as opposed to the group who does not, which as discussed above is more difficult to ascertain.

Volume: Light, medium, or heavy volume of library use is another way to segment. Perhaps a library might settle for serving a few heavy users or many light users. Circulation statistics from computerized systems are rich with volume information. As mentioned earlier, these circulation systems and packages may be designed to offer user information by address or zip code, sex, education level, and type of material used.

Step Three: Marketing Mix Strategy

Most organizations (libraries included) offer limited resources and, therefore, must allocate these resources accordingly. For example, the reference service must support the goals and objectives of the library, but also meet the needs of every individual (or attempt to) who calls in or walks in. Therefore, this third step of the marketing model—which develops product, price, place, and promotion of materials and services and programs based upon market research to various market segments—assists libraries in utilizing these limited funds in an efficient and effective manner.

The marketing mix comprising product, price, place, and promotion is often called the 4 Ps. While the mix is the most visible part of the marketing model, it is not exclusively the most important. Librarians historically participate heavily in the promotion arm of the mix. Little explicit regard is given to aspects of price, place, and product when considering which segments to prioritize service to.

So What Is a Library Product?

Briefly and broadly, a product is defined as anything that can be offered to a market to satisfy a need. Library products can include materials such as books, films, videocassettes, CDs, educational games, software or toys, or Internet access. Products may also be sources such as the librarian's assistance to customers through computer or manual aided searches, or through provision of information and instruction in the use of the library. Library products may also be programs such as outreach, book-talks, story hours, exhibits, demonstrations, ESL classes, or document delivery and interlibrary loan. The list varies from library to library, and from type of library to type of library. The product line must be constantly reviewed and adjusted according to market segment needs.

Hey, I Thought Library Service Was Free, What Price Is Involved?

Price usually describes the actual charge made by an organization, but it can also be the toil and trouble of acquiring it—and libraries may unfortunately offer plenty of that! As described earlier book purchasing may be less costly time-wise to individuals than the free cost of using the library. Time is money. Fees for online searches may be fairly common, while fees for reserves and interlibrary loan are less so. So most libraries—if they do charge—simply charge to recover costs. For the library certainly the most important aspects of price are the cost of the user's time, such as travel time, wait time, inquiry time, and speed of assistance by library staff.

Location, Location, Location...

Place is the third component. This involves how the library makes its products and services available and accessible to its markets. For the public library this might include bookmobiles, storefront libraries, and branches. For the university library this might include centrality of location, hours of access available, locations of remote online catalogs, or satellite facilities. Historically scientific location theory is not applied when choosing a site for a public library. Yet optimal placement of the library facility for optimal use is as critical to the library as it is to a retailer.

Also, an even lesser consideration regarding place is the interior placement of goods and services within the library for distribution. The layout of the library affects price—the user's time—as well as how products may be accessed or promoted.

Consideration of the ease of use of the library's Web site is a growing concern as libraries consider access points. For potential library users this Web site may be the first calling card they see—and based upon their experience they may continue using library services or choose other competitors.

Promotion Is Not Public Relations

Promotion is the fourth component of the market mix. Promotion is sometimes confused with public relations, which is a two-way communication that depends on feedback. Promotion simply articulates what the library is doing and what it is. There are four groups of promotion tools: advertising, sales promotion, personal selling, and publicity. Again the publicity area is a real trouble spot—at least in understanding that publicity is only one single facet of the marketing process, and is not synonymous with marketing. Granted publicity is a very effective and powerful tool when based upon market research and targeted to a particular segment. This confusion perpetuates the belief by the inexperienced that marketing is promotion. The reader of this article is now aware of marketing's complexity and cyclical steps.

Step Four: Marketing Evaluation

The last part of the model is evaluation and measures of productivity. In the last two decades libraries of all types and respective professional organizations are producing evaluation measures. In the past, libraries traditionally measured "input" such as number of volumes, number of staff, number of hours open, circulation, and registrations. Now libraries because of a growing need for accountability and competition for dwindling public funds are measuring output—circulation per capita, volumes per capita, and registrations per capita. Additionally the use of outcome measures is an attempt to measure the impact of library services upon the customers served—this usually entails asking people questions, such as "how did the children's program benefit your child?"

The benefits of continuing attention to productivity are numerous. If the librarian exhibits interest in productivity the staff is likely to approach operations with an eye to greater efficiency.

The evaluation phase is taken one step further. In actuality evaluation is ongoing and implicit within other parts of the model. A formalized activity—the marketing audit—provides a vehicle for this expansion. The audit is something that can occur before an organization markets, during the marketing process, and after marketing begins. It takes a critical look at an organization's performance in marketing. The marketing audit is a comprehensive and systematic review of the organization's internal and external environment, the objectives, strategies, and activities, identifying problem areas and opportunities, and recommending a plan of action for improvement.

SUMMARY

The interesting thing about marketing is that all organizations do it whether they know it or not—of course, with varying degrees of success. For example, libraries, like businesses, search for prospects or in our case, users/customers; develop products (programs, services, and materials); price these (fees, cost of users' time); distribute these (the main facility, branch facilities, bookmobiles, kiosks, Web site and other online venues, as well as distribution within the library); and promote these (publicity, public service announcements, posters, brochures, possibly advertising).

Many nonprofit groups confuse marketing with aggressive promotion unaccompanied by any real improvements of programs and services based on marketing principles. Libraries are famous for general promotion campaigns that reach anyone who will see or listen. For example, one National Library Week slogan was "Go for it—use your library!" While it does have a clear response stated, one wonders if anyone who previously was not a library user became one because of the exhortation to "go for it!"

Marketing is *not* a panacea for underfunding, understaffing, undercompetence by staff, or lack of substance in the collection. Marketing is *not* a substitute for knowing the interests and concerns of potential as well as actual customers. Marketing is *not* just selling what you have in publicity blitz.

Marketing represents an organized way of offering library services that include actual and potential customer interests, communication methods, imaginative design of service and products, and feedback that improves what you are doing.

SUGGESTIONS FOR FURTHER READING

Andreasen, Alan R. and Philip Kotler. *Strategic Marketing for Nonprofit Organizations*, 6th ed. Upper Saddle River, NJ: Prentice Hall, 2003.
Koontz, Christie. *Customer Based Marketing*, a column for *Marketing Library Services*. Medford, NJ: Information Today, 2001–Present.

Chapter 9

Reflections on Creating Information Service Collections

G. Edward Evans

Age and experience don't always translate into great wisdom, but both can provide some "lessons learned" along the way. What follows are some thoughts and reflections that may prove useful to those who will build collections over the coming years. Perhaps these lessons may be of some value to newcomers to the field.

The lessons I have learned have come through teaching, research, and, above all, practice in a variety of settings both at home and abroad. The lessons began for me when I was as a page in a public library and will probably end with my "solo" experience in a museum archive and library. In between, were years of academic library, teaching, and research activities including a stint in a patient/medical library at a Veterans Administration hospital.

Reflecting upon my various experiences in collection development there are a host of lessons, some good, some not so good, and certainly far too many to cover in a short essay. However, there are seven important areas that have been consistent across the various environments that I believe may have long-term value to those interested in collection development now and in the future:

- Know/learn your service community's needs and interests;
- Remember our "product" is access to information regardless of format;
- Expect change and be flexible;
- Think ahead/plan/scan the environment;
- Build relationships;
- Engage in collaborative/consortial activities; and,
- Realize that providing access can be a challenge for a variety of reasons.

UNDERSTAND YOUR COMMUNITY'S NEEDS

One of the great satisfactions during a busy day in a library, archive, or other information service is the pleased/happy look on people's faces when you supply just what they were looking for. Of course today, in many cases, it's not a matter of face-to-face interaction; nevertheless I have found you do get something of the equivalent smile in the form of thank you e-mails. Sometimes what you give them comes as a surprise to them, because they were unclear about just what they needed or were doubtful that the information might actually exist. A thoughtfully developed collection can, and more often than not does, assist in generating very satisfied users.

Certainly no single information service is able to supply all the information needs of every person every time. Each service has, or should have, a clearly defined mission that links its activities to the interests of a larger institution/organization/community be it public or private in character. No information service can or should stand completely alone, not even national libraries. None have the resources—people, time, equipment, or money—to collect and preserve all the information society generates even for a short period of time. Those facts bring us back to the happy/satisfied smiles on users' faces. You achieve such satisfied smiles or thank you e-mails by thoroughly getting to know and understand your service community in all its aspects. Achieving this takes time and effort on your part as well as from others.

Before undertaking a study of a service community you should devote some thought to how you will view/define a few key words—normative, felt, expressed, and comparative needs. A sound collection development plan will incorporate all four need types; however, understanding their differences is essential in employing them in the best mix for your service community.

Depending solely on *normative needs* (expert opinion about what is needed) is something newcomers to collection development have a tendency to do. Focusing on such needs does reduce the pressure on you to get to know and understand the service population as well as a way to justify a decision in case of a challenge to something you have added to the collection. (The latter point is something you will very likely encounter if you spend any amount of time in the field, and being able to point to experts' opinions provides at least a sense of protection. More often than not, it is just a sense rather than real protection.) Clearly when the service supports the activities of a group of specialists (R&D staff, doctors, or lawyers, for example) depending on their opinions is the appropriate approach. However, even here, getting to know the relatively small and more or less homogeneous population allows you to anticipate their requests. Nothing builds goodwill and support like having a specialist come to suggest an acquisition and being able to hand the person the desired item. Those successes almost always come about through knowing the community needs and interests.

In terms of public libraries, normative needs ought to play a role, albeit a modest one, in collection building. Special and, to a lesser degree, academic libraries make greater use of such needs. There is often a substantial difference between what experts *think* people need, or should need, and what people want and will use. If you drift too far from what community actually wants, you and your library risk losing critical support at budget time, especially in tight times.

In a sense, the published/online reviews of information packages—books, journal videos, e-resources, etc.—feed into the concept of normative need. Presumably reviewers are selected for their expertise, and thus their opinion(s) carry important weight when making an acquisition decision. School media centers and public libraries make substantial use of reviews.

Felt needs are almost the opposite end of the need spectrum. They arise from within the community as it assesses its circumstances. A felt need may or may not be realistic or even "good" for the community. You should be cautious in weighing the importance of strongly articulated felt needs—small highly vocal groups can sometimes drown out larger but less organized community groups. Allowing the volume of requests for a category/topic to solely determine selection decisions is generally not a good idea. Certainly they play a role in the selection process, but they can become a driving force that ultimately limits the overall value of the collection(s) to the entire community. Probably the most common occurrence is where what people use/borrow becomes the key decision factor. What can happen is a small percentage—around 20 percent— of the service community will account for the vast majority of use (80+ percent). When you allow that usage to drive the collection building process, slowly but surely you exclude low use or nonusers interests. The basic key is to try to represent all felt needs.

The foregoing also relates to *expressed needs*. We have all experienced instances where someone says something and then acts in a way that is contrary to what was said. Expressed needs are reflected in what is done, not said. A very simple example of the difference between felt and expressed needs in the library context is where people claim that "classic literature" is what they read and that libraries should stock that type of material. However, looking at data about what they buy or borrow, and presumably read, one finds it is almost all genre fiction, at least for public libraries. A sound goal for a collection is to have a balance based on felt and expressed needs and not drifting too far toward one side or the other. Going too far either way can damage community support when you may most need it.

There are times when some benchmarking (*comparisons*) may pay big dividends. Looking at what other like services make available to their communities can provide some guidance for your collection building activities. It can, at times, be useful in gaining increased budget support for collection development. (Over the years I responded to numerous requests from collection development colleagues about collection size, utilization data, and allocations for acquisitions. I responded because they had responded to similar requests from me.) When gathering such data, you must keep in mind no two services are identical. You are seldom able to fully transplant others' service approaches to your service and expect to have identical outcomes. However, such data does provide food for thought and reworking others' ideas and approaches to fit your service community does work. Knowledge about similar collections is essential for collaborative efforts—more about that later.

Gaining an understanding of your service community takes time and effort as well as being an ongoing activity. Some information comes about through daily transactions within the service, such as what is and is not being asked for and used. Today's integrated library systems (ILS) can generate vast amounts of data about user behavior that can and should feed into the collection building process. Transforming that data into useful information requires careful thought and a plan to handle/collect the most useful data. Other information comes from outside the service and requires a formal project (needs assessment, community analysis, and information audit are some labels for this process), especially when the focus is on identifying and gaining an understanding of the nonuser component of the community. Each project requires its own set of questions, some examples are:

- What are the most important felt needs within the community?
- What are the most significant normative needs?
- Which needs are the most relevant for the service to address given funding realities?
- How will you reconcile multiple valid needs as well as conflicting needs?
- Which of the underserved groups should be given priority and how should we establish those priorities?
- How will the new approach(es) fit into the existing service structure and how realistic is it to expect additional funding to address both the new activities and any necessary adjustments to existing service?

WHAT TO COLLECT?

Although we are near the end of the first decade of the new century there are still a few people who think libraries are just places to find books and magazines on the shelves. The idea that libraries for the most part have transformed themselves into information centers just has not occurred to such people. Very likely many of them have not visited a library in many years. (Unfortunately, all too many of these people are in positions to control funding for libraries. Not an insignificant number of those truly believe the Internet has made libraries irrelevant, or at best museums for books that no one really needs or much less reads.) The view that libraries equal books, while unjustified, has been around throughout most of my career.

When I began working in libraries—long ago and far way—the public library system where I worked did have a "recorded music" department (the records were noncirculating) down at the central building. I still recall the look on the face of the lady on the other side of the desk when I asked about what jazz recordings they had—"Young man, we only have classical music!"—let your imagination be your guide to the look that accompanied that statement. We have come light years from that concept, especially in public, school, and community college libraries. The distance may not be light years for academic libraries but they too have made notable progress.

By the time I started my first full-time professional work in a library, and as a collection development staff member, there was progress within the profession regarding the need to collect all formats. However, the same could not be said for those that issued checks and audited accounts. We had to rework any order for nonprint items into a form that looked like a book or journal order; if we didn't, the order came back with the note "an unauthorized request." The reworking of the order information wasted a substantial amount of time. My department head as well as the director were rather ahead of the times as they frequently said "we're not just in the book business and those——are wasting our time and theirs." (Both the department head and director were also sticklers for knowing the community and the collection. You got to go on buying trips only as long as less than 10 percent of what you purchased duplicated existing holdings or failed to match identified needs. Getting to spend the day in San Francisco or Berkeley buying items for the collection was always a great treat.)

Even in my last two full-time positions, there was a curious resistance to the idea that libraries are in the information rather than book business. The first instance was at a prestigious private east coast university. Based on interviews with all the faculty members, doctoral students, and curators, the primary service population of the library I was responsible for, it was clear there was a universal desire to have a collection of documentary videos in the library. To my surprise, I learned the library system "only funds book and serial collections." It would be acceptable to build a video collection, but only with outside funding. And further, that the system would not assist in seeking such funds. With senior faculty support, raising the funds proved to be easy and we started building the collection. (Note: the views of that library system have since changed and it now supports the acquisition of all formats.)

The most recent experience (early 1990s) was where the library had a "book" and "journal" fund and a nominal budget ($1,000) for "other media." All that was necessary was to get faculty, senior administrators, and a few library staff members to stop thinking about categories and thinking of a materials budget. This was vitally important as we were starting to acquire e-resources (moving funds from "books" or "journals" in order to subscribe to a database brought back memories of the first full-time job). It took a few years but as the concept of "information" become more apparent to senior administrators, the "materials budget" became a reality. However, as late as 2005 there were still a few senior faculty members who asked me, "What is my book budget for this year?" They did indeed mean books as they would occasionally ask if there was any money to buy a video or subscribe to a database.

Dynamic, highly regarded information services build their collections around what information formats best meet the needs and interests of their service communities. Assessing new formats for their potential in addressing such needs and interests is an important part of an effective collection development officer's activities. Mistakes will be made (think about those who were quick to jump on the e-book band wagon a few years ago); however, in my view, taking some calculated (thoughtful) risks is one of the hallmarks of a first rate collection development officer.

EMBRACE CHANGE

If nothing else, the most consistent lesson has been that change happens and it's better to embrace it than to fight it. The above discussion of what to collect reflects one of the change factors you will have to deal with—what the collection formats will be in the future is impossible to accurately predict, but change they will. For me, the best example of the impact of change on collection building relates to music recordings. (Yes, e-resources are also a shift in how we expend our funds but, at least for me, they are not as frustrating and don't feel like a waste of funds.)

Let's assume you worked in the music department in that public library system I mentioned earlier from the day Ed Evans asked about jazz recordings until the present. How many times would you have had to purchase a recording of, say Edvard Grieg's *Holberg Suite*, to match the changes in technology? Two, three, four, five, or even more? The answer is at least seven, not counting iPods and online sources—I'm not certain of how comprehensively classical genre is represented on download lists. Certainly you could skip a format assuming you have confidence that the format will be short lived; not a bad assumption when it comes to recorded music. Remember, each time you repurchase the same music in a new format there is just a little less available to purchase new artists/music that are not in the collection. We may indeed encounter similar issues over the years with e-resources—we had our fun with CD towers and tape loads and now there are issues of maintaining Internet connectivity for access to our database subscriptions. However, in these cases the new form brought with it at least some new material/information in addition to the data we had paid for in the past.

Not only do your collections change over time, so does the character of your service community regardless of its type. Research and reading interests constantly shift and the effective collections adjust accordingly. One challenge is how to reflect such shifts while maintaining a coherent collection development plan—you can respond too quickly to an apparent shift that turns out to be exceedingly short term and end up with a great many very small ineffective topical collections. Having an approved, carefully thought-out collection development policy, which you review and adjust periodically, will help in achieving a realistic balance between current and long-term interests.

Many people have difficulty effectively handling change, be it work or purely personal in character. As a collection development officer, you have to deal with changing formats, so perhaps you have a leg up on others when it comes to other workplace changes. This may assist you when it comes to supervising others. Shifting workloads, new/upgraded ILS systems, organizational restructuring, etc., are a fact of information center worklife. Being able to help your colleagues get through what may be viewed as traumatic change by some people will be a great career asset. Understanding the nature of organizational change is an important key element in being able to do so. The "classic" change model consists of three stages—unfreezing, changing, and refreezing. By understanding the change process you should be able to assist colleagues having problems as well as making the experience less traumatic for those you supervise.

ENGAGE IN SCANNING

Scanning/observing your environment is something any good manager does, or should do, all the time. Certainly doing so helps you anticipate developments/changes that may impact your service's activities. Being proactive rather than reactive is almost always a better option. Obviously just engaging in scanning is not adequate, you must devote time and thought to what you are seeing. Once you have done that you can develop a plan of action.

Gaining an understanding of the service community through studies and projects is a form of scanning, assuming this is an ongoing activity. Some years ago, a public library system I was acquainted with more or less ignored population shifts. Over a period of years, some branch libraries saw a low but steady decline in usage; that in turn led to shortening of hours and staffing. What came as a surprise was the news that the city attorney announced the system was discriminating in its service to nonwhite groups. Collections that it developed for one population were seldom very appealing to other groups as they moved into what had been all Anglo areas. That led to lowering usage and, because much of the funding for branch operations was based on usage data, there was less funding to support appropriate adjustments in collection building, service hours, etc. Had ongoing scanning of the environment occurred, the changing demographics would have become apparent long before the city attorney made it a public issue. With recognition of the problem, the system created a plan of action, but it took a good many years to overcome the lack of appropriate scanning much less thinking about the data that existed.

Scanning is, in part, a function of keeping up to date with what is happening in the profession and the world at large. Read the professional journals and, in my view, don't limit yourself to just "your" type of information service or your country. There are a host of good ideas floating around in other types of services and locations that will, with a little tweaking, be suitable for your service and that may even be viewed as innovative in the new environment. Globalization is a word we frequently hear today and perhaps we don't think it has any real application to our work as information professionals. If nothing else, monitoring economic conditions in countries where you acquire substantial amounts of material will help you anticipate changes in monetary exchange rates, something that academic libraries find to be an issue more often than they'd like. I also firmly believe you can gain insight into possible economic shifts in your location by reading and thinking about the implications of what is happening in other regions. (Anticipating and planning for possible budget shortfalls will make necessary adjustments easier, but not any more pleasant.)

Environmental scanning should be a high-priority activity for collection development officers. Tracking information producers' activities and plans will help with your budget preparation. Developing the habit of scanning the environment will also pay dividends in your career long-term as it is a skill all effective managers must develop.

BUILD RELATIONSHIPS

Building relationships is also a useful skill for long-term career purposes. From a collection development point-of-view, one of the most important areas in which to build strong relations is with vendors.

When I taught collection development, most classes had one or two individuals who were working, or had worked, in an acquisitions or collections development unit. Rather often I would get the comment something to the effect that I had a rather positive attitude toward "the enemy" (the vendors). They were the enemy because they increased prices, failed to provide the desired level of service, etc. In most cases, the person holding the "enemy" view really did not understand the issues facing vendors and producers of information.

Yes, vendors do raise prices, but more often than not it is because their costs escalated rather than "price gouging." Not understanding the operating environment of vendors is a leading cause of misunderstanding and one of the best ways I know of to gain such an understanding is by getting to know your vendors on a personal level. Having a cup of coffee or lunch with them is a good way to learn more about their business and its issues.

I always found it easier to resolve vendor performance issues when there was a sound overall relationship. Dealing with a problem as soon as possible rather than building up a "body of evidence" with which to confront the vendor always worked well for me.

At my last full-time job we developed a very close working relationship with our serials jobber. So close in fact, that when the regional office (just a few miles from the library) hired a new person who had no library experience, they would ask if the person could spend a week or two at the library to begin to gain a sense of what libraries really do and how they work. While that type of relationship can develop rarely, just because of physical locations, lesser relationships can pay big dividends.

Additionally you shouldn't overlook the value of building relationships within your parent organization. One very obvious place to establish a solid professional relationship is with the individuals in the business office that you deal with regularly. Again, getting to know its challenges and what information the people there must have to carry out their tasks is a good first step in creating a good working relationship. Most individuals are pleased to explain what and why they do what they do, especially when it may make their work a little easier. Over the years I found it much easier to gain an exception or even a change in policy when I could present it in terms of how the request fit into their context and yet would meet the library's need as well.

Naturally, building relationships with your colleagues in other services is also extremely valuable. Comparing notes on vendors and other collection issues are obvious benefits of such relationships. In today's environment where resource sharing is so important and, I must note, easier to do than in the early days of my career, having strong personal relationships across service types makes consortial activities so much more effective. They can also provide mentoring opportunities both as mentor and mentee.

SUPPORT AND ENGAGE IN CONSORTIAL/COLLABORATIVE PROJECTS

No service is an island unto itself and never has been. Early efforts at resource sharing were several and ambitious in character; most failed for technical reasons but a few because of people issues. Today, the challenge of knowing who owns what and its availability is almost nonexistent due to online cata-logs. Even delivery of the material is less of an issue. State-wide networks that offer access to materials are fairly commonplace. A number of consortia exist that are negotiating lower prices on e-resources for their members.

The biggest challenges for such projects are people and funding. Funding is never as much as we would like and price increases present additional pres-sures. One way to expand resources is through grants, especially for efforts that cut across service types. To secure such funds means someone(s) must prepare the request, which is often easier than getting agreement on what and how much to ask for. This gets us back to the people challenge and relation-ships.

My consortial experiences have been mostly in my later positions where you are dealing with other senior service managers (directors). One reason for this was the experiences involved creating resource/cost sharing projects; as such they required senior people who could make budgetary commitments. At this level and with the type of project, even with prior professional contact and work, personality, trust, and shared beliefs issues were extremely critical. Needless to say developing those critical traits takes time working together. One project was solely based on "volunteer" efforts by individual directors and with no outside funding. A problem was that much of the work fell to just a few members out of a larger group. (It was not that others would not have liked to do more, but they did not have enough staff at "home" to shift any of their time to consortial work. We understood those limitations and maintained their involvement because of the belief we would all gain something in the long run regardless of how the work was shared.) The bottom line is we grew from a group of twelve to more than ninety institutions because the early group had strong personal relationships and group belief in the project's long-term value to all our institutions. Without those relationships and belief, the project would have died like so many other resource sharing projects had in the past.

PROMOTE ACCESS

My final lesson is that you should never forget that information services exist to provide people with access to the information they need and want. Sometimes in the hustle and bustle of daily work it is easy to forget why we are doing what we do. When unused, a collection is just so many objects and really of little or no value. Only through use does it become a vital asset to anyone, much less to the service population. Having the right items, at the right time, in the right format is the essence of a valued collection.

Sometimes providing access is more of a challenge than you might expect. Almost every service I've worked in had at least one instance of where who has or should have access to what became an issue. Today, most public and school libraries face the issue of Internet access and how to filter that access. They also face more than their share of complaints about this or that item in the collection from individuals as well as formal groups. In both cases, there is more than a little element of politics involved as well as philosophical differences in personal beliefs. The idea of presenting a balance of views on controversial topics is a challenging one, especially if doing so could cost you your position. (As I mentioned earlier, just having a review of an item by an expert is seldom all that you need to justify an acquisition when it is called into question.) Having in place, before a challenge arises, a process for handling complaints is one of the best ways to have some protection and promote full access for one and all.

For academic and specialized information services there is another type of limiting access that comes into play. Services with archival collections often have "restrictions" on who may access, or in some cases, when a collection may be accessed. More often than not such restrictions are imposed by the donor of the collection. Certainly a collection development officer should try to keep such restrictions to a minimum, but often you will not get the collection without the restrictions. Think carefully about the value of the collection to your service population and its relationship to the service's mission and goals before accepting such collections. It may be better to suggest a different service in some cases.

There is another form of access restriction that a few services are having to address today and the pressure is likely to increase in the coming years. Many native groups in the United States are demanding control over their cultural patrimony, even when it comes to materials that have been in the public sphere for more than 100 years. "Culturally sensitive" materials can be published and unpublished as well as print, audio, films, or photographic materials. How to handle this issue is especially difficult for individuals who believe strongly in freedom of access. You may expect to handle such requests in more and more academic libraries, especially those located near large populations of native people or known for their strong collections in the area of native studies.

Providing access and being an advocate of free access is part of being a collection development officer. Most of the time it is of no real concern, but when the issue does come up it can be stressful. Having well-thought plans for handling the matter and having a strong support network of colleagues will make it more manageable.

SOME FINAL THOUGHTS

Being able to develop useful collections is a lot of work, but it is also fun and rewarding. I know those of you who go down this career path will face some hurdles and challenges I never experienced. I do hope that whatever those are they will be, in the long run, just as rewarding for you as my challenges have been for me.

Best wishes for your career and may you build great collections, whatever their format may be. Never forget the primacy of your stakeholders' interests and needs.

SUGGESTIONS FOR FURTHER READING

Atkinson, Ross. "Six Key Challenges for the Future of Collection Development." *Library Resources & Technical Services* 50(4) (October 2006), 244–251.

Briscoe, Peter M., Alice Bodtke-Roberts, and Nancy E. Douglas. "Ashurbanipal's Enduring Archetype: Thoughts on the Library's Role in the Future." *College & Research Libraries* 47(3) (March 1986), 121–126.

Genco, Barbra. "20 Maxims for Collection Building." *Library Journal* 132 (September 15, 2007), 32–35.

Chapter 10

Organization and Representation of Information/Knowledge

Arlene G. Taylor

A basic drive in humans seems to be to organize. Psychologists tell us that babies' brains organize images into categories such as "faces" or "foods." Small children do a lot of organizing during play. With some individuals the need is much stronger than with others. Those who operate on the maxim, "A place for everything and everything in its place," cannot begin to work until the work surface is cleared and every stray object has been put in its place. That is, such a person has to be "organized" before beginning a new project. But even those whose workspaces appear to be cluttered or chaotic have some organization in their heads. Such persons usually have some idea, or perhaps certain knowledge, of what is in the various piles or collections of "stuff." Regardless of one's personal style, however, human learning is based upon the ability to analyze and organize data, information, and knowledge.

We organize because we need to retrieve. Kitchens are organized so that cooking equipment is easily accessible and foodstuffs and spices can be used as needed. Workplaces are organized so that appropriate records or tools are retrievable and work can be done. Learning processes are organized so that relationships among ideas can be used to assist the learner in recalling the learned material.

Retrieval of information is dependent upon its having been organized. Information is needed in all aspects of life—for example, for health reasons, to understand each other, to learn about one's relationships, to fix things that are broken, or simply to expand our knowledge. Some of this information has already been assimilated and is in one's knowledge store, while other information has to be sought. If it is not organized, it is difficult, if not impossible, to find. So we have all kinds of tools that are organized to aid in the process of finding information that we need: telephone books, directories, dictionaries, encyclopedias, bibliographies, indexes, library catalogs, museum catalogs and databases, and archival finding aids, among others.

Organization of information also allows us to keep usable records of human endeavors for posterity. Libraries, archives, museums, and other types of institutions have been doing this for many years. There are also commercial enterprises that have put together collections for the purpose of sale, rather than collecting for posterity.

INFORMATION OR KNOWLEDGE?

There is a running argument between those who believe we are organizing information and those who believe we are organizing knowledge. It seems to me that I can use my knowledge to write a book, but until you read that book, understand it, and integrate it into your own knowledge, it is just information. On the other hand, the book would be a representation of my knowledge, although it would be an imperfect representation, in the sense that some concepts might not be explained as clearly or as fully as I truly understand them. I believe we organize information so that others can find it, read or otherwise absorb it, and use it to add to their own store of knowledge. But it is also fair to say that we organize representations of knowledge.

THE NATURE OF THE ORGANIZATION OF RECORDED KNOWLEDGE

This chapter addresses the organization of recorded information, as other means are necessary to "organize" information that has only been spoken, heard, or thought about. Recorded information, however, includes much more than text. Video and audio recordings, pictures, cartographic representations, and Web pages are all examples of recorded information that is not just "text." Therefore, instead of using words such as *book* or *item* to refer to the organizable unit of information, the term *information resource* is used in this chapter.

Ronald Hagler, in his book, *The Bibliographic Record and Information Technology*, has identified six functions of bibliographic control.[1] His listing reflects the purpose of his book, that is, the emphasis is upon the work of librarians in their collection of mainly printed resources. However, the list, presented and elaborated below, with wording altered to be inclusive of all recorded information, reflects the major activities involved in the organization of recorded information.

1. *Identifying the existence of all types of information resources as they are made available*

A book may be published or a Web site may be established, but if no one knows of its existence except the person(s) involved in its creation, it will be of no informational use to anyone. Existence and identity can be made known in many ways: publishers' announcements, e-mail announcements, reviews, subject-related listings, to name a few. Most publishers create catalogs listing their publications along with abstracts for them. Reference tools such as *Books in Print* are products of this activity. Some online journals send regular e-mail announcements, outlining contents, to let readers know when a new issue is available. Some news organizations allow people to sign up to receive e-mail announcements about new information available at the organization's Web site or about how to order recordings of special programs, and so on.

2. *Identifying the works contained within those information resources or as parts of them*

In the majority of cases one information resource is equal to one intellectual or creative work. However, in some cases a single information source may comprise a collection of short stories or a grouping of artistic images, etc., of which each individual story or artistic image may be considered to be a work in its own right. The level at which the works or resources are described depends upon how much *granularity* is desired. A Web site that is all about a famous person may have individual digitized works by the person, biographical material, accounts of the person written by contemporaries, accounts of events contemporary to the person's lifespan, and other parts. The writings about the person and the events may be important works in their own right and may need to be identified separately.

3. *Systematically pulling together these information resources into collections in libraries, archives, museums, Internet communication files, and other such depositories*

The activity of creating collections has been thought of traditionally as the province of institutions such as libraries, archives, and museums. But collections have always been created in many other situations, e.g., personal collections made up because of an intense interest in a particular kind of information, office collections of internal information and information needed to carry out the work of the office, university departmental collections of materials needed for teaching in a particular discipline, etc. Now it is easy to make these collections known publicly through lists provided at Web sites.

Collections often include electronic resources not held locally. Many institutions purchase the right to allow the users of their collections to search a resource online. Some resources are accessible only online. Others are also available in print. Part of the organizing process is determining whether such resources need to be added to one's collection in some permanent way.

4. *Producing lists of these information resources prepared according to standard rules for citation*

Lists created in the process of describing information resources include bibliographies, indexes, library catalogs, archival finding aids, museum databases, and Web directories. These are important to the retrieval of individual information resources because if one is looking for a known item, especially a tangible one that requires a specific physical location, it is necessary to find it listed somewhere. Such lists may be in print or electronic form.

5. *Providing name, title, subject, and other useful access to these information resources*

The activity that adds the most value to the usefulness and retrieval potential of a collection is the provision of name, title, and subject access points to the descriptions of the information resources. Keyword access can be provided more or less automatically and "on-the-fly," that is, any information in electronic form can be found by searching for a word that appears in the electronic information resource. However, as the size of the collection being searched increases, results of keyword searches become less and less satisfactory. More satisfactory retrieval comes from being able to search for names, titles, and subjects that have been constructed, usually by humans, to bring together variant forms and related terms. If a person has been identified by different forms of a name, and if that name is developed by this process (called *authority control*), then a search for one form of the name will retrieve information resources related to the person regardless of which form of name appears in a particular resource. If a work has been given different titles in its different manifestations, a search for one of the titles will retrieve all. Similarly, if a system uses controlled vocabulary for subjects, a search for a word with more than one meaning (which encompasses most English words) will allow differentiation among the various meanings and will direct one to broader, narrower, and related terms. It will also bring together under one term all the synonyms that may be used to express a concept.

Authority control is of little use unless retrieval systems are designed to take advantage of it. Therefore, a major part of organizing information is designing systems for searching and display that will allow information-seekers to find easily what they need and want.

6. *Providing the means of locating each information resource or a copy of it*

Location of information resources has been, for at least a century, a value added by institutions with collections. The catalogs or other lists created in these institutions give information on the physical location of the information resource. In many library online catalogs, circulation information is available so that if an item has been taken out of the library, that information is conveyed along with the location information. Bibliographic networks (e.g., OCLC—Online Computer Library Center) allow one to find out which institutions own a particular item. Many library, museum, and archival catalogs are available on the Internet. One can learn from these which site owns an item, whether it is on loan at a particular locality (usually a library, because archives and museums generally do not circulate items from their collections), and often whether a resource is on order and when it is expected to arrive.

Traditionally, bibliographies and indexes do not give location information. Bibliographies list information resources that exist somewhere, but seldom tell where. Indexes give the larger information resource in which a smaller work being listed can be found (e.g., the journal in which an article can be found), but do not give the physical location of the larger information resource. All of this is still true for tangible resources, but for electronic resources found on the Internet, it is becoming more common to give a location (e.g., the URL) in any listing that includes the electronic resource. However, the instability of URLs makes it difficult to keep them current.

ORGANIZATION OF INFORMATION IN DIFFERENT ENVIRONMENTS

There are many environments in which there is a desire to organize information so that it will be retrievable for various purposes and so that at least some of it will be kept for posterity. The ones to be discussed here are libraries of all types and the Internet (including digital libraries).

Libraries

As mentioned earlier the process begins with collections. Collections in libraries are created through the process called collection development, discussed in the preceding chapter. When new materials arrive for addition to the collections, physical entities have to be arranged in some fashion. They may be placed on shelves in the order in which they come in, or they may be placed in some more meaningful order. They could be placed in alphabetical order, the way that many fiction and biography sections are arranged. Most, however, are arranged by classification. Classification of materials is part of the process of cataloging, which is usually the first activity following receipt of the materials.

Cataloging involves:

- creating a description of the item;
- choosing certain names and titles to serve as access points for finding the description in the catalog;
- doing authority work on those names and titles;
- analyzing the subject matter of the work;
- choosing subject headings and classification notations to represent the subject content;
- and, for physical items, creating call numbers (location devices), usually by adding a Cutter number to the classification notation to make a unique set of letters and numbers to identify the particular physical item.

Most records thus created are encoded with the MAchine Readable Cataloging (MARC) format so that they can be displayed in the Integrated Library Systems (ILSs) that most libraries have. Let's look at the processes involved in cataloging in a little more detail.

Description

First is the process of creating a description of the item. The purposes of creating a description are:

- to present the characteristics of an information resource;
- to give enough information about an information resource to identify it uniquely and to distinguish it from every other information resource;
- to aid in evaluating or selecting (e.g., Is the original manuscript of a book needed, or will a printed copy do? Is the 8th ed. as good as the 9th ed. for my purposes? Is a vinyl LP acceptable or can I only play a CD?); and

- to provide a filter that serves as a surrogate for a full information resource so that users do not have to examine a multitude of complete (e.g., full text) resources in order to find what is needed.

A description is the beginning of what is often called a "surrogate record" or "metadata." In order to provide a description, it is first necessary to determine the unit to be described. What is the "catalogable" unit? Information resources may contain one work each or one resource may contain many works. For example, a music CD may contain a Brahms symphony, followed by a Schubert symphony, each played by a different orchestra. And each work may appear in multiple expressions (e.g., the Schubert symphony in textual musical notation vs. the performed version). Further, each expression may appear in multiple manifestations (e.g., the musical notation published at the time of its composition vs. the photocopy of it printed 100 years later). It is also necessary to distinguish resources that are complete in one physical package, or in a set of volumes, from resources that are meant to continue indefinitely, such as a monthly journal.

The profession has descriptive schemas that are used to provide descriptions so that they will be standardized and therefore interchangeable and usable in online systems. The most-used bibliographic and general metadata schemas are the:

- ISBD (International Standard Bibliographic Description);
- AACR2R (Anglo-American Cataloguing Rules, Second Edition);
- Dublin Core; and
- MODS (Metadata Object Description Schema).

There are also domain-specific metadata schemas that suit the needs of particular communities. For example, EAD (Encoded Archival Description) and VRA Core Categories for Visual Resources meet the needs for describing archival materials and visual resources, respectively.

Access and Authority Control

The purposes of providing access points are:

- to identify (e.g., an entity known to the user);
- to collocate (i.e., bring together related information resources);
- to aid in evaluating or selecting (e.g., Has this author written something newer on the subject? Which of several works with the same title do I want? What level of subject treatment is needed—a whole work on the subject? a chapter? a paragraph?); and
- to locate a copy of the information resource represented.

Some additional purposes of providing *name* and *title* access points, in particular (reserving discussion of subject access points for a little later), are:

- to facilitate the retrieval of names and titles that are imperfectly remembered;
- to facilitate the retrieval of names and titles that are expressed differently in different information resources;
- to facilitate the retrieval of names and titles that have changed over time;
- to collocate expressions and manifestations of works; and
- to collocate works that are related to other works.

These purposes are accomplished by providing authority control for access points. All name and title access points need to be under authority control so that persons or entities with the same name can be distinguished from each other, all names used by a person or body will be brought together, and all differing titles of the same work can be brought together. Current practice dictates either the establishment of a "heading" for each name or title as an access point or the provision of pointers to draw different representations of names or titles together. Headings are kept track of in authority files. If pointers are chosen as the method for authority control, the Resource Description Framework (RDF) provides one model for linking variant forms. The profession has various standards for the creation of name and title headings.

Subject Analysis, Controlled Vocabularies, and Classification

Regardless of whether controlled vocabularies or classification or both are to be applied to an information resource, it is necessary first to complete a conceptual analysis of the resource. What is it about? It is through determination of the "aboutness" of resources that we can provide for collocation of resources that are of a like nature and contain similar and/or related information. Once we have completed a conceptual analysis, we can translate the analysis into controlled subject access points or classification notations to be added to metadata records. Additionally, the conceptual analysis can be used either for the purpose of storing together resources with like subject matter or for placing metadata records into conceptual hierarchies.

The purposes of using controlled subject terminology are:

- to provide subject access to information resources in a catalog or index;
- to collocate surrogate records for information resources of a like nature;
- to provide suggested synonyms and a syndetic structure to aid a user in subject searching; and
- to save the users' time.

A number of controlled vocabularies are in existence in the form of subject heading lists, thesauri, or ontologies. Some controlled vocabularies of a general nature are:

- LCSH (Library of Congress Subject Headings);
- FAST (Faceted Access to Subject Terminology); and
- Sears List of Subject Headings.

Some specialized controlled vocabularies are:

- MeSH (Medical Subject Headings);
- AAT (Art & Architecture Thesaurus);
- Thesaurus of ERIC (Educational Resources Information Center) Descriptors; and
- Inspec Thesaurus (INSPEC once stood for Information Services for the Physics and Engineering Communities, but has now evolved into the word "Inspec").

Ontologies are specifically intended to be used with online resources, particularly on the Web. Some of these are:

- OWL (Web Ontology Language);
- WordNet®; and the
- UMLS® (Unified Medical Language System).

The purposes of classification (or categorization) are:

- to categorize information resources into knowledge organization schemes;
- to collocate information resources by subject and/or form/genre;
- to provide a logical location for similar information resources; and
- to arrange and retrieve information resources and/or their surrogates.

A number of bibliographic classification systems exist. The most commonly used ones are:

- DDC® (Dewey Decimal Classification);
- LCC (Library of Congress Classification); and
- UDC (Universal Decimal Classification).

There are also "taxonomies" that usually consist of subject-specific categorized lists of terms. Unfortunately, it is somewhat confusing that lists of "taxonomies" found on the Web often include classification schemes, subject heading lists, Internet directories and gateways, as well as the subject-specific categorized lists. Taxonomies are often proprietary to the organizations that created them.

Encoding

Metadata records must be encoded in order to allow for data transmission. Each part of a record should be encoded separately so that each part may be identified, parsed, and accessed separately and may be displayed in a meaningful way. Encoding also allows for integration of many languages and scripts.

Encoding is accomplished by assigning tags, numbers, letters, or words (i.e., codes) to discrete pieces of information in a metadata record. In actual work situations, the encoding is often set up like a "shell" into which the pieces of information are inserted as into a workform. Standard codes are used so that records will be interchangeable. Some standard encoding schemes are:

- MARC (MAchine Readable Cataloging)
  - MARC 21 (now used by most English-speaking countries for their library bibliographic records);
  - UNIMARC (designed for international interchange among several different countries' versions of MARC, but also adopted by some countries as their official MARC version);
- SGML/XML (Standard Generalized Markup Language/eXtensible Markup Language)
  - DTDs and XML Schemas
  - TEI (Text Encoding Initiative)—for encoding literary texts;
  - HTML/XHTML—for encoding Web pages;
  - EAD (Encoded Archival Description)—for encoding archival finding aids;
  - MARC DTDs and XML schemas—for encoding MARC 21 records;
  - ONIX (ONline Information eXchange)—for encoding publishers' records.

These encoding standards constitute a kind of container for single metadata records. The next level of container holds more than one record and can provide a means for linking together metadata for different kinds of resources (e.g., metadata for resources that are linked with metadata for persons and organizations responsible for them and, perhaps, linked with metadata for other information resources). One such framework is the METS (Metadata Encoding & Transmission Standard) schema developed to hold metadata aimed at managing, preserving, displaying, and exchanging digital objects.

Processing and Physical Location

Physical items have to be "processed" so that they can be housed with the collections. This involves removing or adding book jackets, placing security strips in or on items, placing call number labels and barcodes on the items, sending an item to the conservation/preservation department if it is an older item that is not in good shape, etc.

It is important to get users of a collection from the useful description(s) they have located in the catalog to the actual copy of the information resource(s) in the collection. This may be done by an accession number (number assigned by the order in which entities are added to a collection), by a call number (usually consisting of a classification notation and some kind of copy notation), by a URL, or by some other means. The notation on the item or resource must match the notation given on its description so that users can get from a description in the list to the information resource desired.

System Design

At times, it can be unclear where the process of organizing information ends and that of system design begins. In a display of surrogate records from a retrieval tool, both aspects come together to present to the user the information sought. This set of results combines features of the organizing process (description, forms of headings, etc.) and features of system design (labels, screen layout, etc.) in the presentation of the information. When the information is clear, easily retrieved, and well presented, the user does not notice system design or organizing elements. It is only when there are problems or confusion that these elements become an issue.

In the print world, system design was not separate from the process of creating surrogate records. Cataloging rules often included principles for what information to include in surrogate records and also standards for placing those records into a cohesive catalog. Of course, the term *system design* was not used for the process of deciding how print tools would be arranged and laid out. The same people who created surrogate records also controlled the display of those records. They did not think of themselves as system designers. Yet, some print tools were and still are quite sophisticated finding and collocation systems. They could be sophisticated because the designers knew the contents of the surrogate records intimately. As the tools became automated, the task of design was taken on by people who understood computers, but often had little or no knowledge of the contents of the records that would make up the system. System design is a necessity for the retrieval of organized information, whether it is or is not done by the same people who create surrogate records. It can be a design that simply displays, in no particular order, every record that contains a certain keyword. Or, it can be a design that displays records in a sophisticated way to show relationships among records and among works, as well as responding to requested search words.

Online Catalogs

Until recently the online catalog continued to contain records only for items physically held by the library system. As libraries have entered into cooperative relationships, this principle of showing "what the library has" has eroded. In "union catalogs," which contain records from more than one library, the concept was expanded to "what at least one of the cooperating libraries has." More recently, the addition of Internet resources has meant that a number of catalogs now contain records for "what the library can give access to," including "what the library has."

Online catalogs also can be "gateways" to outside systems such as bibliographic networks (e.g., OCLC) that can tell where an item may be found if it is not in the local catalog. The item can then be requested through interlibrary loan. In addition, bibliographic and text databases can be accessed from a catalog gateway. Many of these have become document delivery systems. A major addition to online catalogs has been access to the World Wide Web. Many libraries are cataloging Internet resources that seem to be important for the users of that catalog, and a URL in a catalog record can be hyperlinked to the Web for immediate access to the information resource represented.

The Internet

The Internet has been likened to a library where all the books have been dumped on the floor and there is no catalog. For several years efforts have been made to find a way to gain some control over the Internet; however, one cannot yet say that it is organized. There is so much change so fast that efforts begun may be out of date in a few months. At the end of the 1990s it was estimated by a number of Internet specialists that a Web year was 6 to 9 weeks. In other words the amount of change that happens in society in a year happened on the Web in 6 to 9 weeks. With the fall of the "dot com" milieu and with other stabilizing factors, the rate of change has slowed. Nevertheless, getting a handle on organization is still a challenge.

Several different approaches are being taken in the attempt to organize the Internet. Libraries have attempted to use traditional means for the organization. Some librarians, for example, have compiled bibliographies of Web sites. Some of these bibliographies eventually have become gateways to the Internet. Librarians have been part of the team of people who have been working on a metadata schema called the Dublin Core. In OCLC's Web interface for cataloging, called Connexion, cataloging can be done either in traditional MARC/AACR2 format or in Dublin Core format. An important feature of Connexion with regard to organizing the Internet is its provision for development of pathfinders for certain subjects.

Much work on organizing the Internet has been done by persons other than librarians. Search engines, for example, have been developed by computer and programming specialists. Most people appreciate search engines, even though they may be frustrated that the search engines are not more selective and precise. Most programs or agents (e.g., robots, spiders, etc.) sent out to find sites to add to the indexes of search engines are able to index text only; graphics and pictures can be recognized as such, but cannot be interpreted unless they have textual labels. In addition to that, those programs cannot analyze a site's purpose, history, policies, etc. In order to improve the situation, work on various kinds of metadata is ongoing and important, although at this time, misuse of metadata (e.g., addition of keywords that are popular words but have nothing to do with the content of the site) has kept search engines from making much use of it. Properly used, though, metadata can include information about nontextual parts of a site, information about the site's purpose and history, information about the contents of the site, and so on.

Although some believe that organizing the Internet is impossible, the parts of it that are important for retrieval and for posterity will be brought under organizational control. It is human nature, and the principles learned over centuries of organizing print information can be used to speed the process of organizing electronic resources. The current effort to create a "Semantic Web," wherein data on the Web will be defined semantically and linked to relevant data for the purpose of more effective discovery of information, is a case in point.

Digital Libraries

The Internet has given us the means for creating digital libraries and for making them accessible. Digital libraries vary greatly in content and methods of organization; all have some kind of organization, although not necessarily traditional library organization. Just exactly what can be called a "digital library" has been a matter of debate. Throughout the 1990s there were many experiments that were referred to as digital libraries. For example, at the simplest level were collections of links to resources related to a particular subject. But "digital library" quickly came to mean collections in which a site provides digitized information resources with an architecture and a service for the retrieval of such resources. By the mid-1990s it was recognized that a digital library must contain an organized collection, which may be partly physical, but is at least partly or wholly electronic; it is not exclusively a set of pointers to other material; and it must be created for a particular audience, group of users, or community.

Moving into the twenty-first century, Borgman stated: "Digital libraries are an extension, enhancement, and integration both of information retrieval systems and of multiple information institutions, libraries being only one."[2] She emphasized that digital libraries are for communities of users and that they are really extensions of the physical places where resources are selected, collected, organized, preserved, and accessed, including libraries, museums, archives, and schools. This was echoed in a white paper sponsored by Sun Microsystems, which defined a digital library as "the electronic extension of functions users typically perform and the resources they access in a traditional library."[3] This paper emphasized the importance of digital libraries in the growth of distance learning. Distance alternatives for lifelong learning require that libraries evolve to fit this new paradigm or become obsolete.

Organization of digital libraries is being accomplished with such tools as metadata, XML/RDF schemas, ontologies, and taxonomies. Provision of access to digital libraries is increasingly through "portals" that give access through a unified user interface to disparate sets of information sources. Portals provide users with a way to locate all the information content that they have the authority to access.

Information Architecture

Information architecture provides a way of organizing digital libraries and other information spaces on the Internet. Just as architects must determine the needs of the people who will use a space and then create a pattern that will fulfill those needs in order to design buildings or other structures that will serve people's needs in addition to being beautiful, so must information architects determine the uses to which information will be put and create patterns for paths to finding needed information in addition to creating attractive interfaces to the information.

Information architecture, then, is much more than Web design, but its development and emergence as a "field" is closely associated with the creation of Web sites. Dillon defines information architecture as "the term used to describe the process of designing, implementing and evaluating information spaces that are humanly and socially acceptable to their intended stakeholders."[4] He says he purposely leaves the definition open so that organizational, blueprinting, and experience aspects can all be covered. There is still disagreement in this emerging field about what is covered, but there does appear to be some agreement upon a desire to manage documents and provide easy access to information designed for user needs and experience, including interface and navigation systems as well as useful and pleasing graphic design. Strategy and design phases of information architecture require a thorough understanding of the theoretical underpinnings of the organization of information, including understanding of metadata, provision of access points with all the attendant relationships among them, subject approaches by categories, classification, or alphabetical labels, and a system design that will allow display of results in a logical and usable fashion.

CONCLUSION

Organization of information among humans began as soon as language developed sufficiently for information to be passed from person to person. In oral traditions information was organized in people's minds, and in recorded information traditions, ways of identifying information resources were developed at least as early as clay tablets. Current retrieval tools, including bibliographies, catalogs, indexes, finding aids, museum registers, search engines, and library portals, represent the latest state of progress in organizing information that humans have achieved so far. Arrival at this current state of organization has taken centuries. We cannot know what organized information will look like in another 50 years or even 25 years. I believe, however, that the principles of organization that have developed over the last several hundred years will not be thrown out but will continue to evolve into the organizing principles of the future.

SUGGESTIONS FOR FURTHER READING

General

Gladwell, Malcolm. "The Social Life of Paper: Looking for Method in the Mess." *The New Yorker* (March 25, 2002). Retrieved January 02, 2008 from http://www.gladwell.com/pdf/paper.pdf.
Taylor, Arlene G. *The Organization of Information*, 2nd ed. Westport, CT: Libraries Unlimited, 2004.

Organization of Information in Libraries

Taylor, Arlene G. "The Information Universe: Will We Have Chaos or Control?" *American Libraries* 25(7) (July–August 1994): 629–632. Retrieved January 02, 2008 from http://www.pitt.edu/~agtaylor/articles/TaylorInfoUniv.pdf.

Organization of Information in the Internet

Berners-Lee, Tim, James Hendler, and Ora Lassila. "The Semantic Web." *Scientific American* 284(5): 34–38, 40–43. Retrieved January 02, 2008 from http://www.sciam.com/article.cfm?articleID=00048144-10D2-1C70-84A9809EC588EF21.

Lynch, Clifford A. "Future Developments in Metadata and their Role in Access to Networked Information." In Wayne Jones, Judith R. Ahronheim, and Josephine Crawford (eds.), *Cataloging the Web: Metadata, AACR, and MARC 21* (ALCTS Papers on Library Technical Services and Collections, no. 10.). Lanham, MD: Scarecrow Press, 2002, pp. 183–187.

Organization of Information in Digital Libraries

Borgman, Christine L. *From Gutenberg to the Global Information Infrastructure: Access to Information in the Networked World.* Cambridge, MA: MIT Press, 2000, chapters 2 and 6.

Information Architecture

Wyllys, R. E. "Information Architecture." [Reading prepared for] Information Technologies and the Information Profession, Graduate School of Library & Information Science, University of Texas at Austin, 2000. Last updated 2004 February 18. Retrieved January 02, 2008 from http://www.ischool.utexas.edu/~wyllys/ITIPMaterials/InfoArchitecture.html.

11

Information Retrieval: Designing, Querying, and Evaluating Information Systems

Judith Weedman

Design is at the core of professional work. Herb Simon—computer scientist, cognitive scientist, economist, and Nobel prize winner—wrote a book exploring the nature of professional design in 1969 that still is very influential for people who study design in disciplines as varied as architecture, engineering, and information systems.[1] What professionals do in their jobs, he says, is to take an existing state of affairs, a problem, and transform it into a preferred state, a solution. Information professionals design Web sites, story hours, instructional materials, specialized collections of photographs, search engines, and corporations' intranets. They may have full responsibility for the design, or they may work as part of a design team, depending on the scale (and budget) of the project.

Information professionals also use information systems—they search the Web for hard-to-find information, they provide reference services for doctors, they conduct corporate intelligence to find information about a business's competitors, and they help children learn to use the library catalog. (Notice that in these activities as well, an information problem is being transformed into a solution.)

Evaluation is intricately connected to both of these activities. It's an essential part of design—one must evaluate both the competing systems and the system being developed. Evaluation is an everyday act for librarians deciding which database to use for a search for a patron, or what electronic services the library should subscribe to for the current fiscal year. We evaluate the collections we develop and works that may be added to the collection, we evaluate the reliability of a huge range of sources of information, we evaluate the "find-ability" and usability of information on the Web.

This chapter introduces these three essential ("*constituting the intrinsic, fundamental nature of something*") spheres of information work.

DESIGN: HOW DO YOU ORGANIZE YOUR CLOSET?

Introduction to Design

If you live in Michigan, chances are you have your winter clothes separated from your summer clothes. (But what do you do with clothes you mostly wear in the spring or fall?) If you live in southern California, somehow the distinction between winter clothing and summer clothing just isn't so clear. Maybe your clothes are divided into work clothes and leisure clothes. (That distinction often isn't terribly clear either!) Or "good" clothes and everyday clothes.

And how far do you carry your organization? Do you start with a summer/winter division, and then within each seasonal group put slacks together, shirts together, and sweaters together? Or if you separate your work clothes from leisure clothes, do you then arrange each group by color? If you have a pair of slacks, a shirt, and a jacket that make up an outfit, do you keep all three pieces together, or do you put the slacks with other slacks, the shirt with your other shirts, and the jacket with jackets?

The choices you make about hanging clothes in your closet may not be fully articulated, but chances are they express something about how you decide what to wear. If your choices are often governed by temperature, it's likely (though not certain) that your fundamental organization will be by the warmth or coolness of the clothing. If temperature doesn't have a lot to do with the clothing you decide to wear on a given day, you may have your things arranged by when you wear them—to work, to social events, to outdoor activities. Do you think "shall I wear pants today or shall I wear a skirt?" or do you think "shall I wear blue today or do I feel more like browns and yellows?"—if you most often make your choices based on color, then you may tend to put all the similar colors together, whereas if you consistently make your choices based on type of clothing, you may use that as the basis for your grouping. Or maybe you just do it however your mother taught you.

Or you may be the kind of person who doesn't particularly arrange your closet at all, but the clothes you wear most often tend to migrate to the most easily accessible part, while the clothes you rarely wear move further and further to the back.

The design of an organizational system for your bedroom closet is not that different from the design of an information retrieval system. You make, consciously or not, choices about how to group your clothing, usually based on how you go about finding what you want to wear. You also make choices about whether or not to create subgroups of clothing, and what to do with clothing that doesn't fit into the categories you set up. In the same way, a system for retrieving information requires decisions about groups and subgroups, and what to do with things that don't really fit the system, so that users can pull together (aggregate) the appropriate information-bearing entities.

"Information-bearing entities?" Information professionals work with all kinds of things—books, scholarly journals, digital images, dolls, XML files, collections of presidential papers, MP3 files, picture books for children, and corporate reports, among many, many other things. Rather than trying to enumerate them, "information-bearing entities" is a catch-all term used to include them all. Or, even better, "documents" (fewer syllables). While "document" has a strong flavor of text, it is often used to include all media that can contain information. Suzanne Briet, an influential French information scientist in the 1930s–1950s, defined a document as "evidence in support of a fact."[2] She argued that an antelope in a zoo, in contrast to one in the wild, has been placed in a socially constructed knowledge-promoting institution, can be employed as evidence supporting various facts, and is therefore a document. I use "information bearing entities" and "documents" in this way, to refer to any entity that can be used to provide information, although I wouldn't necessarily include antelopes. (Or then again, I might.)

In information science, "information retrieval" and "document retrieval" are often considered to be two different things; at other times information retrieval includes both finding documents and finding the information they contain. I'm using the term in this second way, to include both.

Design is creative work; it also requires a thorough understanding of several bodies of practical knowledge. This section on design has five subsections. First, we'll briefly examine the nature of design work in general. Then we will look at the some of the specialized bodies of knowledge required for design of information retrieval systems: defining the problem to be solved and understanding those who will be using the system, representing documents in ways that make them findable and usable, and some mechanics of how IR systems work. The last subsection addresses work that runs through the design process from beginning to end: evaluation of the design.

Design as Professional Practice

Design work is some of the most interesting and challenging work that information professionals do. It requires in-depth knowledge of who will be using the system you design, and what their needs and abilities are; it requires in-depth knowledge about what you're designing; and it requires creativity, insight, logic, and high tolerance for uncertainty. In design, there is rarely one perfect solution. It's not a mathematical problem where if you follow the steps correctly the right answer will drop out at the end. Rather, design requires multiple decisions and compromises, and you can never be sure that you couldn't have designed the system better if you had worked on it longer.

Design has been called a "wicked problem."[3] Wicked problems are those that are ill-structured, have no stopping rule, and do not have a finite number of solutions; creating a solution is a process of inquiry, of interacting with the materials of the situation to see how they respond. "Tame" problems, by contrast, have a clear mission and one can tell when the problem has been solved. In design, the solution depends on how the problem is defined, and, as Rittel and Webber write, "one of the most intractable problems is that of defining problems (of knowing what distinguishes an observed condition from a desired condition) and of locating problems (finding where in the complex causal networks the trouble really lies)."[4] In turn, and equally intractable, is the problem of identifying which of many possible solutions is the best. Some of what we call design, of course, is applying solutions that have already been found for similar problems, and those design problems are comparatively tame. But truly original design work is fascinatingly complex and difficult.

What we now call information retrieval used to be called "information storage and retrieval"; people are lazy, and over time, it came to be just "information retrieval," sometimes including both the storing and retrieving processes and sometimes just the retrieval part of the process. This section addresses the design of systems that store information (which will later be retrieved), not just because a system has to be designed before it can be used or evaluated, but because understanding how a system is designed is crucial to understanding *how* to use and evaluate it—or, as I tend to recite as a mantra in my classes, "how you store it determines how you can retrieve it."

Defining the Problem to Be Solved

Problem definition grows out of the beginnings of the design project—who wants an IR system to be designed and why? What are the goals for the system? Who will the users be and what are their characteristics? Will the goals or market for the system evolve over time? What are the best guesses about what future needs from the system will be?

One important aspect of the wicked problem of defining the problem is learning everything you can about the people who will be using the IR system and why they will be using it. There are studies published about the information needs of some user groups (though you can't just assume that the results fit your particular population). Depending on the amount of time and money you're investing in the system, you may want to distribute questionnaires to some members of the user population, interview some to get more in-depth understanding, or have focus groups talk about what they would want from the information system. There are research techniques called "think-aloud protocols" in which people use their existing information systems and talk about what they're doing and why they take each step—this kind of in-depth analysis is very expensive, but yields rich understanding of search behaviors and information needs. For really large projects, the anthropology technique of ethnography may be used—participant observation as your users go about their work, observing in close detail the factors that affect it. Research methods classes teach the best way to get the most useful information through each of these techniques. The cost and complexity of the requirements analysis you do should match the cost and complexity of the system you are involved in designing. The most commonly made mistake is to assume that because you've worked with a particular population already, you know what their needs are. Assumptions make a shaky foundation for design.

Representation: Metadata

As a clearer understanding of the information problem emerges, an idea of potential solutions also emerges. If information is going to be stored, it has to be represented in some way so that it can be found and retrieved. Representation is a central part of our discipline and profession, and it takes many forms. Web designers use labels to indicate where a link leads. The navigation system for a Web site is a representation of what may be found there and a path for getting to it. Cataloging in a library is creating representations of the library's materials for the catalog—subject headings, a Dewey Decimal or Library of Congress Classification System class number. The MARC record (the electronic format used by online library catalogs) has fields for representing the author, the title, and other attributes of the document. Taxonomists create subject headings or classification systems that are used to organize information on Web sites. Work with representations such as these raises linguistic, sociological, and philosophic questions about what it means to say that something "is" an X, what it means to give a name to something. In their book *Sorting Things Out: Classification and its Consequences*, Bowker and Star look at various classifications we use in everyday life—racial classifications and classifications of diseases, for instance—and how the way that we group things affects what we know and think about them.[5]

The representation of a document in an information system is called "metadata." The best definition of metadata I've found was written by the National Information Standards Institute (NISO). NISO identifies, develops, and publishes technical standards to manage information; these standards guide the design of information systems. NISO's definition of metadata is "structured information that describes, explains, locates, or otherwise makes it easier to retrieve, use, or manage an information resource."[6] The information in a library catalog record, meta tags on a Web site, records in a database, and the labels on file folders are all forms of metadata. Metadata does many different things—it provides identification information such as author or title, it may provide a record of exhibits in which a work of art has been shown, it may provide information about permissions and authentication that govern who has access to the data. A lot of different kinds of information are involved in making it easier to "retrieve, use, or manage an information resource."

Subject metadata is the organizational system that allows a user to aggregate documents that are relevant to an information need about some topic. Subject representation is usually done with controlled vocabularies (standardized sets of searchable terms such as subject headings or descriptors), natural language (searching text from the document itself—this can be the full text, or selected parts such as title, abstract, and author), or classification (hierarchical or faceted categories that allow you to place documents with other documents about the same topic). Many information systems use two or all three of these—libraries, for instance, have both subject headings and a classification system. Each technique has advantages and disadvantages. Controlled vocabularies create a great deal of precision in searching because they standardize what terms are used to express concepts; on the other hand, a person or computer has to create the controlled vocabulary and assign it to the appropriate documents. Natural language doesn't require human processing, but the inconsistencies and subtle nuances of everyday language mean that documents that are relevant will be missed (because you searched for "balance" but the author of the document used "equilibrium") and that documents that are not relevant will be retrieved (because you wanted the element mercury and the system couldn't discriminate that from the planet Mercury).

There is also a new approach to subject metadata, the utility of which is being debated: social tagging. Social networking systems like Flickr and deli.cio.us allow people to choose their own labels or subject headings for their documents. Search on "kittens" on Flickr and you will find a huge collection of appealing pictures of (mostly) people's pets. Cloud tags allow users to see what tags are used most often by other users, and they can then, if they wish, use those same tags. Why would they? So that their pictures will be grouped with the others for anyone who searches on that tag. If I add a tag to my picture of a kitten that says "kitten," a lot more people will find my picture than if I tag it "Muffin" or "cutie." These vocabularies are called emergent vocabularies, because they take shape as users converge on certain preferred tags for particular subjects. It's a completely open question at this point whether people will choose tags so that others can find their documents, or whether they will tag only to enable themselves to find their own documents. To the extent that people do converge on the same tags, emergent vocabularies may prove to be very effective (for the same reason that controlled vocabularies are effective—because you can count on a term to retrieve what you want).

There is a great deal of interesting work going on in this area right now; one of the more extensive projects is steve[7]—a collection of digital photographs of art objects from museums such as the Denver Art Museum, the Guggenheim, the Cleveland Museum of Art, and the Los Angeles Museum of Art. They are experimenting with social tagging, also known as "folksonomy," as a way to increase access to works of art.

Social tagging is a really interesting blend of the controlled vocabulary and natural language approaches—the goal is for tags to converge and become a sort of voluntary controlled vocabulary, yet it depends on participants who are free to assign whatever tag they wish to their documents, or no tag at all. The utility of a folksonomy depends completely on how each individual user decides to do his or her own tagging.

Search Engines: A Few of the Mechanics

Another critical part of an information retrieval system is its search engine. How does it create a match between what you want and the representations of the appropriate documents? With a file cabinet system, the search engine consists of your own eyes, brain, and fingers—you look at the labels on the file folders in the cabinet and decide which file is most likely to have the information you want within. With an electronic database such as a library catalog, the search engine matches the string of characters you type in to strings of characters in the records for the documents, and displays the ones that match. In a full-text document system, the words of the documents themselves (sorted into alphabetical order for faster processing) are searched to find matches to the character string you typed in as your query. Some search engines have an additional feature that sorts the documents after they're retrieved into order according to which match your character string best; this is true of Internet search engines such as Google and Yahoo. The assumption is that the more closely the character strings in the document match the character string in your query, the more relevant the document will be. Often, this assumption is accurate.

What does it mean to say the character strings in one document match your query better than those in another document? Search engines that provide relevance ranking are "partial match" systems, that is, unlike the search engine in a database or library catalog, they will retrieve documents that match part of your query, even if they don't match the entire query. (This is why you can search for "fly fishing Sierra Madre" and retrieve records about fly fishing in the Sierra Nevada.) Since some of the matches aren't exact, this provides a basis for saying some matches (the ones that match exactly) are better than others (the ones that match only partially). The procedure for ranking documents contains several different kinds of "decisions." One is the ranking of exactly matching documents higher than partially matching documents. Another is ranking documents that many other sites have linked to more highly than documents that fewer or no Web sites have linked to. A third algorithm ranks the documents depending on where in the document your desired character string resides—if it is in the title or in a section heading, the document will be ranked higher than if it is found in the last paragraph. Some search engines even include font in the algorithm—if your character string is in a larger font or brighter color than the rest of the text, that document will be ranked higher than a document with the character string in the ordinary font. Other factors that may be included in the ranking criteria include how closely the words in your query occur together in the document, and how many times they occur in the document. There are algorithms (sets of rules executed step-by-step) that direct this processing and then determine the order, based on a combination of all of them, in which the documents will be displayed. The exact algorithms are not published, since the accuracy of the algorithms in determining relevance is what gives a search engine its competitive edge over the others. All of these algorithms are based on the assumption that a short string of characters can be an effective proxy for meaning.

What is a search engine actually doing? In most electronic databases, it is not searching the records in the database to match your query. As the records are entered into the system, all the words from each field of the record are sorted into an index—called an inverted file—in alphabetical order. Searching an alphabetical index is much faster than searching each record to see if the character string occurs there. The same thing is true, on a much grander scale, of Web search engines; Web sites are indexed and it is that index that is actually searched.

Search engine design is done in our field and in others such as computer science. It is also done commercially in corporate laboratories such as those of Google or Yahoo and in government agencies. Since 1992, the National Institute of Standards and Technology (NIST) and the U.S. Department of Defense have sponsored TREC (Text REtrieval Conference), a yearly workshop in which designers run their experimental information systems on a large data set provided by NIST, and thus have a chance to test their systems' performance against others. NIST has also sponsored large-scale evaluations of retrieval in Chinese and Spanish.

One of the interesting dimensions of Internet search engines is that in addition to creating an index to the documents' words, they need some technique for finding the documents in the first place. (In a database, there is a finite—though often very large—number of documents, all of which are included in the character string matching process.) This has, of course, become a very important area for design. Web search engines do not include all of the documents on the Web. They use Web crawlers or spiders, software that contains complex algorithms for finding Web sites and determining which sites will be indexed. Thus these algorithms need to be able to identify "good" sites, since if a search engine returns a lot of junk to its users, they won't remain users for very long. Design of Web crawlers is a very fast-moving area; not only do market forces of competition stimulate change, but designers of Web sites have been quick to find ways of increasing the likelihood that a site will be found and indexed, forcing search engine designers to create ways of recognizing such manipulation. So there are two design domains involved here–the design of algorithms for the crawler, and the design of Web sites in such a way that they will be crawled.

Evaluation in Design

Evaluation is essential throughout the design process. Early conceptions of the system may be evaluated by asking potential users for their reactions to the designers' initial ideas and by creating graphics that will give them a sense of what the system will be able to do. Designers try various approaches and see the results (often through "thought experiments," sketches, and other quick approximations early on), and gradually close in on more solid conceptions of the end product. As the conceptions grow more solid, prototypes may be built. Alpha and beta testing are useful for even small-scale projects. Alpha testing is usually done in-house on early, incomplete versions of the system, to find problems before the development has gone too far. When the system is closer to being finished, beta testing by people from the intended user population finds problems that don't show up until heavier use is made of the system. If you're designing a subject vocabulary to use in an image database, a test on a representative sample of your images will allow you to find gaps or overlap; having some of your users search for images they need will show up other areas where additional work is needed. System developers for companies that market to libraries often ask librarians to beta test their product; libraries may load their catalogs or part of them into the system for a period of time, or make a database or search engine available to library patrons. This has an obvious advantage for the library, since it puts them on the leading edge for that technology, but of course the disadvantage is that the system is not likely to work perfectly; your job as a beta tester is to break it, so that the designers can fix the problems before they take it to market. As with the requirements analysis stage of design, the alpha and beta evaluation stages can be as quick-and-dirty or as complex as the situation warrants.

QUERYING

How You Can Retrieve It Is Determined by How It Was Stored

There are two fundamental things you need to know to search effectively for information. The first is that you have to make your search fit the system. There is more difference between information systems than you would probably expect, and a search that fails in one system may work quite well in another. This means that the better you understand the design of the system, the better you will be able to retrieve what you need. The second fundamental is that there are strategies for searching, and professional searchers usually have to try more than one strategy to get good results, except for very straightforward queries.

Fitting Your Search to the System

Internet search engines have led us to believe that we can type one or two words into a little box and find what we need. Often this is true. Because there is so much information on the Web, probably any word in the dictionary (and many that aren't) will retrieve something. And sometimes that's sufficient; we're looking for a definition or a little information about a topic, or a photograph of the Colorado River, and most any source that provides that will suffice. Especially when searching for information that is widely established and well known, retrieving everything about the topic isn't necessary (or desirable!). But when you need information that is complex, when the need for accuracy is high (for instance, information about drug interactions with herbal supplements), or when you need varying expert opinions, then more specific (exact) retrieval becomes important. Does your search engine allow you to specify that two words must occur together as a phrase to be retrieved? (*Public libraries* is a very different topic from *public use of private libraries*.) Does your search engine allow you to require that one or more of your terms must be present for documents to be retrieved? (Generally, the documents that contain all of the terms in your search will be ranked highest, but documents that contain fewer or only one of the terms will also be retrieved.) Can you require that only documents from the domains ".gov" or ".edu" be retrieved? (This may eliminate a great deal of spurious information from sites that are .com or even .org.)

Awareness of how social tagging works will make your searching of sites like Flickr and deli.cio.us more effective; it's important to know that choosing any term as a tag, and even providing a tag at all, is completely optional. If you know that there may be documents out there about kittens that are labeled kitty or baby cat, you will know to try alternative terms as well in your search if you need to be thorough.

And, of course, there are many other information systems that contain information not available on the Web. Databases contain many fewer documents than does the Web, and there is a level of quality control in the processes used to select which journals (or other documents) will be indexed. The need to fit your search to the system is even higher with these databases. Do you want to search the controlled vocabulary (that will often give you the best results, since it is consistent and assigned by indexers), or do you want to search the full text of the document (that will give you broader retrieval, but many "false drops" because words have many meanings, and may occur in a document without being its central subject). What is the default search?—this is, if you don't specify which field(s) to search, which field(s) is the database searching? If journal titles are included in the default search, for instance, you will get articles that are not directly about the subject, when a journal name contains a word that's present in your query. Names can be a particular challenge in databases. In libraries, we've become accustomed to authority control, linking all versions of an individual's name so that you don't miss any of his or her publications. This is rarely done in databases, however, and never on the Web. For instance, if you follow her output over her entire career, the author we know as "Nancy Van House" appears as many different people:

> In *Social Science Citation Index*, her name appears in five different ways (note that this database uses first and middle initials only, not full names, and no punctuation):

> Vanhouse N
>
> Vanhouse NA
>
> Vanhousedewath N
>
> Dewath N
>
> Dewath NV

> In the Educational Resources Information Center (ERIC), she also appears in five different ways:

> Van House, Nancy
>
> Van House, Nancy A.
>
> DeWath, Nancy A.
>
> DeWath, Nancy V.
>
> DeWath, Nancy Van House

> In *Library and Information Science Abstracts* (LISA), her name appears in ten different ways, only three of which overlap with ERIC.

> DeWath, N. V.
>
> DeWath, Nancy A.
>
> DeWath, Nancy V.
>
> House, N. Van
>
> House, N. A. Van
>
> Van House, Nancy A.
>
> Van House, N. A.
>
> Van House De Wath, Nancy
>
> Wath, N. V. De
>
> Wath, N. Van House De

This is a total of seventeen different names that need to be searched if you want to be sure of finding everything by this author! Some of these variations are because her name appeared in different forms in different publications; others are simple dirty data—mistakes made when the records for the publications were created. Some are alternative forms provided by the database (although Van House herself doesn't use any of those alternative forms). You need to know how to examine the inverted file for the database to be sure of finding all versions of her name. You also need some detective skills to notice that DeWath sometimes occurs with Van House and might be another last name; nothing directs you automatically from Van House to search for DeWath.

Search Strategies

It must be clear at this point that a major part of a search strategy is knowing the structure of the information in the database. But there is more to it. One of the things a good searcher has to know is what each information resource contains. Google and Yahoo do not index all the same Web pages, although there's a great deal of overlap. (Do a search on jux2.com to compare the output from Google, Yahoo, and MSN.) Clusty8 indexes much less of the Web than do Google and Yahoo, but it sorts your results into subsets of the subject, rather than mixing all approaches to the topic in one undifferentiated list. If you do a search on "information retrieval," for instance, the subsets are software, books, search engines, images, and so on. Of two business databases, one may be a very good source of information on companies, another may be excellent for thoughtful analyses of business topics. Selecting the right information resource for the question is a critical part of using information systems.

Once the right information sources are selected, strategies must be designed to fit each of them. Do you want a broad search that retrieves everything possible about your subject? Do you want a couple of quick facts? Or do you want the most authoritative work on the subject? The searches will be different for each, even if they're conducted in the same database. Are you looking for research on the topic, or popular magazines' discussions of the research? If you search on "dude ranches," you need to notice that many are now referred to as "guest ranches" or "working ranches" and change your search accordingly. (Nobody wants to be a "dude" in the old cowboy sense of the term. It was an insult.) You need to know how to structure a search on steroids so that you retrieve articles about their physiological effects rather than stories about their abuse, and vice versa. Very few professional searchers find the information in a single search; a searcher needs to be very observant about how language is being used and how topics are combined, and then try several approaches, often in different resources, to be sure of getting the best possible results.

There are a variety of search tools available. Books have A–Z indexes; many Web sites have recently begun adding them because they increase findability within the site. Databases generally allow Boolean searching, which allows you to specify alternate terms for a concept, and to *and* together concepts to precisely define your interest. Web search engines are still very limited in their functionality compared to standard databases; most users don't realize this because the variety (and quantity!) of data that they can retrieve is so great. But there is no way to indicate, for instance, in a Web search, whether you want works authored by John Steinbeck or works about John Steinbeck; in any database, this is a simple discrimination. Web search engines are adding features constantly. Most now offer Boolean searching. Web directories are another tool, hierarchical classification systems somewhat like the Dewey Decimal System or LC Classification, with links to sites providing information in that area. To use them, you start with a very broad category and drill down through narrower categories until you find what you want.

Each of these tools has its own set of strategies for getting the best results; as noted (several times) earlier, understanding the structure of the tool and of the representations is critical for doing effective searches.

EVALUATING: HOW WELL IS IT STORED?

How effectively does the search engine identify the documents you will want?

The key to evaluating an information system is relevance—does it retrieve information the user wants and avoid information the user doesn't want? "All and only" is a phrase frequently used in symbolic logic and philosophy. Bill Maron, Professor Emeritus at UC Berkeley and one of the pioneers of search engine design, appropriated it for information retrieval; his wonderfully succinct definition of what an information system should do is to retrieve "all and only the relevant information."[9] The word relevance has been used in various places throughout this chapter. Relevance is found in the same location as beauty—in the eye of the beholder. It is thus extremely difficult to assess. A great deal of research has been done on how users decide that a document is relevant or not, and there have been numerous attempts to define what relevance means. Despite the lack of ability to pin this concept down firmly, it is essential to the evaluation of information systems.

The two most frequently used measures of information system performance are based on this concept of relevance. One is recall—how close the system gets to retrieving all of the relevant documents. The other is precision—how close it gets to retrieving only the relevant documents. Almost any nontrivial search will retrieve some irrelevant documents and miss some relevant ones. Maximizing the ability to discriminate between relevant and irrelevant documents is the goal of information system design.

Just as there are many components to an information system, so there are many aspects to evaluation. Each part of the system can enhance or degrade the operation of the system as a whole. The underlying document collection can be evaluated (is it complete? is it up to date? are the works authoritative?).

While we don't normally evaluate the user, or the user's need, we do evaluate whether that need is appropriate to the information systems that we have access to. In this chapter, we'll only discuss the evaluation of the representations of the document, of the representations of the need, and the process that is intended to bring them together.

How the document is represented affects the ability to retrieve it. In systems using a controlled vocabulary, that vocabulary may be rich and complete, or it may be shallow and sparse. A controlled vocabulary is good if it enables the user to "say" what he or she wants. For instance, one may talk about "children" or one may talk about "infants, toddlers, preschoolers, adolescents," etc. How should this concept be represented in the database? Should "children" be a controlled vocabulary term that includes everyone from birth to 17 or so? Or will people want to be able to search for children of particular ages and separate the documents about infants from those about older children? The answer will be different for different situations. For a database of documents about education, being able to specify age is very important. For a database of newspaper articles, it may be much less important, and the word "children" may be good enough. The ability to discriminate the documents that are valuable to the user from those that are not and aggregate them is central to the value of the information system. Concrete knowledge of both the users and the subject domain are important in evaluating as well as in designing an information system.

Evaluation of a Web site's representation of its content has an aspect not present with other information systems: its effectiveness in being found by a Web crawler.

Search engine optimization (SEO) is the process of evaluating a Web site to determine how likely it is to be crawled and ranked appropriately and suggesting improvements. A Web site that search engine Web crawlers don't find is useless to anyone outside its own local users. And if the Web site was designed to sell a product, or provide customer service, or to disseminate information, being retrieved—and ideally being in the top 10 on the list of retrieved sites—it is essential to fulfilling the purpose of the information system. Words have a great deal to do with the findability of a site. The words that are in meta tags, those in section titles and descriptions, the density of keywords, where they are located on the page—all of these will affect whether a Web crawler indexes the site or not. There are also technological features that make a site more or less likely to be displayed and ranked as relevant. SEO has good guys and bad guys. The good guys use legitimate means to fully represent what information the site has, so that it will be crawled in the first place, and will appear appropriately high in the relevance rankings when people search. The bad guys of SEO manipulate the vocabulary and technological features in ways to make a site be retrieved and ranked highly for many searches, whether it is relevant to the user's query or not.

Designers of search engines, in turn, are always doing research on how the Web crawler's algorithms can recognize attempts at manipulation. As search engines get smarter, unethical SEO becomes more difficult and new manipulation techniques must be devised. Search engine optimization is a fast-changing niche for information professionals, and it is currently important because many Web sites were designed before a lot was known about how to maximize their findability. Both Google and Yahoo now make guidelines available to Web designers for legitimately optimizing their sites. As Web designers become more knowledgeable about search engine optimization, optimization techniques will be incorporated into the design of the Web site in the first place, and professionals who evaluate and retrofit Web sites will have less work to do.

The other important issue with Web sites as sources of information is their usability. Usability has many aspects—the clarity of the site's layout, the extent to which labels are unambiguous, the extent to which external links are kept current, the amount of information found on each page. It refers mostly to the interface of the Web site, but also includes underlying structure. Jakob Nielsen has written extensively about usability and has made a great deal of his work available on his Web site.[10] Peter Morville's book *Ambient Findability* addresses both item-level issues (how easy it is to find information within a Web site) and system-level issues (such as search engine optimization).[11]

Just as a document is represented in an information system, so a user's need has to be represented in a way that the system can process. It is much more difficult than it seems like it should be to turn a complex desire for something that a user may not be able to completely define into a query that will come close to retrieving all and only the relevant documents. Information professionals often serve as search intermediaries, doing that translation for the client. Just as an information retrieval system can be evaluated by determining precision and recall ratios for searches, so can the searches themselves be evaluated according to the precision and recall of their retrieval.

The ability to retrieve relevant information is dependent upon a complex mixture of the design of an information system, its contents, and the skill of the searcher in formulating appropriate queries. Each factor has an effect on the effectiveness of the others.

CONCLUSION

As more and more of human knowledge (and ignorance) is available on the Web and through other media, ways of representing it are changing. Retrieval depends on two things: the ability of the searcher to construct an incisive query and the ability of the designer to incorporate features that will result in the query retrieving documents with the desired attributes. This is of obvious importance in the business world where profit depends on sales of a product or service. It is equally important for anyone who wants his or her information to be useful.

The area of design, use, and evaluation of information systems incorporates technology, understanding of human behavior, and the ability to use language in nuanced ways. Patrick Wilson, a philosopher in the field of Library and Information Science, wrote that information professionals are engineers in system design—but engineers who also have human/social/behavioral knowledge as part of their discipline.[12] This combination of design knowledge and social knowledge allows us to explore information needs at many levels and to create systems to meet them.

SUGGESTIONS FOR FURTHER READING

Bowker, Geoffrey and Susan Leigh Star. *Sorting Things Out: Classification and Its Consequences*. Cambridge: MIT Press, 1999.

Boxes and Arrows: The Design behind the Design; Journal Dedicated to Discussing, Improving and Promoting the Work of the Information Architecture Community. Retrieved January 02, 2008 from http://www.boxesandarrows.com/.

Hock, Randolph. *The Extreme Searcher's Internet Handbook*. Medford, NJ: Information Today, 2004.

Krug, Steve. *Don't Make Me Think: A Common Sense Approach to Web Usability*, 2nd ed. Berkeley, CA: New Riders Press, 2006.

Leonard, Will. Thesauri and Vocabulary Control: Principles and Practice, 1992. Retrieved January 02, 2008 from http://www.willpowerinfo.co.uk/thesprin.htm.

Morville, Peter. *Ambient Findability*. Sebastopol, CA: O'Reilly Media, 2005.

Nielsen, Jakob and Hoa Loranger. *Prioritizing Web Usability*. Berkeley, CA: New Riders Press, 2006.

Norman, Donald A. *The Design of Everyday Things*, 1st ed. New York: Basic Books, 1988.

12

Reference Service: The Personal Side of Librarianship

David A. Tyckoson

Reference service. Personal assistance provided by members of the reference staff to library users in pursuit of information. Synonymous with *information service.*[1]

Reference staff. All library staff members whose assigned duties include the provision of information service.[2]

Reference work. 1. That branch of the library's services which includes the assistance given to users in their search for information on various subjects. 2. The work of the Reference library. 3. Any authoritative Reference source—database, web site, publication etc.—compiled to be referred to rather than for continuous reading.[3]

There are many definitions for reference service. Whether we call it information service, reference service, reference work, or some other more modern name, reference service focuses on two specific factors: the provision of personal service to library users by library staff. Reference is personal—each user receives assistance specific to his or her individual needs. Reference is also interactive: a service provided directly by the staff of the library requiring an interaction between the user and the staff. Whereas other aspects of the library focus internally in areas such as building collections and creating search tools, reference focuses externally on the library user. It is reference service that links the user to the library in a very individual and personal way.

This individual assistance to users is a very complicated process. Since each user is seeking something different, the reference librarian needs to be able to adapt to a wide range of subjects, skill levels, search tools, and information sources. Personalization means that anyone can request anything at any time, requiring the reference librarian to be flexible, adaptable, and a quick thinker. To our users, we are those nice people who help them. To ourselves, we are lifelong learners who are constantly required to absorb new resources, new searching skills, and new subject areas.

The reference librarian is the human face of the library. When our users interact with us, we represent the entire organization in their minds. A good experience with a reference librarian equates to a positive experience with the library. On the other hand, a bad experience with the reference librarian may leave the user with the impression that the library is not a useful institution. The success of reference is measured by its ability to help users with their individual needs in such a way that they will continue to value the library as a whole.

However, this was not always the case. In fact, the idea that library staff would interact directly with library users is a very new one in the profession. Despite the fact that reference service has been around for all of our lives, it is a relatively new phenomenon. Understanding why reference service was developed helps us understand its importance in libraries today.

ORIGINS OF REFERENCE SERVICE

Although reference is a standard feature of every library today, this has not always been the case. In fact, reference service has been in existence for only the most recent six percent of the history of libraries. In terms of the history of the profession as a whole, this is a very short time. Reference is definitely the new member of the suite of library activities.

Historically, the role of the library in society can be divided into three primary functions. Each is a very complex process in and of itself, yet it is a process that can be defined in relatively simple terms. Without any one of these three functions, libraries as we know them would not exist. They build upon each other to create the modern library environment.

Each of these functions aimed at a specific audience: the community that the library serves. Libraries are not independent organizations that sit isolated within society. Libraries are designed to support the needs of very specific, defined communities. Public libraries serve the residents of specific geographic areas. Academic and school libraries serve the students, faculty, and staff of specific educational institutions. Medical libraries serve the staff and patients of a specific hospital or clinic. Corporate libraries serve the employees and management of a specific business entity. Law libraries serve the attorneys and staff of a specific law firm. In each case, the needs of the community are supported by the library in very different ways. The three functions of libraries must directly serve their parent communities in order to be successful.

Historically, the first function of libraries is to build and preserve collections. From ancient times, libraries have accumulated collections of materials of interest to the communities that they serve. Those collections were created as a resource for the community and were available to those who had the power, authority, and skill to use them. From the Great Library of Alexandria two millennia ago to the Library of Congress today, the collection serves as the collective intellectual utility for the community. Although the formats of those collections have changed dramatically over time, from scrolls and clay tablets to books, microfilm, DVDs, and electronic databases and Web sites, the library collection remains central to the function of the library today. A library without a collection cannot adequately serve its parent community.

The second function of the library is organization. We not only collect materials, but we build tools that help our users (and ourselves) find specific information contained within those collections. The origins of the organization function are fairly simple. When library collections became too large for the librarian to remember all of the resources that they contained, librarians began to develop tools to find materials within those collections. Catalogs, indexes, bibliographies, and other tools were designed to lead the librarian to the sources within the library's collections. This practice began in a widespread sense in the sixteenth century and became more refined over the next several centuries. Author main entries, subject headings, the catalog card, the Dewey Decimal System, periodical indexes, keyword searching, OCLC, html, xml, and metadata are all components of this function of the library. The tools become more complex, but the function remains the same.

The third function of the library is service to users—the function that today we commonly call reference service. Whereas collections form the internal center of the library and organization connects those internal materials to the external users, reference is a function that begins with the user. Unlike the other two functions of the library, reference service began at a very specific time and place and in response to a very specific need. It also signified a dramatic change in the role and nature of libraries within their communities.

Before the mid-nineteenth century, libraries were entirely the domain of the elite within any given community. Libraries were of little interest to the common resident for a very simple and basic reason—the majority of the working class and the poor did not know how to read. Education, and particularly the ability to read, was reserved for the wealthy. For most of human history, the common people in any community lacked this most basic skill. Since reading is a critical skill for any library user, the institution of the library was irrelevant to the majority of the people in the community. As a result, most of the community had no interest in the library.

However, during the nineteenth century the concept of universal education was taking hold. Universal education was the idea that all citizens should be educated with certain skills, including the ability to read. This concept was first proposed in New England in the mid-nineteenth century and spread across North America. Children of all backgrounds were beginning to be educated—and beginning to read regularly. However, books at that time were disproportionately expensive, so the availability of reading material in the average home was extremely limited (often to the one book found in most households, the family Bible). During this same time period, several communities considered the concept of a library that would be available to all of its members—what we now call the public library. Boston was the first community to open such a library (in 1854) and it was an immediate hit. During the first year that it was open—and at a time when the idea of taking books home from the library was brand new—every volume in the Boston Public Library circulated an average of 1.5 times. The people had clearly demonstrated a strong desire for libraries and reading. There was only one problem—most people had no idea how to use a library.

Within a couple of decades of the opening of the first public library, the need for service to users had been established. This was widely discussed at the inaugural meeting of the American Library Association in 1876. Samuel Swett Green[4] is widely credited as publishing the first paper about reference service, but there is little doubt that he was not alone in recognizing and proposing a means for dealing with that need. By the 1880s, direct service to users was an established feature of public libraries. Over the ensuing decades, the concept of service spread to academic and special libraries. Today, it is highly unusual to find any library that does not offer reference services to its users.

It is important to note that public libraries and reference service arose out of the democratic ideals (small "d") of the nineteenth century. The concept that everyone in the community, from the wealthy elite to the most recent immigrants, should have equal access to library resources is one of the foundations of modern library science. Libraries continue to be one of the most inclusive institutions in modern society, offering their resources to everyone who walks through the door, calls on the phone, or connects to the Web portal. This is all a legacy of the initial idea that we should help our users.

WHAT IS REFERENCE SERVICE?

In the initial discussion of Reference Service in 1876, Samuel Green identified four service roles for librarians. Although the tools that we use today are vastly different from Green's era, those four objectives remain at the heart of what we call reference service today. Green's four functions of reference service were:

Instruction. The first function that Green mentioned was teaching people how to use the library. This was a natural reaction to the fact that the "new" public libraries had many people coming in who had never used a library before, were not sure what libraries contained, and did not know how to use the catalogs and indexes that librarians had created to find what they wanted. What those users did know is that they wanted to read and that the library was their community's gateway to the world of reading. Green recognized that librarians needed to instruct these new library users in the ways of the library.

Over time, those new library users did learn how to use the library. As they learned how to use a library, they became more independent and did not always need the librarian for assistance. However, other groups of new library users constantly came through the doors. New immigrants, former slaves, and generation after generation of children all saw the same opportunity in the library and all needed to learn how to use that resource. In addition, waves of new tools, resources, and technologies arrived, requiring the reinstruction of those who already knew how to use the library. As a result, instruction remains one of the main functions of reference librarians to this day.

Question Answering. Traditionally, the common popular image of the reference librarian is of someone who answers questions for users. Users come in with specific information needs and the librarian finds the best reference book, database, or Web site that contains the answer to that need. In the film *Desk Set*[5] starring Spencer Tracy and Katharine Hepburn (and still the best library-themed film ever made, in this author's humble opinion), the fictional librarians answer a wide range of factual questions, from the names of Santa's reindeer to the type of automobile driven by the king of the Watusi tribe. To many library users, the reference librarian is exactly this: a wise sage who knows where to find the answer to just about any question.

Which came first, the reference book or the reference librarian?

Unlike the chicken and the egg, this question has a clear answer. As public libraries became popular, they contained two kinds of books: those that could be checked out and those that were kept in the library for referral. These books commonly became known as "reference" books. When librarians were hired to help people, those librarians also used the reference books and soon became known as "reference" librarians.

Green discovered the need for this role of the reference librarian very early on. Users would come in with specific questions and the librarian would help them find an answer. In those days, access to information sources was very limited. Books were disproportionately expensive and reference books were even more expensive than other books. The average citizen could not afford to buy many books (if any) and there were very few alternative sources for information. As a result, the library and the reference librarian became the foci of the factual information universe within the community. Out of necessity, reference librarians became the gatekeepers to the world of factual information.

Over time, it has become much easier for users to find factual information on their own. By the second half of the twentieth century, the price of books had dropped dramatically (as measured in terms of the percentage of personal income) and more and more people owned basic reference tools. Encyclopedia salesmen convinced the baby boom generation that every house needed an encyclopedia in the home so that their children would succeed in school. The most comprehensive single volume factual reference work, the *World Almanac*, was priced at under $10.00 per copy. Consumers became interested in information and began to have it available for themselves in their own homes. They no longer needed to rely strictly on the library for information from dictionaries, atlases, almanacs, encyclopedias, or similar works. If they had a question, they simply looked up the answer themselves whenever possible.

And then the Internet was created. Suddenly, more information was available to more people at no direct cost than at any time in human history. Over a very short time frame, the entire world became wired into a network of information sources far more comprehensive than any library collection had ever owned in the past. As information consumers joined that network, the role of libraries for the provision of factual information became even further diminished. As a result, the role of the reference librarian as a fact-giver was also diminished. While society's access to factual information continually increased, the need for the reference librarian to fulfill this need continually decreased.

This does not mean that reference librarians no longer answer questions from members of their community. This function still exists, but the nature of the questions has changed. Since users can answer simple questions on their own, the type of question handled by reference librarian has become much more complex. Most of the questions that reference librarians work on today do not have single, factual answers, but have multiple, complex components that lead to multiple potential answers.

For example, consider the following two related questions:

How much wine is produced in the Napa Valley of California each year?
   What makes California's Napa Valley wine so good?

The first question seeks a simple, quantitative answer that can be found in many sources, including a search on Google, Yahoo, or any other popular search engine. The second question requires a detailed analysis of a number of complex issues, including soil chemistry, climatic conditions, plant genetics, business patterns, historical factors, and even personal taste. The first question can be answered in a matter of seconds with a simple search, whereas the second may take hours of searching through a wide range of resources in order to even begin to comprehend the factors necessary to consider in developing an answer. It is quite possible that the second question will never be answered completely because the conditions that lead to an answer are constantly evolving. There are many answers to the second question (including the potential negative answer that Napa Valley wine may not be that good), none of which is definitively correct or incorrect. There are many pathways to information about the second question, all of which lead to reasonable responses. The role of the reference librarian is to work with each user to determine which pathway is most appropriate for their individual needs.

The question answering role of the reference librarian has shifted over time from specific, factual questions to broader, inexact subjects. As a result, the role of the reference librarian has shifted from providing specific answers to serving as a research counselor. We don't answer questions much any more, but we guide people through the process to determining what an answer might be. The constant is that we still work with users to help them find resources to answer their questions.

Reader's Advisory. The third role that Green identified for the reference librarian is to advise users on what to read. In his time, the new users of the library wanted to take advantage of their education, wanted books to read, but did not know which ones would interest them. The librarian became an advisor, telling readers which books were good, bad, or indifferent and matching the readers' interests to the books' contents.

In Green's day, this function was literally "guiding the reader to good works," with "good" implying morally and spiritually uplifting material. The democratic nature of libraries has expanded the range of materials recommended to readers over the years. The problems of another fictional film librarian, Marian Paroo (Marian the Librarian of *Music Man*[6] fame), highlight the importance of reader's advisory services. Marian recommended Balzac, which was deemed too racy by some of River City's community leaders. This fictional fight for intellectual freedom mirrors real fights that librarians have endured over the years. Today we support the rights of readers to have access to any and all resources of interest (within a few legal restrictions). The American Library Association's *Freedom to Read* statement was published in 1953 (incidentally, four years before the first performance of the *Music Man*). That statement reinforces librarians' support of the readers' right to have access to what they want, even if it is not part of the mainstream culture. (See Appendix D for the full statement.)

"Reader's advisory" is often associated with public libraries and fiction collections. The stereotypical example of a reader's advisory question is:

"I really liked the latest Marcia Muller mystery. Do you have others like that?"

The librarian will then recommend other authors who have certain traits in common with the one mentioned by the user. These might be novels that take place in the same time period, in the same geographical location, or with the same types of characters. Although some librarians can do this from memory, various tools are available to help the rest of us with this type of request. Print resources such as the *Fiction Catalog*[7] and online resources such as *NoveList* aid the reference librarian in making sound recommendations to users. Some library catalogs and Web sites now have recommendation software built in, as do many commercial Web sites. Amazon.com and other online retailers who use a "customers who bought this will also like this" feature have ventured into reader's advisory services as part of their business plan. One librarian (Nancy Pearl, author of the *Book Lust* series) has even become an action figure as a result of her skills in providing reader's advisory services.

However, reader's advisory is more than just recommending pleasure reading. At its core, it is the skill to recommend the specific resources that best fit the users' needs. Whenever a reference librarian recommends a database, Web site, book, or journal, this is a form of reader's advisory. One of the skills of the reference librarian is our ability to evaluate and prioritize the content, usability, and validity of information sources. When we translate this into recommendations for our users, we are performing reader's advisory services.

Marketing and Promotion. The fourth role of the reference librarian that Green identified was to promote the library within its parent community. This aspect of the reference librarian's duties is often the least visible, but one of the most important. Winning the support of the community that the library serves ensures that the library will receive the funding, political support, recognition, and general goodwill to continue as an institution. In practice, libraries are not consistent in their promotional activities, with some doing tremendous jobs and others doing very little. Public libraries tend to have a greater emphasis on promotion than academic or special libraries, which have a more captive audience. However, all libraries need to continuously remind their constituencies of their ability to serve their needs.

What is most interesting about Green's original functions is that he saw the mere act of helping people—teaching them how to use the library, answering questions, or suggesting reading material—as a means of promoting the library. The fact that the users had direct, personal access to the librarian gave the librarian a more human presence within the community. The image of the librarian shifted from someone who selected and managed remotely to someone who was a real person who could help real users with real information and reading interests. The fact that the librarian became personalized with the introduction of reference service greatly increased support for the library because the members of the community actually knew the librarian as a person, not a figurehead.

This type of promotion by performance remains with us today. In an increasingly impersonal world, where many services are handled by recordings and machines, the reference librarian remains one of the very few professionals that any member of the community may consult on a personal level, usually on a drop-in basis without an appointment at any time of the day that the library is open. By remaining an accessible and helpful person, reference librarians continue to build good will for their libraries. The democratic ideal of service to all in the community ensures that the community will support the library. Reference service does not quite market itself, but most library users who receive reference service will support the library as an institution.

Much has changed over the 100+ years since the idea of reference service was first introduced. Today there are more libraries, with bigger collections, supporting a wider range of users, and with much higher degree of technology than in the nineteenth century. However, the same four functions that Green emphasized back then remain the focus of reference service today. Instruction, answering questions, recommending resources, and promoting the library within the community remain the core functions of reference service.

Five Good Reference Books

No chapter about reference service would be complete without the inclusion of a few standard reference sources. As more and more information has become available electronically, the need for reference books has decreased tremendously. Although reference librarians do not rely upon reference books nearly as much as we did 20 or more years ago, some reference books are still useful. This is a personal top five list.

1. *World Almanac and Book of Facts*. (New York: World Almanac, annual). Still the best single volume compilation of factual information ever published.
2. *World Book Encyclopedia*. (Chicago: World Book, annual). This is the best encyclopedia for looking up factual information. The *Britannica* and *Americana* may have more background material, but the *World Book* is the one to use for quick answers to questions.
3. *Statistical Abstract of the United States*. (Washington, DC: U.S. Bureau of the Census, annual). The best place to find out how much of anything is happening in the United States, including comparisons to other places throughout the world.
4. *Guinness Book of Records*. (New York: Facts on File, annual). From the fastest car to the most hot dogs, this book tells the who, where, and when any record was set.
5. *Famous First Facts*. (New York: H.W. Wilson, 2006). Like *Guinness*, but telling about the first instead of the most.

TOOLS OF THE TRADE

Reference work has always been associated with the specific information sources that are used by reference librarians. In fact the name "reference librarian" is derived from the phrase "reference books." In early libraries, reference books were those resources that could not be checked out, but which users could only "refer" to in the library. When librarians began helping users answer their questions, they naturally used these same books to do so. When Melvil Dewey formed what was then the first multilibrarian department to help users at Columbia College (now Columbia University), he chose the name "Reference Department" and called the staff "reference librarians"— names that are still in use in many libraries today.

For most of its history, reference service continued to be defined by the physical information sources that reference librarians used (i.e., reference books). Reference librarians were trained in the intricacies of encyclopedias, dictionaries, indexes, abstracts, almanacs, directories, chronologies, and other publications that were designed to present factual information in a concise, clear format. An entire branch of the publishing industry grew up around the need for reference works, producing ever-more specialized resources. Publishers such as Macmillan, World Book, and Gale derived a significant amount of their income catering to the needs of reference librarians. In a somewhat symbiotic relationship, they published the reference books that reference librarians consulted when helping their users.

The electronic revolution changed all that. From the introduction of electronic databases through services such as Dialog and BRS in the 1970s to CD-ROMs in the 1980s and the Internet in the 1990s, more users had more access to more information than at any previous time in human history. Information that was previously only available in reference books in the library became available to anyone with a computer anywhere in the world. Users and librarians suddenly had less need for traditional reference books. During the past decade, the image of the reference librarian has finally been liberated from being linked directly to specific information sources. Although some reference books are still used (but not nearly as frequently as in the past), the primary tool of today's reference librarian is a computer with an Internet connection.

However, books and computers are not the only technologies that reference librarians use in their daily activities. Since the creation of reference service, a wide range of tools have been developed that assist the reference librarian. In roughly chronological order, some of these technologies are:

- Typewriter
- Telephone
- Radio
- Microfilm
- Photocopier
- Fax Machine
- Television
- Computer

- Printer
- Floppy Disk
- Modem
- Videotape
- CD-ROM
- E-mail
- World Wide Web
- DVD
- Instant Messaging/chat
- Wireless
- USB devices

Each of the technologies above has affected reference service to one degree or another. However, if we look at the essential nature of those technologies, we can divide them down into two major categories:

Storage/Reproduction	Communication
Typewriter	Telephone
Microfilm	Radio
Photocopier	Fax Machine
Computer	Television
Floppy Disk	Modem
Printer	Email
Videotape	World Wide Web
CD-ROM	Cell Phones
DVD	Instant Messaging/Chat
USB storage devices	Wireless

Over the years, reference librarians have integrated each of these technologies into their services. The storage and reproduction technologies provide access to information that otherwise might not have been available in the library. With each advancement in these areas, librarians have been able to collect and distribute more and more information. Microfilm (and later, computers and electronic storage devices) allowed reference librarians to obtain materials that otherwise would have been available in only one place (or at most only a few libraries). These technologies allowed for the wider distribution of information to libraries and the communities that they served.

The communication technologies allow librarians to reach out to users who are not physically in the library building. These services, which we commonly call remote reference, have grown tremendously as technology has enabled reference librarians to reach out to ever wider audiences. Although remote reference has existed from the beginnings of reference service when users would write letters to libraries and await an answer, its use was not widespread due to the long time lag between the request and the response. The modern version of this is e-mail reference service. While many libraries offer e-mail reference services, the volume of traffic has never reached anticipated levels.

Due to the asynchronous nature of e-mail communication, e-mail reference is really just like traditional mail but with faster delivery.

The telephone is the technology that really allowed remote reference services to flourish. By calling on the phone, users are able to talk in real time to a reference librarian and get an immediate response to their question. Although telephone reference does not allow for the visual display of information, it does offer an interactive communication medium that allows the librarian and the user to communicate effectively. As the number of telephones in businesses and homes rose over time, telephone reference became more and more popular with library users. Because of the volume of calls received, some large public libraries established separate departments for telephone reference. In some cities, as many or more staff were devoted to telephone reference as were devoted to in-person reference services. Telephone service established the fact that users wanted to contact the library without having to make a trip into the building. As the ease of communication rose and the cost of communication dropped, the number of remote users of the library increased dramatically.

As the technology evolved and allowed us to deliver ever-more comprehensive services to remote users, the types of services provided have also become much more sophisticated. Through Instant Messaging and live online chat, reference librarians are able to offer remote users services that are essentially equivalent to those received by users who are in-person within the library building. The ability to send text, images, and Web links allows the librarian to reproduce remotely the experience of the user in the library. Some libraries use special software that permits co-browsing, in which the librarian can take over the user's computer (or vice versa). OCLC's Questionpoint (http://www.oclc.org/questionpoint/) is currently the most developed and most commonly used software for cobrowsing. With cobrowsing, the librarian can show the remote user the process for finding the desired information on their own computer. This technology brings the instructional aspect of remote reference to the same level as that of in-person reference.

A side effect of the rise of remote reference is the development of consortial reference programs. Since technology allows a reference librarian in one location to answer questions from users located anywhere else, a number of libraries and library systems have created cooperative reference services in which librarians take turns answering questions from any or all of the members. The Library of Congress was instrumental in starting cooperative reference, establishing an international network of libraries that covered all time zones and subjects. This innovative project served as a model for other regional networks to follow. By pooling their staff resources, libraries are able to offer a 24/7 online reference service while only having to staff it themselves for a short period of time. These cooperative reference programs have extended the reach of individual libraries to a statewide, national, and even international level.

From its origins of in-person assistance with books to its current ability to assist anyone anywhere using real-time interactive technologies, reference librarians have continually strived to reach out to serve their communities. And those communities have responded, using the library in-person and remotely. The balance of in-person and remote services is different for each community.

Whether using reference books or Web sites, whether in-person, on the telephone, or cobrowsing, reference librarians continue to use more and more tools to serve their users. As new technologies are developed, reference librarians will incorporate them into their services when those technologies can improve communication with their users.

THE REFERENCE INTERVIEW

Whether answering a question, teaching how to use an information source, or recommending a book or database, the most important part of the reference process is determining the specific need of the user. A reference librarian's knowledge of sources and technologies is useless unless the librarian fully understands the user's question. Before any of the tools mentioned above should be used, the librarian and the user need to arrive at a mutual understanding of what is being asked. The process that the librarian follows to determine the user's needs is often called the reference interview. This is the single most critical aspect of reference service.

The reference interview is necessary for one very simple reason: people rarely ask for what they really want. Most of the time, people ask for a topic that is much more general than what they really need. For example, a user who wants ratings of restaurants in New York might start the conversation by asking for travel books. Similarly, someone who wants to know if a certain purchase is deductible as a business expense would ask if the library has anything about taxes. Or a user who wants to know about the adverse effects of a certain prescription drug may start out by asking for health information. In each case, the librarian who answers the original question correctly does not address the real need of the user. The reference interview is the process of communicating with the user—mostly through questioning—to identify the true information need.

The reference interview is critical to the success of the reference librarian. A correct answer to the wrong question is a wrong answer to the correct question. The reference interview is also complicated by psychological factors. In our society, asking for assistance is often seen as a sign of weakness. Users who come to us for questions—especially those who have not used reference services in libraries before—are often hesitant to do so. Because they are asking for help, they feel as if they are in an inferior position in relation to the expert librarian. The librarian needs to win the user's trust, find out what the real information need is, and direct the user to resources that can address that need. At the same time, the librarian needs to minimize the user's feeling of inferiority and infuse the user with a greater sense of self-confidence about the search process. These factors comprise the interpersonal heart of good reference service.

During the 1990s, the Reference and User Services Association (a division of the American Library Association) recognized the importance of the behavioral factors involved in the reference process and developed a set of guidelines[9] to help reference librarians achieve positive results. The guidelines were revised in 2004 to incorporate specific features related to remote reference service, but the basic concepts remained the same. By following the guidelines, the reference librarian will be successful in interacting and assisting library users. In short, the guidelines help the reference librarian to be successful with the reference interview.

The guidelines are divided into five distinct areas, each of which needs to be successfully navigated in order to conduct a successful reference transaction. The guidelines cover five areas that are critical to reference success: approachability, interest, listening/inquiry, searching, and follow-up. Each of these five factors contributes to reference success or failure in a different way.

1. *Approachability.* Approachability is a fancy term that defines a user's willingness to ask a question in the first place. The best and most knowledgeable reference librarian in the world is useless if people are afraid to ask that librarian a question. The reference librarian needs to create an environment that encourages users to ask questions. Approachability is influenced by a combination of physical and behavioral factors. Some techniques that increase approachability are:

   a. Making eye contact. Eye contact is a nonverbal method of signaling that a librarian is ready and willing to take a question. Eye contact is the single most important factor in approachability.

   b. Smiling. Like eye contact, smiling is an inviting behavior that encourages users to approach the librarian.

   c. Reducing barriers. Physical barriers such as computer screens, piles of books, or desk walls inhibit users from asking questions. If a user cannot see that a librarian is available, that user is unlikely to ask a question.

   d. Greeting and welcoming users. A simple "hello," "welcome," or "may I help you?" breaks the ice and encourages users to begin the reference interview process.

The examples above all involve in-person reference service. However, approachability is equally important for remote users. A user who cannot find the Web link, instant messenger address, or phone number will be unable to ask the librarian a question. These need to be displayed prominently on all appropriate locations. In addition, a complicated phone tree or Web form will discourage users. We need to make remote access as simple and trouble free as in-person access.

2. *Interest.* To engage the user, the librarian needs to show an interest in the user's questions. A librarian who appears bored or disinterested will discourage the user from completing the process, leading to failure. Some techniques for displaying interest include:

   a. Maintaining eye contact during the transaction.

   b. Nodding the head or using other nonverbal signals to indicate that the librarian is paying attention and understanding the question.

   c. Using verbal clues such as "I see" or "that's interesting" or even "uh huh" to indicate that the librarian is following the user's train of thought.

With remote users, the nonverbal cues are not usually available, so an even greater emphasis must be place on verbal communication. When working with remote users, the librarian needs to interject frequently to let the user know that the librarian is still connected and still paying attention.

3. *Listening/Inquiry.* This is the heart of the reference interview. Once the user feels free to ask a question and sees that the librarian is interested and paying attention to the user's needs, the librarian may begin to ask questions to understand, clarify, and refine the question. This the "interview" portion of the reference process. Several different types of questions are frequently used in the reference interview. These include:

a) Open-ended questions. Open-ended questions are asked by the librarian to get the user to expand upon the original query. Open-ended questions are usually asked at the beginning of the reference interview and they provide the user with the opportunity to provide more information to the librarian. Note that these do not always need to be asked in question form (third example below). Some examples of open-ended questions include:

Can you tell me more about that?

What about [user's topic] would you like to find out?

Tell me where you have looked so far.

b) Closed-ended questions. Closed-ended questions are used by the librarian to find out specific details from the user. These are normally asked near the end of the reference interview, when the librarian has a good idea of the information need but still needs to refine the query. Examples of closed-ended questions include:

Do you need current or historical information?

Do you want to find books or journals?

How much information do you need?

c) Neutral questioning. Throughout the reference interview, the librarian will mix open- and closed-ended questions until the librarian and the patron agree that they each understand the query. An important aspect of the questioning process is to keep the questions on a positive level. A question that sounds accusatory to the user may prevent the user from completing the process, resulting in the librarian not knowing the true question and the user not getting that question answered. The librarian needs to maintain a neutral, yet encouraging tone throughout the process. The librarian must refrain from making judgments about the patron or the question being asked. Some examples of questions that can cause problems are (emphasis added in *italics*):

What do you need *that* for?

What are you going *to do* with this information?

Why do you need *this*?

Mastering these questioning techniques is essential to success as a reference librarian. Although the entire process may take place in a very short time period, the use of open-ended, closed-ended, and neutral questioning will enable the librarian to fully understand what the user really needs. In many cases, these questions will also help the users define their needs in their own minds. Many times, users come to the library with only a general idea of their actual question. Through the reference interview, the librarian helps the user define the problem, which helps the librarian determine where to look for potential solutions. Once the question is identified, the librarian can move on to finding resources to answer it.

4. *Searching.* Once the librarian understands the question and the specific needs of the user, then the search for a response can begin. Although searching is not always a behavioral aspect, the librarian does need a sufficient understanding of information sources and how to use them effectively to find potential answers to the query. If the librarian has poor searching skills, no potential answer will be found no matter how well the reference interview is conducted.

5. *Follow-up.* In most cases, questions posed by our users are sufficiently complex that a number of potential information resources might satisfy their needs. The librarian will often get a user started with one resource and check on that user later to see if it was able to fill the information need. If the reference librarian checks back with the user, the librarian can determine if the search was successful. If it was, the librarian knows that the question has been answered. If it was not, the librarian may take the user to another possible source. In either case, the user gets the impression that the librarian cares about the user. Interestingly, follow-up is the factor in the reference process that leads to the highest satisfaction level among users.

MEASURING REFERENCE SUCCESS AND FAILURE

Reference service is one of the most labor-intensive activities provided by most libraries. Using highly paid (at least in library terms) professional librarians to work directly with the public during all (or most) hours that the library is open is an expensive proposition and one that many are questioning in this day and age. As a result, evaluation and assessment of reference services have become important factors in determining whether, how, and when to provide reference service. Several methods have been used for measuring the success of reference service. Four of the most common methods of evaluating reference are: unobtrusive testing, obtrusive testing, willingness-to-return, and a more formal method, the Wisconsin-Ohio Reference Evaluation Program.

Unobtrusive Testing. Since reference is a service that provides answers to questions, one obvious measure of success is whether those answers are correct or not. In the 1970s and 1980s, many studies of the correctness of reference services were conducted (most famously by Peter Hernon and Charles McClure[10]). In these studies, a user would ask a question (most commonly in-person or on the telephone). The user would record the answer provided by the librarian and compare it to the correct answer that was already known to the researchers. The answer was judged as correct or incorrect based on whether it matched the previously known correct response. This method is called unobtrusive because the librarians are unaware that the question being asked is part of the study.

After a statistically significant number of questions had been asked of the reference librarians at a particular library, the researchers were able to give that library a score that reflected its level of accuracy. Interestingly, the libraries that were tested all showed a fairly consistent range in their levels of accuracy. Disappointingly, that range was fairly low. On average, reference librarians were able to provide the correct answer 55 percent of the time. Study after study arrived at this same measure of reference success (or failure). This result came to be popularly known as the 55 percent rule.

For a profession that prides itself on finding answers to difficult questions, this figure was an embarrassment. It led a number of thinkers in the profession (most notably Jerry Campbell[11]) to seriously question the value of providing reference service. Naturally, reference librarians became defensive. They thought that the tests were sneaky and unfair, that they only applied to other libraries and not themselves, or that there was a flaw in the research methodology. Unfortunately, as test after test came back with the same results, it became impossible to ignore the problem of reference accuracy. During the 1990s, reference librarians suffered from a collective crisis of conscience about what we were doing. Unobtrusive testing had demonstrated that the reference emperor really wore no clothes.

Or had it? The problem with unobtrusive evaluation is that it can only measure questions that have single, invariable, factual answers. However, as mentioned earlier in this chapter in the section on the functions of reference service, these are not the kinds of questions that reference librarians receive on a regular basis. With the growth of the Internet and easy access to information, library users can find the answers to these questions on their own and do not need the assistance of a reference librarian. This type of question is asked less and less in most libraries. Most of the questions that users ask librarians are those that do not have specific answers, but that have many possible pathways to a result. Many of the questions do not have answers at all.

The problem with unobtrusive testing is that it measured only a small fraction of what reference librarians were doing. In addition, this fraction was not typical of the needs of most users of the library. Getting a right answer is important when such an answer exists, but most of the time the difference between right and wrong is a matter of opinion and nuance rather than hard fact. This method gathers no information on how the answer is obtained, tells us nothing about the reference interview process, the searching process, or whether the librarian ever really determined what underlying question really was. Other evaluation tools would need to be developed to measure those factors of the reference process. Although unobtrusive testing helped to shock reference librarians out of their complacency with the status quo, it did not mean that the entire service was a failure.

Obtrusive evaluation. In many ways, obtrusive evaluation is the opposite of unobtrusive testing. In obtrusive evaluation, the librarian is followed by an observer who watches the entire process. The observer does not participate, but takes notes on how the librarian interacts with the user, performs the search, and retrieves an answer (if one exists). After the user has left, the observer discusses the transaction with the librarian. The observer reviews the entire process, indicating where the librarian performed well and where the librarian performance can be improved.

Obtrusive evaluation has several advantages over unobtrusive. In addition to the reviewing the answer found in the search (if any), it studies the entire reference process, including the reference interview and the search techniques. Reference transactions are complex behavioral interactions and obtrusive testing provides observational data about all aspects of those interactions.

Unfortunately, obtrusive evaluation also has one fatal flaw—people change their behavior when they know that they are being observed. It is human nature to want to show your best when being evaluated. When the reference librarian knows that there is an observer, that librarian will make an extra effort to do the best possible reference interview and search for information on the topic. This may not reflect that librarian's daily performance, so the observer may not be getting a true display of how that librarian responds to user queries. Observation changes the result, making the data obtained unreliable.

However, obtrusive testing is making a comeback in evaluating online chat/instant messaging reference services. Since many of the software packages used in remote reference keep a transcript of every transaction, reference managers can read those transcripts after the fact to determine how a librarian interacted with a user. Since the observer is not obvious to the librarian and the user, these transcripts are much more likely to display actual librarian behavior and skills than when obtrusive testing is used with in-person reference. By reading transcripts, the evaluator can identify areas in which additional training is needed for the participating librarians.

Willingness to Return. Joan Durrance[12] at the University of Michigan has merged the best aspects of obtrusive and unobtrusive evaluation into a single study, which she calls "willingness to return." In this method, a user with a real question (answer unknown) asks a reference librarian for assistance. The user is also an observer who compares the actions of the reference librarian to a checklist based upon the behavioral guidelines. The user reports back on both the accuracy of the answer and the process that the librarian used to arrive at the answer. The final evaluation is based upon a single factor: would the user return to that same librarian with a future question?

This method takes the best of obtrusive evaluation (observing the entire transaction) and combines it with a measure of accuracy similar to unobtrusive evaluation. Since it uses real life questions, many of the questions used do not have specific factual answers. As a result, this method more closely simulates real-life reference transactions. And since the librarian does not know that this user is part of the study, in the librarian's mind it is a real-life reference transaction.

The most interesting finding from willingness to return studies is that the interaction with the librarian is much more important than the answer to the question. Many users who get a wrong answer (or wrong advice if there is not a specific answer) are still willing to ask the librarian another question if the librarian followed the behavioral guidelines. Alternatively, users who get a right answer may not be willing to return to a librarian who was rude, disinterested, or distracted. Willingness to return studies highlight the importance of the reference interview and the reference process as opposed to answers to specific questions.

The biggest problem with willingness to return studies is that it is almost impossible to get a large statistical sample of evaluations. Since each user can only be an observer one time, you would need a very large number of potential users to conduct a large-scale study. In addition, you are depending on the good will of the users to carry out the evaluation. Users must be open-minded and not bring in any preconceived notions or else the results will be skewed. Willingness to return provides useful anecdotal data, but cannot be used for large scale evaluation of the service.

Wisconsin-Ohio Reference Evaluation Program (WOREP). Originally designed by Charles Bunge (University of Wisconsin) and Marjorie Murfin (Ohio State University) and now run out of the School of Library and Information Science at Kent State University (http://worep.library.kent.edu/), the WOREP is a tool that combines several of the factors of the other three evaluation methods. With the WOREP, the user and the librarian each fill out an evaluation form after the transaction is completed. The forms are processed centrally and the data from each side is matched. The library must pay a fee to cover the processing and administrative costs (currently $1.25 per transaction).

For a transaction to be considered successful in WOREP, the librarian and the user must indicate that the question was accurately and completely answered. If this standard is not met, the librarian is able to indicate why the transaction was incomplete or inaccurate. Typical reasons include insufficient collections, being very busy, and technical problems. From the user's perspective, the form permits ratings of the performance of the librarian on factors such as helpfulness, courtesy, instructional skills. This is the only evaluation tool that combines measures of accuracy and behavioral factors from the perspective of the librarian and the user.

The WOREP also provides baseline data on how other similar institutions have scored, allowing a comparison of performance among peer libraries. Interestingly, the average accuracy rating on the WOREP is also around 55 percent. It seems that we can never get away from the 55 percent rule. However, with its higher standard for measuring success, the WOREP results show that we are doing better than do results from unobtrusive testing.

One of the most interesting factors to come out of reference evaluation is that our users tend to be universally satisfied with our services. No matter which evaluation method is used, library users tend to say very positive things about the library and their experience with the reference librarian. In survey after survey, reference service gets high marks from library users—regardless of whether they found what they were looking for. This emphasizes the fact that users appreciate the personal interaction with the librarian that lies at the heart of reference services.

THE FUTURE OF REFERENCE

Will reference continue to be a standard function of libraries in future years? The fact that users value reference service indicates that it will probably be around for some time to come. Regardless of the definition of reference service that we use, the personal interaction between the user and the librarian will remain at the core of reference services. The tools and the information sources that we use will change dramatically and our users will communicate with us in ways, but we will continue to offer personalized service to members of the communities that we serve.

Five Useful Reference Web Sites

Reference has evolved from print resources to electronic information. As a result, most of the places that reference librarians search for answers are on the Web. Here are five personal favorite reference Web sites.

1. *Google.* www.google.com. The fastest, most comprehensive search tool ever developed. The specialized sections (Google Scholar, Google Maps, Google Images) make it even more useful for searching for specific types of resources. Google uber alles!
2. *Yahoo.* www.yahoo.com. Google is for searching, Yahoo is for browsing. Yahoo still has one of the best directories on the Web.
3. *Wikipedia.* www.wikipedia.org. Wikipedia is the most comprehensive encyclopedia on the Web. It takes advantage of the collective wisdom of its authors to present a wide range of topics never considered by its print equivalents. Yes, we complain that some wikipedia articles are biased and yes, we still use it.
4. *Librarian's Index to the Internet.* www.lii.org. Like Yahoo, but built by some of us. Living up to the claims of its motto: "websites you can trust."
5. *Infomine.* infomine.ucr.edu. Like the Librarian's Index, but for academics. Scholarly Web sites collected and reviewed by librarians.

Note: Each Uniform Resource Locator (URL) was verified as an active link to the appropriate Web page on January 02, 2008.

However, it is possible that society will no longer need reference service at some time in the future. There are three possible scenarios in which reference service will cease to exist in libraries:

1. *Information becomes ubiquitous, freely available, and so easy to find that users no longer need assistance.* Given the ease of access that we now have to information of all kinds, it is possible that all information will some day be available everywhere to everyone. Although the Internet has made information much more available to the public today than at any previous time in human history, users still need help with the tools that retrieve that information. As new tools are created, users will need assistance in learning how to use them. And as the finding of information has become easier, users continue to need assistance in evaluating the information that they find with those tools. Google certainly makes finding easy—but figuring out which of the millions of results are useful takes special evaluative skills. Finally, those users who are not entirely certain

about what they need will still need people to help them formulate their search strategies. Although information resources will become easier and easier to use, it is unlikely that there will be a time when no assistance at all is needed for their users.

2. *Information becomes commercialized to the point that vendors control all access and we are forced to contract with those vendors for everything that we need.* Although in recent history much information has become more freely available over the Internet, at the same time large segments of the information universe have come under the control of private companies. Copyright laws have become more restrictive, extending the rights of those companies for longer and longer periods of time. Intellectual property rights are increasingly being controlled by fewer and fewer individuals and corporations. While it is possible that all information will become someone's intellectual property and that we will need to pay for access, this is also highly unlikely. Even if information does become privatized, the library will continue to serve as an information utility for its parent community. Citizens will be able to use the library to access information that they can not afford individually. In this scenario, reference service becomes even more important because they become the link that community members' need to access the world of commercial information.

3. *Communities cease to value the library as an institution and do not support its historic roles of collection, organization, and service.* Sadly, this is the most likely of the three scenarios to actually occur. In the past few decades, many corporations have closed their libraries. Some university presidents are questioning the value of spending large segments of their budgets on library resources. Funding for public libraries has been voted down in many communities. Those who think that everything that they need is on the Internet may not appreciate the role that libraries play in providing information to their community. It is vital to the library—and to the community—that librarians continue to be successful in Green's fourth function of reference service, marketing the library to the community. When a community no longer values its library, that library will not survive.

Although each of these three scenarios will occur to some degree, none is likely to dominate so much that libraries and reference service will become endangered. For the foreseeable future, reference librarians will continue to teach users about information resources and search tools; answer informational queries and help users determine what they need; recommend resources; and promote the library within the community. We will adopt new information and communication technologies and we will continue to be appreciated by our users. As long as we continue to provide personal assistance to all of the members of our respective communities, libraries—and reference librarians—will continue to thrive. The need for reference books is no longer as critical, but the need for reference librarians is stronger than ever.

Chapter 13

Librarians: The Best Googlers in the World

Linda Main

Do you want to work in an attractive setting, use cool technology, encourage peer teaching and mentoring, and have fun? The following three job descriptions might appeal to you:

Job Posting One

Lead a team implementing technologies such as instant messaging, podcasting, and streaming audio/video for all ages; help guide the continuing transformation and development of the Web site with new and developing technologies such as blogs, RSS, and wikis. Knowledge of Dreamweaver and Contribute is a plus, as is experience conducting usability testing; help develop and implement the organization's digital services; collaborate with other team members to build and promote community, including virtual community; participate in the creation, preparation, and delivery of programs and classes for staff and the public; prepare user information and training materials; plan and present public programs and bibliographies.

Job Posting Two

Lead our virtual reference team, implementing transformative technology such as IM, podcasting, and streaming audio/video; recommend and implement new and developing technologies such as wikis, blogs, etc.; contribute to the development of the organization's Web site; contribute to our virtual services offerings, such as Web 2.0, federated searching, open URL resolver, etc.; provide training and support for colleagues in new technologies; manage our electronic resources and online databases, explore and recommend new on-line resources, and negotiate contracts with consortia and vendors; collaborate with other colleagues to provide community development and outreach, particularly in regard to our virtual services; facilitate planning and decision-making, resolve problems, implement projects, improve customer service and ensure the smooth delivery of services.

Job Posting Three

Professional to deliver techno-savvy reference to an educated, enlightened resort community in SW Colorado; must have strong general reference skills and be an enthusiastic team player; interest in blogging, RSS, wikis, and IM essential.

The above job descriptions are seeking librarians; the people who will get hired will work in the Redwood City Public Library in California, in Wayne State University Library in Detroit, Michigan, and in Wilkinson Public Library in Telluride, Colorado, and they will have an MLIS (Master of Library and Information Science) degree. The MLIS degree is the basic requirement for professional employment in libraries and the information professions.

Librarianship is the second oldest profession in the world—after prostitution. And like the oldest profession in the world, librarianship is an applied discipline—a service industry constantly adapting to the needs of users. Throughout the ages, librarians have been responsible for helping people record their comprehension of themselves and the world about them. To do this they have always been involved with technology. In Assurbanipal's library (668 B.C.E.--626 B.C.E.) the "keeper of the tablets" was trained in the making of clay tablets and in cuneiform writing. He recorded history, geography, tax lists, and myths and legends. He was a graduate of the school for scribes and an expert in cuneiform, astronomy, math, medicine, accounting, and the languages of the time.

Move forward in time to May 2006 to the sands of Uig in the island of Lewis in the Outer Hebrides in Scotland. The local population and visitors gathered to hear Gaelic songs and stories about the surrounding landscape. Instead of being told around a fire or inside a tigh ceilidh the stories are delivered directly to individuals and retold digitally via an electronic handpack called an ipaq. The area has been mapped as a series of "magic circles" using global-satellite-positioning. When people enter these circles the ipaq delivers tales and songs that are relevant to that specific location. Locals and visitors can hear about the area's history back to the Iron Age and find out about the Bornais Broch, the local Fenian legends, the origin of the Brahan Seer's stone, the nineteenth-century evangelical revival, the area's strong connection with the Napoleonic Wars and the discovery of the Lewis Chessmen. This is part of a research project developed by MediaLab Europe in partnership with local libraries. Several of the researchers who worked on the project in MediaLab Europe were librarians with MLIS degrees. This is an example of the oral tradition at work, ancient as humankind, but in twenty-first-century guise being provided by twenty-first-century librarians.

The technology skills that are typically learned in an MLIS program teach you how to enhance user centered services, how to facilitate and promote collaboration among users, and how to effectively locate information on the Internet. These are skills that carry over into every part of our increasingly networked world.

LIBRARIANS IN THE AGE OF BLOGS, WIKIS, AND RSS

Libraries have always been a physical place, source, and resource for their local communities (public libraries) and specialized communities (educational and corporate libraries). They have offered spaces for groups to meet, places for students and researchers to study, events for the education and recreation of the community, reference services, and of course books, movies, and music. They will continue to offer these services.

However as we move to Web 2.0 defined by Tim O'Reilly as an "architecture of participation"[1] the line between what is real and what is virtual is beginning to fade. The kind of interactions that people have daily by phone, text message, and e-mail is being extended online. Being "present" with another person is taking on a new meaning. The Web is no longer a static and mainly one-way medium, where visitors to sites merely read the content fed to them and play no active role. Now users participate and connect to each other using services as opposed to sites. Ordinary citizens have the chance to be publishers, movie makers, or storytellers. However the role of the librarian has not changed. It has merely expanded into a virtual space.

Librarians always have been and still are people who can connect arts and sciences into an integrative world whole—the humanist ideal originating from the Italian Renaissance. They identify interconnected fields of knowledge where those connections exist and more importantly, help people create connections where they do not exist. The twenty-first-century librarian simply does this increasingly in a virtual as opposed to a physical space. The library offers virtual space and digital tools and the librarian helps to make what is created in the space useful. This is the communication side of the Internet. The librarian is also trained in the other side of the Internet, namely how to use effective search techniques to retrieve useful information. Librarians find information that is already there—the trick is that we know where to look; librarians know what kinds of resources will be most appropriate for the person asking the question, how to measure the resources they find, and how to help people find their own resources and evaluate them. Librarians "google" better than anyone else.

THE COMMUNICATION ROLE OF THE TWENTY-FIRST-CENTURY LIBRARIAN

The communication tools of Web 2.0 are:

blogs
wikis

RSS feeds

podcasts

instant messaging

Flickr

vodcasts

mash ups (named after hip-hop mixes of two or more songs, mash ups blend music, video, and images from a number of different sources into an integrated whole).

Twenty-first-century librarians have to understand not only how to use and market the tools of Web 2.0 but also know how to help their patrons use the tools effectively and efficiently. Twenty-first-century librarians have to be able to compare different versions of the same type of software to figure out which will best meet their patrons' needs. They can help the user to avoid using tools to merely provide what George Will calls a more sophisticated delivery of stupidity.[2]

The following section briefly discusses the communication tools of Web 2.0 and provides some examples of how librarians are using the tools to empower and involve patrons.

Blogs

A Weblog or blog is an online diary. It refers to a category of Web site where the content is presented in a continuing sequence of dated entries. The newest entry is typically at the top of the Web page and can be updated at anytime—hourly, daily, weekly, or monthly.

Blogs can be thought of as the unedited voice of a single person or company or as a networked digital paper. NPR (National Public Radio), for example, is using a blog to open up the process of developing a new show (a work in progress) to the public. People are asked to listen to the segments and to offer their comments.[3]

Library blogs are typically building blocks for communicating news and information to users. They are a place to:

List new books, videos, CDs, or DVDs as they are added to the collection;

Review new titles and link them to relevant Internet sites;

Start an online book discussion;

Provide links to author interviews;

List book award announcements such as Man Booker Prize, Children's Book Week awards, Pulitzer Prize winners;

Encourage young adults to discuss Top 10 albums, Top 10 movies, Top PS2, or XBox games;

Engage children to get involved with literature and to discuss what's new and what will appeal to children of different reading levels and ages.

Examples

Madison (WI) Public Library publishes a blog review every day. Readers are encouraged to interact with the reviews by posting comments and opinions. http://www.madisonpubliclibrary.org/madreads/.

Many scientists now use blogs and the number of science blogs is on the rise.Technorati (an Internet search engine that searches blogs) listed over 4,000 science blogs at the end of 2006. Science blogs connect scientists to other scientists, serving as modern-day intellectual salons. They also connect scientists to the general public, offering a behind-the-scenes look at how science is progressing. An example of this is Siphs. Siphs provides a forum for collaboration and information exchange to around 200 biology and biomedical researchers in 30 countries. http://www.siphs.com/.

Yale University Library runs a blog dedicated to emerging surgical teaching and research. http://surgery-update.blogspot.com/.

Wikis

The term wiki originates from the Hawaiian word for quick. A wiki is a group-created Web site. It is an open shared space for collaborative content contribution and editing. Any information added to a wiki can be changed or deleted by anyone. A person with a web browser can insert new pages, include new content in existing pages (text and multimedia), or delete content.

What makes a wiki different from a blog is that it runs software that permits visitors to add new information and, more importantly, edit previous authors' submissions. In contrast, a blog typically allows visitors to post responses to previous authors' submissions. In a blog visitors cannot go back and edit earlier blog submissions.

Don Tapscott in his book Wikinomics discusses how wikis are bringing about a new age of participation in the economy and how many businesses are using wikis to conduct research and development for their products. He uses the term "ideagoris" to discuss this development.[4]

Examples

The librarians at the investment bank of Dresdner Kleinwort Wasserstein set up a restricted access Socialtext wiki to create meeting agendas and post training videos for new hires. Six months after launching, traffic on the 2,500-plus-page wiki was used by a quarter of the bank's workforce and the use surpassed that of the company's intranet.

The Ohio University Libraries Biz wiki contains articles about business reference books, databases, Web sites, and other research guides. It is a library resource to which students, faculty staff, and other librarians can contribute. http://www.library.ohiou.edu/subjects/bizwiki/index.php/Main_Page.

The Princeton (NJ) Public Library has created a book club for its adult readers using wiki software. Once registered, readers can post reviews on the wiki that is called Book Lovers Wiki. http://booklovers.pbwiki.com/.

RSS Feeds and Aggregators

RSS stands for rich site summary or really simple syndication. RSS conveys information that a Web site or blog has been updated and allows quick scanning of the latest headlines. An RSS service consists of a list of items, each of which usually includes a headline, description, and a link to a Web page. RSS news readers allow users to view the selected pages all together in the same place. The news reader automatically retrieves updates and enables users to stay current with new content soon after it is published. E-mail boxes do not fill up; nor is there a constant need to check various Web sites. A blog or Web site posting can even be distributed to individual users via wireless PDAs.

Examples of RSS Feeds Set Up by Librarians

Users post reference questions about political matters (generally United States-based), with answers posted to the site. Feeds such as this give a sense of what interests people in a community. http://nyc.indymedia.org/en/index.html.

Users are updated with genealogy. http://rssgenealogy.com/ keeps up with genealogy.

See what librarians all over the world are doing to feed news and all kinds of information to their communities. http://www.libdex.com/weblogs.html.

Podcasts

The word podcast originates from combining "iPod" and "broadcast." A podcast is an audio program distributed over the Internet. Like a radio show each podcast consists of a series of individual episodes that users can listen to however, whenever, and wherever they want. Users listen when it is convenient.

Podcasts are used by librarians in the following ways:

Training tools for databases and online library resources;

Short, informational episodes about an issue combining voice-over by a narrator/host and interviews with clients;

Weekly updates about what is going on in the library and in the community;

Reviews of new books followed by interviews with users who have read the books.

Examples

The Public Library of Charlotte and Mecklenburg County (NC) regularly holds a joke contest for teens and later podcasts the best jokes. The podcast is called Libraryloft podcast. http://www.libraryloft.org/podcasts.asp.

The Cheshire (CN) Public Library offers a podcast for teens. The podcast is a teen driven cultural magazine featuring teen writers, musicians, reviewers, and commentators. http://www.cheshirelib.org/teens/cplpodcast.htm.

Instant Messaging (IM)

Instant messaging allows online communication between two or more people using typed text sent via computers in real time. It is a very popular medium of communication with teens but also with people who work in or own local businesses or stay-at-home parents trying to find out when for example the next storytime is being held.

Examples

Take a look at Homer Township (Homer Glen, IL) Public Library. http://homerlibrary.org/.

St. Joseph County (IN) Public Library. http://libraryforlife.org/asksjcpl/asksjcpl.html.

Flickr

Flickr is an image-hosting online community. It is a way for people to upload their photos and share them with the entire community of users. Michael Stephens discusses ten ways that librarians are using Flickr.[5]

1. To highlight new materials:
   http://www.flickr.com/photos/westmontlibrary/page2/
2. To show the face of the Teen Advisory Board:
   http://www.flickr.com/photos/michaelsphotos/276656379/
3. To highlight programs and some young library users:
   http://www.flickr.com/photos/sjcpl/156548234/
4. To create a presence in the site itself:
   http://www.flickr.com/people/asheborolibrary/
5. To create an easy virtual tour for users and staff: http://www.flickr.com/photos/11329886@N00/sets/72157594291410121/
6. To promote what your teens are doing at the library and a book sale:
   http://www.flickr.com/photos/thomasfordmemoriallibrary/sets/72057594113917054/
7. To store and use images for Wikis, etc.:
   http://albystaff.pbwiki.com/Processing
8. To share the library's history:
   http://www.flickr.com/photos/tuttlibrary/124369627/in/photostream/
9. To commemorate the first patron of the new bookmobile:
   http://www.flickr.com/photos/homerlibrary/148791618/in/photostream/

10. To celebrate Harry Potter day:
     http://www.flickr.com/photos/60582448@N00/27984592/

Vodcasts

A vodcast is a term used to describe the online delivery of video on demand via RSS.

Examples

The Public Library of Charlotte and Mecklenburg County (NC) produces vodcasts of a program for teens called Fairy Tales Gone Bad @ImaginOn:
http://www.youtube.com/watch?v=Fkn6Dd0eZ88.

The Best Googlers

The volume of digital information available on public and private Web sites will continue to increase. Electronic records (born digital) now make up more than 50 percent of all records created and maintained at institutions. Search tools are struggling to make the contents of the exploding blog and social software accessible. Librarians have the training to explore the rabbit-warrens of content building up in blog servers. They know how to index, abstract, and preserve this new digital content. They know how to use keyword search engines to provide personalized and relevant information about products and services. Librarians are the other half of tagging.

Tagging is where users assign keywords in order to optimize future findability of a link or item. When others see interesting tags they sometimes apply them to their own items or links. A variation of tagging is social bookmarking. This is being used heavily by scientists engaged in research. An example is Connotea, created by the publishing group that owns the journal *Nature*. Connotea can be added to the toolbar of a Web browser. When a scientist finds a relevant reference he or she can save it and add their own keywords. They can then share their bookmark library with colleagues.[6]

Another variation of tagging is rating. Rating has importance for scientists and researchers. An example of this is the development of "true trials" for scientific research in which both sites and sponsors can participate. Investigative sites establish a presence and allow sponsors to contribute to their reputation by rating their performance in clinical trials. Through this rating system, companies can create a database of rated sites for sponsors and provide new opportunities for highly rated sites.

All of the above is part of the *input* part of the tagging process.

Librarians are concerned with the other half of the equation—the *output* part that lets users *find information through tags*. Librarians are trained in data retrieval processes and how to use natural language processing and computational linguistics to read, filter, and interpret content. An MLIS program teaches the fundamental processes of description, classification, information structures, database models, and intermediation. These processes are reflective of information systems of all types, including but not limited to, libraries. Librarians are also taught how to assess conflicting information. For example, one of the structurally inherent problems of a wiki is that there's no guarantee that people adding to existing material actually know what they talking about. Typically all likeminded people go to the same site to see support for their own point of view. This is the echo chamber effect that leads to selective exposure and selective attention. Librarians know how to provide balance. They know what sources are best used for particular purposes by particular individuals.

Following is a sample of the kinds of research and retrieval skills you can expect to learn in an MLIS program. They have relevance for almost every part of our digital world.

Digital asset management in the public and private sector focusing on metadata, workflow, taxonomy, data security, and preservation of digital assets;

Identifying vocabulary design, retrieval requirements, and licensing issues for online digital collections of photographs;

Analyzing digital video collections to identify issues related to access, content, format, and eventual repurposing by users;

Analyzing graphics collections of logos, images, and multimedia assets, and creating project plans for digital asset management implementations including metadata models for these assets;

Digitizing archival, library, and museum materials using digital technologies to provide better access to and sometimes to preserve text, images, sound, and video.

Librarians know how to create, acquire, provide access to, and preserve digitized and "born-digital" cultural heritage materials. Studying the preservation, conservation and restoration history of, for example, the original Domesday Book (1086 C.E.) and its digital equivalent (1986 C.E.) is typically used in an MLIS program as a structural narrative to bridge two preservation paradigms.

Copyright issues permeate the library's digital environment, from virtual reference to full-text book scanning projects to library Web site design. Google book search, digitization projects, and personal copying all depend on generous interpretations of fair use. Librarians need to be well versed in both the newest interpretations and the basics of copyright law. This includes fair use, digital rights management systems, and database legislation.

Librarians are trained to know about the following:

What is fair use, and how is it determined?

How long are copyrights valid today?

How does the public domain work?

What are "orphan works"?

Who owns a wiki?

Who owns a virtual reference knowledge base?

How do you add a creative commons license to a digital object created online making sure that it has the creative commons "code" so that it will show up in user searches?

Which browsers have a creative commons plug-in so that creative commons licensed content can be found?

Do You Want to Play Games?

The library has always played an educational role in its community. It is fulfilling that role in the twenty-first century by embracing games such as FIFA World Cup 2002, Medal of Honor: Allied Assault, Star Wars Jedi Knight II: Jedi Outcast, Tony Hawks ProSkater 3, and WarCraft III. Game worlds are typically organized as a series of levels each associated with a different performance challenge that must be overcome in order to unlock access to the next level. The levels are usually organized in a graduated difficulty progression so that the skills learned on one level form the foundation for the skills learned on the next. This is no different from a well-designed academic course that builds and integrates knowledge in a structured continuum that leads from the beginning to the end; and that involves learning objectives. Students must form hypotheses, make decisions, and troubleshoot problems.

Several libraries host gaming parties. The Santa Monica (CA) Public Library, for example, hosts a regular LAN (local area network) party gaming night where teens come to play the first person shooter game Counterside. A LAN party is a temporary gathering of people bringing their computers to the library and networking them together to play multiplayer games.

The Austin (TX) Public library partners with a software and computer game designer to work with kids to help them build their own computer games. The Ann Arbor (MI) Public Library provides console-style games for youth tournaments. It uses the Nintendo Game Cube Game Mario Kart because it is a racing game without any violence, has broad appeal for both sexes, and works well in a multiplayer environment.

The Carnegie Library of Pittsburgh (PA), the Public Library of Charlotte and Mecklenburg County (NC) and the Rochester Hills (MI) Public Library are taking the lead in using the Wii in the library. The Wii uses motion sensors instead of gamepads with buttons. It is controlled by a wireless signal and can detect motion and rotation in three dimensions. The right-hand controller lets the user point and shoot. The left-hand holds the "nunchuck," which has a joystick for movement. The console can also receive messages and updates over the Internet.

Already one or two job ads are appearing for gaming librarians.

WHAT DO YOU WANT TO LOOK LIKE TODAY?

Libraries in Second Life . . .

As early as 1993 Benjamin Woolley[7] wrote: "There has been a very real shift in the foundations of knowledge-and it is clear in which direction. Reality has left the physical world and moved into the virtual one."

Second Life is a 3D virtual universe that lets people create digital representations of themselves. It is the closest thing to a parallel universe existing on the Internet. Participants see, hear, use, and modify simulated objects .Users access the world from their desktops. All can meet in the 3D world but may be physically located anywhere on the planet. Virtual 3D environments can be created that fit needs for purposeful interaction spaces such as virtual offices, virtual cafeterias, virtual training centers, virtual labs, and virtual team rooms. Virtual classrooms can be programmed in different configurations: informal discussion areas where speakers must queue up and only two or three are allowed to speak at once (but an unlimited number of others can "listen"); and one-way "lecture halls." A Virtual Auditorium can be used for special events and formal guest lectures by speakers from around the world. There are also chat environments for users to communicate with each other. In addition there are avatars.

Avatars serve as the visual representation of users inhabiting the world. All the connected people are able to "move," represented by avatars, "see" each other, "communicate" real-time, and experience the interactive "design" of the environment.

Reuters has opened a news bureau in Second Life. They have appointed a virtual bureau chief, who uses a personal avatar, or animated character, called "Adam Reuters". IBM has opened a business as has Dell. *Wired* magazine has an office in Second Life.

In 2007 libraries also moved into the 3D virtual world and created themselves in 3D formats inside Second Life. InfoIsland Library is a virtual library providing real service to Second Life residents. It receives around 4,000 to 5,000 visitors per day. The library hosts exhibits, offers lectures from real world experts, and the staff answer questions that range from the simple to the complex that involve consulting online databases of various kinds.

In the twenty-first century libraries and librarians link the physical with the virtual world. Lee Rainie,[8] Director of the Pew Internet and American Life Project, listed reasons why the future belongs to librarians:

1. Nobody knows better how to manage information
2. Nobody knows better how to track down information
3. Nobody knows better the importance of information standards— common ways to categorize, sort, and act on things
4. Nobody is in a better position to teach people about information and media literacy
5. Nobody is in a better position to be a watchdog on new systems of sorting information
6. Nobody is in a better position to teach the world about the history and built-in wisdom of credibility-assessment systems
7. Nobody is more empowered by professional creeds and training to articulate the rationale for freedom of speech
8. Nobody is in better shape to play a thoughtful, constructive role in debates about the value of information "property" and the meaning of copyright in an age where it takes a couple of minutes to download a brand new movie

9. Nobody can be as constructive in helping people think through the new norms and even new laws that we need to develop about what information is public and what is private.

This chapter started with job postings and it concludes with a job posting. *We need an agile, imaginative, and engaged staff. We need people who are not afraid of jettisoning traditional activities in favor of new ones. We must have people who can learn constantly, foster change, and create new kinds of collections and services. Some of these people are already in our buildings and virtual spaces; we are hiring others. Required: An MLIS degree.*

Note: Each Uniform Resource Locator (URL) was verified as an active link to the appropriate Web page on January 02, 2008.

SUGGESTIONS FOR FURTHER READING

InfoIsland.org. Retrieved January 02, 2008, from http://infoisland.org. Second Life Library 2.0 blog.

Levine, Jenny. "Gaming and Libraries." *Library Technology Reports* 42(5) (September–October 2006).

Sinha, Rashmi. *A Cognitive Analysis of Tagging*, 2005. Retrieved January 02, 2008, from http://www.rashmisinha.com/archives/05_09/tagging-cognitive.html.

Stephens, Michael. "Web 2.0 and Libraries: Best Practices for Social Software." *Library Technology Reports* 42(4) (July–August 2006).

———. "Advanced Web2.0 for Libraries." *Library Technology Reports* 43(5) (July–August 2007).

Tapscott, Don and Anthony Williams. *Wikinomics: How Mass Collaboration Changes Everything.* New York: Portfolio Hardcover, 2006.

Readers Advisory Services: How to Help Users Find a "Good Book"

Mary K. Chelton

Contemporary readers advisory (RA) services generally include a variety of techniques aimed at one goal—helping readers find what they might enjoy reading. While RA services are usually delivered through reference or information services desks to adults in public libraries, some libraries, such as the Downers Grove (IL) Public Library, do devote separate departments to them, and there is an ongoing philosophical discussion about whether RA should be part of reference, because of the narrow way in which until recently, information-seeking has been conceptualized by library and information science researchers. RA services are also a traditional "backbone" of youth services in public libraries and elementary school libraries. RA services emphasize fiction and nonfiction that reads like fiction, such as memoirs, personal travelogues, and true crime, in part because cataloging and information retrieval systems to find such stories either do not exist, or are too dependent on traditional forms of indexing by genre, theme, setting, or protagonist's gender and occupation to identify or keep up with the factors that make books appealing to readers. The many ways in which authors now constantly blend genres and themes, combined with the multiple formats in which stories are now available to readers, such as audio books, make it difficult for retrieval systems to stay current.

While RA services were once considered a means for librarians to help adults with improving their knowledge and education through guided reading, or for youth services librarians to take young people up increasingly difficult reading ladders, both of these early conceptions have been largely supplanted by the more egalitarian idea that readers should be assisted to get what appeals to them unless they specifically request self-improvement assistance. This can become problematic for librarians who still feel the need to "recommend" rather than "suggest" titles to people, or for youth services librarians enamored of literary award winners, because doing so is now considered an inappropriate professional attitude for RA services providers. Contemporary RA librarians see themselves as being on equal footing with readers and that doing RA work demands that they pay better attention to readers' preferences.

The theoretical foundations of contemporary RA services are found in reader response theory and various theories of popular culture such as cultural capital, the nature of cultural products, and the interpretive communities who interact with them, as discussed by Louise Rosenblatt,[1] Herbert Gans,[2] or Pierre Bourdieu.[3] For Rosenblatt, reading literature is a means of self-exploration, broadly defined, with the assumption that literary aesthetics are secondary. Unless the book has meaning for the reader, all the rest is useless. Reading is also viewed as a very social activity, whether through the influence of readers on each other as Catherine Ross[4] has shown to be a method used by avid readers to identify titles to read, or as Elizabeth Long[5] suggests, as a process of how people "construct themselves with materials from a vast cultural storehouse" in reading groups.

The various practices that make up readers advisory services range on a spectrum from those highly interactive, such as the face-to-face encounter or reading discussion groups, to those that are not interactive, like merchandising, which depend on the strategic use of space and browser behavior to put books and readers together. What all of them depend on is an understanding of readers and reading behavior, so this understanding can be used for whatever technique is chosen. There is no one way to do RA services, and most libraries would be hard pressed to do everything all of the time, but the problem is to conceptualize the service broadly enough so something along the spectrum is being offered. Some noninteractive RA practices, such as lists and displays are more often thought of as collection-promotion or reading motivation activities, and others, such as author visits and talks are regarded as programs, but regardless of what they are called, they should not be omitted from the readers advisory services repertoire.

THE FACE-TO-FACE READERS ADVISORY ENCOUNTER

While there are many other techniques used by librarians to match books and readers, the face-to-face encounter gets endless attention because it so troubles librarians who simply do not know what to do when they get an RA query. Their fear is magnified by a pervasive myth among librarians that, unless the librarian being queried has read the book or genre someone is interested in, the librarian cannot make a suggestion. This is patently false and has become a frequent and unjustifiable excuse for lack of service, especially since many print and online RA reference tools such as NoveList[6] exist to help librarians with RA questions. RA practice demands no less rigor than the documented use of resources that is standard for reference librarians. Even when disregarding this myth, however, there are some common mistakes made in face-to-face RA encounters.

Librarians trying to answer RA questions frequently misuse the online public access catalog, either using it as a crutch while trying to think, or mistakenly thinking it will magically cough up an answer when the cataloging embedded in an OPAC inevitably is not specific enough to help with RA questions, especially about fiction, until *after* the librarian knows what the reader wants. RA questions are only minimally bibliographic, and a rush to the OPAC that exists primarily to answer location and ownership of bibliographically verified titles, is usually fruitless.

Besides this "OPAC dependence," librarians frequently compound their mistake by assuming the reader has not read anything else by the identified author, or worse, that the author only writes the same kind of book all of the time. Many popular genre writers experiment with genre blends or may write several different kinds of stories under the same name. Examples include Nora Roberts, John Grisham, and Lois McMaster Bujold.

Beyond these mistakes, though, is the one where the librarian assumes without asking that the reader is in the mood for an identical reading experience, when he or she may want something entirely different. It is wiser to find these things out before rushing to suggest another book by the same author. The most egregious mistake, however, is where librarians just excuse their own ignorance as if the fact that they don't read a certain author or genre naturally means they cannot help anyone who does. Excusing one's ignorance is as unacceptable in readers advisory services as in reference.

Since many readers cannot say exactly why they do or do not like a particular book, the librarian trying to help them should ideally ask them either to describe a title they've loved and enjoyed, or if not that, one they've loathed, to get some idea of what the person enjoys. Then find out if they want another similar title, and if so, whether they want something else by that author if it exists; if not, what are they in the mood for at that moment. It should be pointed out also that if someone likes a particular genre, the librarian should ask what kind of romance, mystery, science fiction, etc., the person likes. Genres are neither monolithic nor homogeneous, with numerous subcategory preferences among their readers. In fact, one of the greatest SF writers, Ursula K. Le Guin, called genre "only a word that a Frenchman can love".[7]

APPEAL CHARACTERISTICS

Joyce Saricks[8] has identified several intrinsic characteristics of fiction that appeal to people, and Neal Wyatt has done the same for nonfiction. These characteristics usually have nothing to do with literary merit, although complex and beautiful writing do appeal to some readers. For many though, appeal is found in characteristics like the pacing of the plot, the depth of characterization, how the storyline is laid out, what "frame" (i.e. setting, mood) the book possesses, what kind of experience the reader is in the mood for, how hard he or she wants to work, what type of book he or she is interested in, or what desired learning experience the book offers.

OTHER INTERACTIVE RA TECHNIQUES AND SERVICES

Presenting books to readers in groups through book talks or oral book reviews has long been a staple of RA services, whether the presenter is a librarian or a visiting author or more recently, thanks to the National Endowment for the Humanities and the ALA's Public Programs Office, a humanities scholar. The book talk with a motivational "hook" is used in youth services, whereas librarians are often asked to present or "review" books for adult groups, usually reader and discussion groups of one type or another. Sometimes this involves leading a discussion and at other times, the groups use the librarian's presentation to decide whether to read the book individually or to use the book for their particular group's discussion. In some cases, book group discussion leaders as well as less experienced librarians may use the librarian's presentation to learn how to present and lead discussions themselves. In fact, having an annual workshop for book group discussion leaders is a wonderful RA service in and of itself.

A reading group is basically a group of adults who meet at regular intervals to discuss individual books or themes in books previously agreed upon. They meet in private homes, libraries, online, or face to face, as time and format permit. They can include both men and women or be intergenerational or specifically multicultural in composition. They can also be genre-specific, such as the Super Sleuths one on mysteries at the Lucius Beebe (MA) Memorial Library, or the Murder Most Sweet one at the Nevins (MA) Memorial Library. Groups may have a designated discussion leader, an invited leader, or rotate the leadership role among themselves. While reading groups may exist outside library sponsorship, they almost always need library support at one time or another. In some cases, they fall under library sponsorship. The permutations are as varied as the groups themselves.

There are a variety of RA services that can be offered to reading groups by libraries, besides sponsoring one in the library itself, as many libraries do. The first is just to maintain a list of all the reading groups that are active in the library's community so that interested readers can find out how and where to join one. The Suffolk County (NY) Cooperative Library Association maintains such a list, for example. Besides its own branch-sponsored book clubs, the San Antonio (TX) Public Library lists online book clubs for interested users on the library Web site. The Westport (CT) Public Library supports over seventy-five reader groups by supplying books and helping with titles for discussion, with a staff member dedicated to the service.

Another service is a list of resources and Web sites for reading group organizers and discussion leaders, so that groups can use and benefit from each other's experience with successful themes and titles for discussion as well as easily find already published reading guides for selected titles. It is particularly helpful if this can be maintained on the library's own Web site, such as the one on the Lucius Beebe (MA) Memorial Library's Web site www.wakefieldlibrary.org/index.htm

Whether it is called a "city-wide book club" or a "state-wide reading campaign," if the reading program follows the model started by Nancy Pearl, then Director of the Washington Center for the Book in 1998 with Russell Banks' book, *The Sweet Hereafter*, this type of program involves people in a community coming together through the reading and discussion of a common book. It embraces the notion of "civic unity" through common reading. By getting community members to talk with each other, such programs hope to foster intergenerational literacy, and also to foster community and discussion.

The main reason such programs have been successful, in addition to meticulous planning and attention to detail, is because of well-organized related programming that crossed normal community boundaries. These have included exhibits, author visits, scholarly lectures, arts programming such as music, films, or drama from the period of the book, unusual speakers such as psychologists (Arizona's focus on *Animal Dreams*, e.g.) or actual convicted felons (Peoria (IL) for *A Lesson Before Dying*), outreach to existing book discussion groups or assistance to new ones, and the involvement of college and secondary school teachers.

A reading and discussion guide prepared by the planning librarians provides the key to the chosen book for readers, as well as to the project as a whole. Such a guide may include a summary of the project, a calendar of events, biographical information on the author and the historical context for the book, original or reprinted critical essays on the book, reviews of and quotes from the book, suggested follow-up reading and resources, and sponsor credits and acknowledgements.

NONINTERACTIVE READERS ADVISORY SERVICES

Lists and Bibliographies

There are basically three types of lists or bibliographies for readers: topical, thematic, and readalike. Lists, whether paper or electronic, can be used by themselves or in conjunction with a display, or with an RA program or related community event. In fact, *NextReads*,[9] an offshoot service of NoveList's e-mail and indexing capability, and *BookLetters*,[10] a commercial book notification system for libraries, both specialize in e-mails of topical and new book lists in various categories. Many libraries now do both paper and electronic versions of lists to take advantage of the service and promotional opportunities on their own Web site home pages. Lists are intended to help readers select books they might like by limiting choice and focusing attention. They also save librarians' time by informing and empowering readers directly. In fact, it is important that lists be placed in the books listed to save the reader's time as well as the librarian's. Don't just dump a pile of lists on a table or low bookshelf somewhere. All lists should also be offered online in a downloadable format, either on the library's own Web site, or by e-mail to users who sign up for it.

Displays

Libraries are ideal browsing sites for many readers, even if they only come in for a specific title or bit of information. Unfortunately, many libraries are still organized as if everyone knew exactly what they wanted as soon as they came in the door, or as if the librarian had to be able to find any particular item in its spot on demand. This is an uninformed view of our users' actual behavior because it does not take into account that being in the library itself might change someone's idea of what they wanted when they came in. This is why displays are tools for the reader's adviser. RA services exploit the opportunity the library presents to attract browsers.

Displays can be done with or without lists and vice versa, but they do reinforce each other when necessary. For example, a list can be published on a library's Web site either following or preceding a display. If a display is quite popular and dynamic, a list can offer future choices to readers for books in circulation. Displays can also be organized by topic, theme, and readalike or potpourri. The conceptual underpinnings of their content are less important, except for readalikes, because they exploit the strategic use of space and the psychology of impulsive attraction.

Merchandising

Merchandising takes displays one step further. The technique exploits impulse attraction for browsers by placing materials readers would not otherwise see in specific strategic locations. When books are merchandised, librarians do not have to worry about theme, topic, or appeal factors. They just need to keep stuff displayed face out in the magic spots. This is not rocket science and should be easy once you realize that merchandising surrounds you in retail establishments. Only in libraries do we seem myopic enough to ignore it! One has only to read Marion Nestle's *What to Eat*,[11] especially the section on supermarket arrangement, or Paco Underhill's *Why We Buy*[12] to understand the power of this technique and what we miss by not using it fully. The four magic spots are (1) front end; (2) ends of stacks; (3) point-of-circulation; and (4) high traffic areas.

The Front End

The "front end" is the first 10–20 feet of space one walks through going into a store or in this case, a library. Mall bookstores specialize in having "front ends" that sort of spill into the larger corridor of the mall as a "come-on" to potential customers; however, attractive though this is, the technique is often not feasible in libraries. Larger bookstores usually feature remainders and displays as one walks in, with all the new stuff for sale displayed face-out as near to the security gates inside the inner front door as possible. This is the model libraries can most easily use, without risking the security of the collection. Depending on the architecture of the building, if there is a "dead zone" between the outside front door and an inside one, such as frequently found in supermarkets and discount stores as well as large bookstores, that users quickly stroll through without noticing anything in it, Underhill himself points out that it is important not to put anything there, but to use subsequent space as soon as possible.

Many libraries waste front end space with community flyers, ongoing book-sale items, historical collections, art displays, etc., when prevailing consumer behavior models suggest that this prime merchandising space would be much better used displaying the collection and making materials easier for browsers to find.

Ends of Stacks

Library users may enter a library for a specific item, but in the process of finding it, they have to walk past the ends of many other aisles. It would be unheard of in a retail establishment not to take advantage of the ends of aisle shelves—the endcaps or ends of stacks. Only in libraries do we waste this space with interminable iterations of the ALA Read posters, or only with the call numbers or alphabetical letter designations of what is there. One library in my experience had such expensive wood shelf ends that they would put nothing there, obviously feeling that admiring rosewood would somehow lead users to truth. It certainly did not help them find any materials of interest. Even better, there are commercial fixtures designed specifically for endcap displays that can be added to existing shelves or written into furniture specifications for new or refurbished libraries, which can easily be found with a simple Google search of "bookstore fixtures."

Point-of-Circulation

This spot is called "point-of-purchase" in retail settings. It's where you pay for a product prior to exiting a store, and where you check out prior to leaving in a library. Along with the front end space near the incoming door, nearly everyone has to go through or past this spot, which makes it a prime merchandising area. Put materials on or near it, as well as lists and brochures promoting materials. Just having a table on either side of the checkout line with books displayed face out will spur impulse checkouts. There are also tabletop fixtures to display materials.

Ideally, point-of-circulation would include the use of slatwall with fixtures or face-out display on regular bookshelves behind the circulation desk. Too many libraries put reserve books there with ratty-looking paper tags banded around them, when they could be as easily placed under the circulation desk. This is a waste of prime space to display materials!

High Traffic Areas

These are spots where lots of people have to walk in the building, and the display need be nothing other than a return book cart or tabletop so people cannot miss them. Some libraries use displays that look like pyramids with several tiers around which the books are displayed face out.

Librarians frequently ask how they will know where any particular item is if someone wants it when confronted with a suggestion to merchandise the collection. Most circulation systems have a "location" field that can be changed, but merchandising works so well that in truth, the book may go out before anyone gets around to changing location. The real problem with merchandising is that it works so well that the "spots" need attention or the displays in them become haphazard, or disappear entirely because everything—except possibly the last remaining item—has been taken. There is some sort of psychological resistance to taking the last thing. Merchandised displays demand constant attention if you want to do them well. Putting new staff in charge of them in rotation with other staff is a great way to get newcomers to know the collection.

USING TECHNOLOGY IN READERS ADVISORY SERVICES

Listservs and Websites

Librarian-instigated listservs have existed for some time, the most notable being Dorothy-L[13] for mysteries, named after author Dorothy Sayers, and Romance Readers Anonymous,[14] which was started by two academic librarians who loved the romance genre. Both lists include readers, authors, publishers, as well as librarians. Fiction-L,[15] started by Roberta Johnson while still a library school student, is hosted by the Morton Grove (IL) Public Library. It assists RA librarians with difficult RA questions, generates readalike lists, and encourage discussions of RA issues. GNLIB-L[16] allows disscussions among librarians, authors and and publishers of graphic novels. While nonlibrarian readers can subscribe to the latter two lists, discussion is dominated by professional issues.

Web 2.0 technology offers many opportunities to enhance RA service. For example, a library-based "wiki" can use the collaborative energies of librarians and "expert" fan readers to create and edit readalike lists quickly. Weblogs (blogs) offer the potential for librarians who have become trusted sources for readers to augment their comments on certain books and authors and invite reader responses to the comments, thus creating a discussion online. Online asynchronous book clubs sponsored by many libraries already exist and weblogs offer a new variation on how to do it.

Even older technology like e-mail offers libraries the opportunity to notify readers when favorite authors or types of books are available, and there is no reason why libraries should not use links and lists of author Web sites to help readers keep up, in much the same way Barnes & Noble notifies their customers of new arrivals. Several commercial companies are already trying to figure out how to sell such services to libraries.

CONCLUSION

Readers advisory services are enjoying a renaissance in public libraries, buoyed by technology. While there are still collaborative, organizational, and training issues to be resolved, such as how to work with local bookstores, where the service best fits organizationally, and how to hire a staff competent to deliver RA services—something difficult to do when many schools offering MLIS degrees are more interested in information science—public library interest in such services is not diminishing.

In much the same way library users suffer from "search fatigue" from unsuccessful keyword "googling," they also suffer from too many entertainment choices in a media-saturated culture. A skilled librarian who can suggest or call their attention to something they might like to read, regardless of format, becomes a very valuable asset to their quality of life.

SUGGESTIONS FOR FURTHER READING

Gans, Herbert J. *Popular Culture and High Culture: An Analysis and Evaluation of Taste.* New York: Basic Books, 1974.

Long, Elizabeth. *Book Clubs: Women and the Uses of Reading in Everyday Life.* Chicago: University of Chicago Press, 2003.

Nestle, Marion. *What to Eat.* New York: North Point Press, 2006.

Rosenblatt, Louise. *Literature as Exploration*, 5th ed. New York: Modern Language Association of America, 1995.

Ross, Catherine S., Lynne E. F. McKechnie, and Paulette M. Rothbauer. *Reading Matters: What the Research Reveals about Reading, Libraries, and Community.* Westport, CT: Greenwood, 2006.

Saricks, Joyce. *Reader's Advisory Service in the Public Library*, 3rd ed. Chicago: ALA, 2005.

Underhill, Paco. *Why We Buy: The Science of Shopping.* New York: Simon & Schuster, 1999.

Wyatt, Neal. *Readers' Advisory Guide to Nonfiction.* Chicago: ALA, 2007.

Chapter

15

Research

Ron Powell

INTRODUCTION AND DEFINITION OF RESEARCH

When librarians and other information professionals state that they are engaged in research, they are often referring to "library research" or the utilization of a strategy for identifying, evaluating, and accessing or obtaining information held by libraries and other information sources. As valuable as this activity is, however, it is not true research, even though it may be conducted in support of true research studies. Indeed, all research should build on research and knowledge that precedes it and that foundation is typically developed through library research or a similar process. Such background information is often presented in the related literature/research section of a research report.

Many librarians and other information professionals are, however, involved in true research and, in fact, make the bulk of the contributions to the research literature in Library and Information Science (LIS). But what is this kind of research, as opposed to library research? Actually there is no one definition of research, in part because there are different types of research. *Webster's Seventh New Collegiate Dictionary* provides the following broad, generic definition: "studious inquiry or examination; especially: investigation or experimentation aimed at the discovery and interpretation of facts, revision of accepted theories or laws in the light of new facts, or practical applications of such new or revised theories or laws." Research is also often thought of as a process that leads to the dependable resolution of problems or things about which we want to know more.

PREVIOUS LIBRARY RESEARCH

Having just made a distinction between library research and true research, it is ironic that much of the earlier research that was conducted by librarians and that was about libraries and related matters was often referred to as "library research" even if it was thought of as true research. But such library-related research should not be confused with the library research/information-gathering process identified at the beginning of this chapter. And, unfortunately, much of the early so-called library research did not meet all of the criteria for good true research. Much of it took the form of biographies, case studies, and histories and too many of those did not represent the kind of rigorous research that we more routinely see today. The historical research, for example, tended to rely on too few, if any, primary sources and to glorify the subjects and institutions being studied. And in general, the early library research relied too heavily on opinion, did not produce generalizable results, did not build on previous related research, was methodologically unsophisticated, and did relatively little to build a theoretical foundation for the LIS field. However, there were a number of early studies that were methodologically sound and that made important contributions to the development of the LIS profession.

CURRENT LIS RESEARCH

In contrast to the earlier library-related research, current research in the LIS field tends to be more rigorous methodologically and, as a whole, employs a greater variety of research methods, including a number of methods borrowed from other fields. In fact, one of the first things that the would-be LIS researcher (or any researcher for that matter) must do after settling on the research problem or topic is select the research method(s) to be used in resolving the problem. The researcher must first decide upon the broad research methodology or approach to be utilized for the study, and in this regard, the most fundamental options are basic research and applied research.

Basic research, also referred to as pure, theoretical, and scientific research, is mostly concerned with creating new, generalizable knowledge. For many years basic research, especially if quantitative in nature, has tended to follow the scientific method of inquiry. This approach usually involves the following steps: statement of the research problem, identification of relevant theory, development of one or more hypotheses to be tested, methodological design of the study, and collection and analysis of the necessary data.

Applied research, on the other hand, is more concerned with the solving of specific problems in real situations and often is indirectly concerned with the practical application and testing of the findings of basic research. Much of the earlier library-related research was more similar to applied research than to basic research and dealt with such things as the evaluation of book collections and the assessment of various library procedures. In short, applied research is usually more pragmatic in nature than is basic research. However, the two approaches are not necessarily dichotomous. As was just noted, the results of basic research can lead to practical applications and applied research can serve as the foundation for more theoretical research.

A major type of applied research is *action research*. It is especially pragmatic and is less concerned with validating the findings of basic research than is applied research. Action research is conducted much the same as is applied research but is even less concerned with taking the steps necessary to produce generalizable results. Another type of research that is often viewed as applied research is *evaluation*, or *evaluative research*. In an age of reduced financial resources and a greater need to be accountable, it is increasingly common and important for librarians and other information professionals to assess the quality and effectiveness of their organization's resources and services. Evaluation research uses many of the techniques common to applied, and basic, research but there are numerous types of evaluation research, characterized more by their objectives than by any unique techniques. Evaluation research can be broadly categorized as formative and summative. The former type of evaluation examines how well a program or service is working and is conducted while the program is underway. The latter is more concerned with the outcome or effects of the program or service and is conducted upon completion of the program. More specific types of evaluation research include:

- Input measurement: the measurement of the resources that are assigned to an organization such as, in the case of libraries, books, journal subscriptions, staff, space, and budget.
- Output/performance measurement: the measurement of what is produced or accomplished by an organization, such as the number of books circulated and the number of reference questions answered.
- Process evaluation: process indicators are similar to performance measures but focus more on the activities and procedures of the organization than on its products. For example, a library might be more concerned with assessing how books are acquired and maintained than with how often they are used.
- Impact/outcomes assessment: the measurement and evaluation of how the resources and performance of an organization affect the users of those resources. In an academic library setting, outcomes might include better papers, more learning, and more research.
- Service quality: this process represents an attempt to assess the quality of a library's services as reflected by the difference between a library user's expectations for a library's services and his or her perceptions of the quality of the library's services.
- Benchmarking: an attempt to assess the quality of a library's services by comparing them against an external standard such as the performance of highly regarded peer libraries.
- Standards: the use of guidelines or recommended practices to assess a library's quality or performance.
- Cost analysis: the use of cost-related techniques to determine whether monies are being spent in an optimal fashion. Such techniques include cost-effectiveness studies and cost-benefit analysis.

Evaluation research studies often employ the same data-gathering methods and techniques that are used in other applied, as well as basic, research studies. They include the collection of statistics, questionnaires, interviews, observations, diaries, consumer panels, and document delivery tests.

After the researcher decides whether to conduct basic or applied research, he or she must decide whether to take a quantitative or qualitative approach, or a combination of the two. Simply stated, *quantitative research* is concerned with things that are numerical or that can be quantified. Quantitative research methods are usually highly structured and, if designed properly, are well suited to testing hypotheses and producing generalizable results. *Qualitative research* methods, on the other hand, focus on observing events and behaviors from the perspective of those engaged in the activities being examined and tend to take a more natural approach. Qualitative methods are particularly useful for investigating complex phenomena and for taking a relatively holistic approach to the resolution of a research problem. Qualitative LIS researchers use modified versions of some of the techniques common to quantitative research, but they have also borrowed a number of techniques and methods from fields such as anthropology and sociology. A quantitative study of the performance of reference librarians might, for example, measure the number of reference questions answered correctly while a qualitative examination of that issue might focus on how the reference librarian communicates with the patron.

RESEARCH METHODS

Having decided on the general methodology or approach to be followed for the research study, the researcher must next identify the methods and techniques that he or she will use to gather the necessary information or data. What follows is a brief overview of several of the research methods often used by LIS researchers.

Survey

Survey research methods have been and continue to be among the most frequently used methods in LIS research. They are perceived, accurately or not, as a relatively easy research method and are well suited to determining the present status of phenomena. In addition, they are quite appropriate for studying a large number of geographically dispersed cases and for examining personal factors. Surveys tend to be quantitative in nature and are often used to describe the characteristics of some population. However, it is often difficult or impossible, or not necessary at any rate, to collect information from or about every member of the population of interest. Therefore, the survey researcher often selects a sample of the population from which to collect the appropriate data. The characteristics of the sample may then be generalized to the full population so long as steps have been taken to ensure that the sample is representative of the population.

One of the data collection tools most frequently used to gather information for a survey is the questionnaire. Other common survey data collection tools or techniques are the interview and observation. Tests are also often used, especially when educational factors are being studied. There is a bit of a trend to employ more than one technique in a study (triangulation), as doing so tends to increase the validity and reliability of the data. Certain types of interviews and observations lend themselves more to qualitative studies than do questionnaires.

Experiment

Experimental research methods have also been employed by LIS researchers for many years, but have never been as popular as survey methods. Similar to the survey, the experiment is well suited to dealing with contemporary phenomena and quantitative data but in contrast to the survey, the experiment is considered to be an excellent method for testing causal relationships between or among factors. In a typical experiment, at least one independent variable is manipulated, other relevant independent variables are controlled, and the effect of the independent variable(s) on one or more dependent variables is observed. Such a method requires more control over the research setting than the survey and other research methods are able to provide. There are a number of specific experimental designs available to the researcher, but those strongest in internal validity are best able to rigorously test a causal relationship. Those designs strongest in external validity tend to be the designs most capable of producing generalizable results, but internal validity is usually of greater concern to the experimental researcher than is external validity.

History

The research method perhaps used the longest by LIS researchers is the historical method. The earlier historical research conducted in LIS was often referred to as "library history." Unfortunately, however, many of the earliest historical studies in LIS were limited to merely describing past historical events in their order of occurrence. In contrast, true historical research, or historiography, not only describes historical events, but it attempts to put those events into their broader context, interpret their meaning, examine possible relationships, and even identify general principles that can facilitate describing the present and planning for the future. More recent historical research in LIS comes closer to that model than did the earlier library history. LIS researchers often engage in historical research, but library practitioners are more likely to conduct *bibliographical research*. Bibliographical research, while an important scholarly activity, is not considered to represent true historical research. However, descriptive bibliography is more closely linked to historical research than is the compilation of subject bibliographies.

Case Study

The case study has been about as popular with LIS researchers as have been the survey and historical methods. The case study is characterized by the limitation of a study to a single individual, event, program, or organization (though some case studies consider multiple cases), weak internal and external validity (therefore not well-suited for testing causal relationships and generating generalizable findings), and the use of multiple data gathering techniques and multiple sources of data. The case study is appropriate for investigating phenomena that involve numerous factors and relationships that exist in the real world. Similar to historical methods, the case study tends to be qualitative in nature, but often considers quantitative data as well. The case study is frequently employed as an exploratory technique.

Focus Group

The focus group can be thought of as a research method or as a special type of interview or data collection technique. In other words, a focus group can be designed as a stand-alone study or as the tool for collecting data for a study, usually a survey. In contrast to a more conventional survey, the focus group does not make the generation of generalizable, descriptive data its major priority. Rather, the focus group is an unstructured type of interview and is more concerned with exploring the feelings, attitudes, and behavior of a fairly small group of participants. Librarians have found the focus group to be quite useful for learning more about patrons' views of the library's resources and services, but it must always be remembered that it cannot be assumed with much confidence that the thoughts, etc. of the people in a focus group are very similar to those of the people in the complete population.

Delphi Study

The Delphi study or method is a procedure for developing a consensus among a group of experts or at least individuals qualified to express opinions on a given topic. The participants in a Delphi study are often asked to make predictions related to the topic. In a typical Delphi study, the researcher will review the related literature on the topic, develop, for example, a list of relevant issues, identify and recruit the group of "experts," and then send a copy of the list to each participant asking him or her to delete, revise, or add items to the list. The researcher will continue to send revised lists to the participants until they indicate that they are content with the latest version, or in other words a consensus has been reached. At least three or four such rounds are usually required in order to reach a consensus.

Content Analysis

The research methods briefly described thus far are methods that are quite common to a number of disciplines, especially those in the social sciences. The next three research methods to be considered represent methods that are more unique to the study of library resources and services. For example, *content analysis* is essentially a systematic analysis of the occurrence of words, phrases, concepts, etc. in books, films, and other kinds of materials. Content analysis is another technique that can be treated as a stand-alone study or as merely the data collection procedure for a study. This method has been used, for example, to determine how frequently racist terms appear in certain textbooks and to examine students' perceptions of library research.

Bibliometrics

Bibliometrics is a special type of documentary research method used to measure certain aspects of written communication and to quantify bibliographical data. Related terms are scientometrics, informetrics, and librametrics. Bibliometric studies have been used, for example, to describe how the literature of a subject area is distributed in its journals. A common type of bibliometric research is *citation analysis*, which is concerned with who cites whom in the published literature. The applications of citation analyses have included the improvement of the bibliographic control of literatures, the identification of the core journals of a subject area, the tracing of the growth of and spread of ideas in a literature, and the evaluation of library collections. Bibliometric methods are now being applied to Internet-based research as well.

Comparative Librarianship

Comparative librarianship may refer to a research method or a subject matter. As a subject, comparative librarianship is concerned with phenomena in LIS that can be compared, often on an international or at least regional basis. For example, how classification practices vary in different countries might be the topic of a study in comparative librarianship. When treated as a research method, the focus would be on the process of comparative analysis carried out in the study. The data for such a study are usually gathered with standard tools such as questionnaires and interviews. The analysis process itself tends to view practices, procedures, etc. within a broader context such as relevant geographical, historical, or political factors.

Qualitative Methods

The research methods considered so far are quantitative in nature or represent a mix of quantitative and qualitative techniques. Quantitative methods still predominate in the LIS research literature, but as is true of other researchers in the social sciences, LIS researchers are increasingly turning to a variety of qualitative methods. In 1999, Powell[1] examined the research literature of the previous several years in the social sciences and LIS and thereby identified numerous qualitative methods that were being used. Those qualitative methods, with brief definitions, follow:

- Ethnography—the observational study of a cultural group in its natural setting over an extensive period of time.
- Grounded theory—the process of analyzing data that will lead to the development of theory based on a specific situation but that will be useful to the discipline.
- Phenomenology—an examination of how participants actually perceive their specific, concrete experiences and realities.

- Hermeneutics—a method that is closely related to phenomenology and that is concerned with the meaning of words and narrative.
- Reflexivity—emphasizes that the interpretation of ethnographic statements must take into account the origin and nature of the ethnographic document (e.g., a diary).
- Symbolic interactionism—a process that takes into account that people create shared meanings through interactions.
- Discourse analysis—an examination of the formal talk, or discourse, among members of an institution.

Other methods that appear in the qualitative research literature include case study and historical method, both of which were considered earlier, and biographical method.

Technology-Centered Research

As libraries and other information agencies have become more technology intensive, there has been more research that focuses on issues affected by information technology or that utilizes information technology as part of the research process. Some of the relatively traditional social science research methods continue to be quite useful for examining procedures, services, and use as affected by information technology. For example, questionnaires, interviews, observations, and experiments have been used to examine online catalog use. And to a lesser extent, techniques such as *protocol analysis*, which makes it possible to record and analyze the thoughts of users as they carry out subject searches in the online catalog, have been used in such studies. On the other hand, techniques that facilitate the investigation of the use of information technology by utilizing the technology itself are now being used in some studies. *Transaction log analysis*, for example, makes it possible to examine unobtrusively the computer records created as patrons use an online catalog and other electronic resources and services. Similar techniques, referred to as Web log analysis, are being used to study information retrieval on the Web. Such techniques may also be used in conjunction with other data collection tools such as questionnaires.

DATA ANALYSIS

As was indicated earlier when describing the scientific method of inquiry, the researcher must analyze the data, whether quantitative or qualitative, after collecting it. At the very least, it is necessary to organize and summarize the data. In quantitative data analysis, this process generates descriptive statistics. If the quantitative researcher wishes to generalize characteristics of a sample to its population or test hypotheses, it will be necessary to employ inferential statistical analysis as well. Qualitative researchers are able to analyze their data using techniques such as content analysis and the constant comparative method.

THE RESEARCH REPORT

While the analysis of the research data may be seen as the final step of the formal research process, the researcher's job is not really complete until he or she has communicated the results of that research. Doing so first entails the writing of the research report. This report should be a straightforward document that clearly, precisely, and efficiently describes the research study and its findings. The research report should be well organized and follow a standard format and bibliographical style. Ideally, in order to reach the widest audience possible, the researcher should attempt to publish the report in an appropriate professional journal. At the very least, the researcher should see that the results of the research reach the audience most likely to be interested in and benefit from that information. That might be accomplished via publication in a library newsletter, professional association bulletin, or an electronic discussion list. "The research report, regardless of format, is what communicates specific information to an audience, adds to the general body of knowledge, and hopefully stimulates further research."[2]

RATIONALE FOR RESEARCH IN LIBRARY AND INFORMATION SCIENCE

Growth of the Profession

Virtually every definition of profession indicates that it should have a solid theoretical base of knowledge as its foundation; it follows that if a profession is going to advance, its practitioners must be engaged in creating new knowledge relevant to that profession. The development of a profession needs to build on the most current knowledge—knowledge that is based on solid research, not merely assumptions, rules-of-thumb, and past practices. In other words, basic research is crucial if the field of library and information science is "to solve professional problems, develop tools and methods for analysis of organization, services and behavior, to determine costs and benefits of our services, and most importantly, to establish a body of theory on which to base our practice."[3]

Management

As was noted earlier, the results of research, both basic and applied, often lead to applications for the improvement of practices in actual information agencies. The application of research findings can improve decision-making, produce better insights into professional issues, and result in more meaningful services and resources.

Evaluating Research

All members of a profession, including library and information science, should be engaged in reading and evaluating the results of research even if they are not inclined to conduct their own research. As was stated above, a profession should be based on a solid body of theoretical research. But a profession is not likely to benefit from such research unless its members are able and willing to critically read, evaluate, and understand the reports of research. In other words, practitioners cannot appropriately use the results of research unless they can critically consume those results. A recent study[4] found that almost 90 percent of LIS practitioners in the United States and Canada regularly read at least one research journal, nearly 62 percent regularly read research-based articles, approximately 50 percent occasionally apply research results to professional practices, and 42 percent occasionally or frequently perform research related to their job or to the LIS profession.

Improved Service to Patrons

Yet another reason for information professionals to be knowledgeable of, if not involved in, research is that doing so better equips those professionals to serve the needs of information users, especially researchers. If the information professional knows the basic process that a researcher follows, then he or she is better able to anticipate and meet the needs of that researcher. It is even reasonable to assume that a researcher is more likely to turn to an information professional for assistance if he or she realizes that the professional has an appreciation of the research process.

Personal Growth

There are also personal benefits that can be realized by the information professional involved in research. For many librarians, especially those in academic institutions, research activities are necessary in order to be considered for promotion, merit salary increases and, in some cases, tenure. An understanding of the research process and the criteria for good research proposals can be useful for those engaged in applying for grants, even nonresearch grants. The involvement of an information agency and its staff in research can even improve staff morale and strengthen the agency's status within its larger community or organization. And last but not least, it is believed that the study and conduct of research can improve an individual's ability to think critically and analytically—skills that also improve one's ability to be an effective professional and leader.

CONCLUSIONS

Research in LIS is still relatively young and has not been as rigorous or as plentiful as would be ideal. LIS research would no doubt be stronger if LIS professionals were better prepared to engage in research but, unfortunately, a research methods course is required in slightly less than 40 percent of the LIS programs accredited by the American Library Association (ALA). The study cited earlier[5] found that only 47 percent of the respondents had taken a course on research methods at the master's level, and 59 percent of them reported that their master's degree programs had not adequately prepared them to conduct research. However, LIS programs do not bear the entire responsibility for teaching research skills; and, indeed, many professional associations, libraries, and other information agencies provide some training opportunities in research methods.

The shortcomings of education in research methods are exacerbated by the fact that most students view LIS programs as primarily practical and professional in nature and not concerned with imparting academic skills such as research methods. Some LIS master's degree students seem to begrudge having to devote one of their courses to the study of research methods. But there are encouraging signs. The quality and quantity of research-based articles appearing in professional journals are on the rise. ALA's Office for Research and Statistics continues to be quite active, and as of 2003, the Research and Statistics Assembly of the ALA had twenty-nine member units. The Association of College and Research Libraries recently established a Research Mentoring Program for member librarians. The Special Libraries Association has been advocating for the greater utilization of research. The "Vision Statement" of the American Society for Information Science and Technology calls for placing more value on research. The fourth national Library Research Seminar was held in the fall of 2007.

In conclusion, it appears that research in LIS is increasing and improving while incorporating more multidisciplinary and qualitative methods. And the growing demands for accountability and assessment and the need to address the issues related to the newer information technologies will only add to the pressures to do more and better research. In short, there is mounting evidence that future LIS researchers will be well equipped and motivated to investigate the problems facing the field of Library and Information Science.

SUGGESTIONS FOR FURTHER READING

Gorman, Gary E. and P. Clayton. *Qualitative Research for the Information Professional: A Practical Handbook*, 2nd ed. London: Facet, 2005.

Powell, Ronald R. and Lynn S. Connaway. *Basic Research Methods for Librarians*, 4th ed. Westport, CT: Libraries Unlimited, 2004.

Shera, Jesse H. "Darwin, Bacon, and Research in Librarianship." *Library Trends* 13 (July 1964), 141–149.

Williamson, K. *Research Methods for Students and Professionals: Information Management and Systems*, 2nd ed. Wagga Wagga, Australia: Centre for Information Studies, Charles Sturt University, 2002.

Chapter 16

Learning and Using Evaluation: A Practical Introduction

Charles R. McClure

In the day-to-day management and long-term planning of libraries and information centers (hereafter referred to as libraries) there is a critical need to employ a range of ongoing evaluation and assessment activities. A critical approach to questioning why library services and activities are being done the way they're done, describing the quality and impact of current library services, and how the library can best serve its community of users now and in the future are only the beginning points on the horizon for learning and using ongoing evaluation efforts.

Evaluation is the process of determining the success, impact, results, costs, outcomes, or other factors related to a library activity, program, service, or resource use. Typically such library evaluation can be summative—done at the end of program or service—or it can be formative—done on an ongoing basis to monitor a program or service. At its best, evaluation provides input for planning and decision-making, provides high quality qualitative and quantitative data describing library activities, and serves as a basis to constantly assess and improve library services.

Evaluation is a *process* that assists library decision makers and others by determining:

- The amount or the extent to which a service, program, or resource is provided;
- The degree to which individuals are satisfied with a service, program, or resource; and
- The quality or impact of those services, programs, or services.

Evaluation is especially useful because it can assist libraries to better provide services, programs, and resources that meet the needs of its clientele. It is also useful as a means of providing these services, programs, and resources at least cost while still maintaining high quality or impact. Given the struggle to obtain adequate resources, librarians must be certain that they are using available resources wisely and to best meet community information needs.

An organizational culture is comprised of shared values and behaviors by the people who work in that organization. Organizational culture also includes the notion that there are shared goals and expectations as to the "appropriate" ways in which individuals interact with their colleagues, appropriate ways to complete tasks, and appropriate ways in which the organization is presented to others. Typically, the individuals, themselves, encourage the acceptance of these values, behaviors, and expectations. A library with an evaluation culture is one that constantly assesses how well the library meets its goals and objectives and provides quality services.

The purpose of this chapter is to discuss the importance of and need for evaluation in libraries and to encourage librarians to have a clear sense of why evaluation and self-assessment are important. Given the complexity of today's information management and services delivery environment, librarians must be able to assess the degree to which a particular resource, service, program, or activity meets library goals and objectives and ultimately improves the quality of services to the library's community. Without ongoing and meaningful evaluation the library profession will not be able to attack and resolve successfully the issues and challenges of today or the future.

LINKING EVALUATION TO PLANNING

Although this paper's emphasis is on evaluation and not planning, it is important to recognize that they are linked. Planning is a disciplined effort to produce fundamental decisions and changes that shape and guide what the organization should be and what it should be doing. At its best, planning identifies current trends affecting the organization, considers possible goals and strategies, integrates information technology planning with services planning, takes a user perspective on what services are needed and why, and considers future implications of present decisions.

Planning typically sets priorities for what is most important for the library to accomplish in both the short term (1–2 years) and the longer term (3–5 years). Typically a library plan includes a mission and/or vision statement, a needs assessment process, goals and objectives, specific programs or strategies to accomplish the objectives, and some type of evaluation process to determine the degree to which the goals and objectives were accomplished. Planning is making *choices* of what to do and what *not* to do.

Ongoing evaluation activities inform the planning process. For example, if an evaluation of a digital reference service finds that the costs to complete one digital reference transaction is twice the cost of completing one in-person reference transaction, then the overall goals and objectives for providing reference services may have to be reconsidered. Successful planning requires regular assessment of the degree to which a plan's goals and objectives are accomplished. Stating goals and objectives without determining the degree to which they were accomplished is like taking a test and never knowing how well you did on that test. In short, planning and evaluation are the two sides of the same coin—each contributing to a successfully managed library.

IMPORTANCE OF EVALUATION

There are a number of reasons why evaluation is important and important to different library stakeholder groups. It:

- determines the degree to which service objectives are accomplished and the degree to which these objectives were appropriate for the library;
- assesses how well services support larger organizational goals, e.g., is the library assisting in the accomplishment of university (or local government) mission and goals?;
- monitors the status of services and operations to produce trend data that assesses the service over time;
- obtains community input for planning and development of current and future services;
- justifies and shows accountability of services to governing boards, government officials, local community members, and others;
- compares the relative costs and benefits of one service versus other or similar services to assist decision makers where to best allocate resources;
- provides input for planning and the selection/development of future services for specific target audience groups;
- assists the organization to determine the types of staff training that might be most needed and appropriate;
- informs governing boards as to the nature, needs, and success of library services;
- identifies those aspects of library services that are successful and those that need to be refined or newly created;
- educates the staff as to costs, benefits, impacts, and problems related to the operation of the library;
- provides information and data that can be used by local advocacy groups to promote the importance and impact of the library; and
- forces the organization to think in terms of *outcomes . . . what are the outcomes of these services and are they what you want?*

Ultimately, however, evaluation is important as a validity check, that is, "are library services, programs, and activities as successful as they might be and how could they be improved?"

The importance of evaluation has grown in recent years because of the various new information technologies that are available for libraries. Applications include a broad array of choices as to hardware, software, telecommunications, and integrated library systems (ILS). Which of the technologies are best for any one particular library? How will they improve the quality and usefulness of information services for the community? Will staff have increased productivity as a result of these technologies? Purchasing innovative information technology is not the same as deploying it successfully to improve services. Thus, ongoing evaluation of these new technologies is essential and will continue to require significant time and knowledge.

The degree to which evaluation will be successful in a library depends on a number of contingencies. To what degree does library staff have basic and advanced knowledge and skills related to conducting evaluations? If there is limited knowledge and skills available, then a range of staff training activities should be considered. Another factor to consider is the amount of time and other resources that library administrators can provide to support staff involved in evaluation efforts. The complexity of the organization and the types of evaluation needed are additional factors. There must be administrative support (both moral and resources) for staff to conduct evaluations. And lastly, staff need to see that the results from an evaluation were actually implemented into the library's planning process or somehow "made a difference" in how a particular service or program operated. All these factors affect the degree to which library evaluation is successful.

Evaluation is important because it also forces librarians, community members, governing board members, and others' attention on specific assessment criteria:

- **Extensiveness:** How much of a service, program, or resource the library provides (e.g., number of reference transactions per week, number of remote sessions per week). Note that extensiveness criteria answer only "how much" and do not address quality or impact.

- **Efficiency:** The use of resources (usually measured in terms of time or money) in providing services, programs, or resources (e.g., average time per reference transaction). Efficient services, however, may not be effective, e.g., the time per reference transaction is very quick (very efficient) but resulted in the wrong answer (not effective).

- **Effectiveness:** How well the information service, program, or resource meets specific objectives of the library or the user (e.g. success rate of identifying and accessing the information needed by the user). Effectiveness criteria require that service goals and objectives are known before the degree of effectiveness can be determined.

- **Service Quality:** How well the service, program, or resource is provided (e.g., does the service meet organizational or user expectations?). Service quality is often difficult to assess as different stakeholder groups may have very different expectations of what constitutes "quality" services.

- **Impact:** How a service, program, or resource made a difference in some other activity or situation (e.g., the degree to which users enhanced their ability to save time, resolve a problem, or identify new and innovative applications/services). Impacts are often called outcomes. Outcomes typically determine the degree of change in a person's knowledge, skills, attitudes, or behavior.

- **Usefulness:** The degree to which the services, programs, or resources are useful or appropriate for individual users (e.g. did the service assist or solve problems for different types of user audiences?). Once again, usefulness may depend on values and expectations of the user in that a service that is useful to a senior citizen may not be useful to a young adult.

There are other assessment criteria, but for most librarians, these criteria offer a useful overview of factors that can be considered when developing an evaluation. In other words, when thinking about conducting an evaluation what does the evaluator want to know as a result? Information about efficiency? Impacts? Appropriateness of the service for a specific user group? As discussed later, the planning process for conducting an evaluation can help the evaluator better manage how the evaluation will be conducted and ensure that the resultant evaluation data is the data needed to answer basic service, program, resource allocation, or other questions.

THE EVALUATION PROCESS

Although space limits the extent to which we can detail the evaluation process in this paper, the basic component parts can be discussed. Those listed in this section are intended only as an introduction, additional detail can be found in a number of other excellent sources noted at the end of this chapter.

Know Your Context

It is important to consider the larger institutional perspective toward planning and evaluation. What are the university's or local government's perspectives and requirements for planning and evaluation of library and information services and how do these perspectives and requirements affect the library? How will library planning and evaluation be best integrated into the larger institutional efforts in this area? Are there specific performance measures or evaluation questions that are of special interest to the larger institution? Existing larger institutional goals should help frame evaluation efforts within the library.

It is useful to begin slowly and to understand the scope of the evaluation. Libraries with little experience in this area would do well to identify a relatively small number of areas for evaluation and first work on these rather than a broader set of areas. What level of effort is the library willing to commit to this effort? If there are limited staff available, then the scope should be relatively small, the number of services to be assessed limited, and a recognition that there will be a learning curve for individuals involved in the effort. Finally, ensure that adequate time and resources can be committed to the evaluation effort before beginning.

GET ORGANIZED

Getting organized and planning for the evaluation should be carefully considered. Will an individual be in charge? Will there be a committee that will have this responsibility? How will the evaluation be integrated with other library activities?

If library administrators determine that a staff committee should be appointed for such an effort, membership should be based on:

- High level of interest in evaluation;
- Knowledge of basic data collection techniques and evaluation methodologies;
- Good interpersonal communication skills;
- Experience with a range of different services and resources; and
- Ability to work with various individuals inside and outside the library.

Further, it should be very clear who will serve as the chair of the committee, who that chair reports to in the organization, and that the committee will be a *working* committee.

The issue of "who is in charge" is critical for the success of the data collection effort, especially if the evaluation effort will include a consultant.

An early task of the person in charge of the evaluation (or the chair of the committee) is to reach agreement on what will be evaluated, why they need to be evaluated, the time line for the assessment, the budget needed to do the assessment, and the specific goals of the assessment. Defining the scope of the evaluation is essential as the effort must be manageable and clearly defined. Use of project planning software to "task out" responsibilities of specific individuals, the activities for which they are responsible, and the time line for these activities of the evaluation is an excellent strategy.

Thinking about the preparation needed to conduct the evaluation and how the process can be handled as efficiently as possible *before* the effort begins can help ensure that the library staff:

- Uses its time as wisely as possible in the data collection process;
- Collects high quality and useful data;
- Integrates that data into other library data;
- Can draw upon the data for future purposes through a management information system; and
- Uses the data to improve overall library decision-making, planning, and meeting community information needs.

The statistics that result from describing programs and services have great value to the library. Taking time to prepare adequately to conduct the data collection process will increase that value.

Agree on Methods and Measures

There are a number of different methods and approaches that can be used as a guide for assessing library services. There is no need to reinvent the wheel given the extensive amount of work that already has been done in this area. The evaluation committee/library staff may wish to review the basic approaches and measures highlighted in figure 1 at the end of this chapter.

There are many different types of measures that can be used in an evaluation effort.

Performance measures are a broad inclusive term used to measure how well a service or program has performed. For example, "correct answer fill rate" is a performance measure of the success with which library reference staff provide the correct answer to a reference question to a patron. Another performance measure is "repeat visitors to the library's Web site" that shows how many times a visitor came to the library's Web site more than once over a specific period of time.

Output measures are those that are indicative of the results that come from a program or service or other library activity. In reference services, one output would be reference transactions; in cataloging it might be books cataloged; for a Web site an output could be page views.

Outcome measures are indicative of impacts or outcomes from the service, program, or library activity. An outcome from bibliographic instruction classes might be improved grades in freshman English class. An outcome from using the library's Web page might be obtaining employment.

Measures are not quality standards, which are specific, measurable, expectations of the *desired* quality of some service or activity. They define the level of quality or performance that an organization is willing to accept as representing quality for that particular service.

The use of quality standards is important because they:

- Encourage staff to discuss and agree upon what constitutes "quality" for a specific service;
- Provide clear guidance as to the quality "targets" that are acceptable;
- Recognize that there may be differing acceptable levels of quality for different types of services; and
- Provide a basis for rewards and demonstrating accountability.

Performance measures differ from quality standards. A performance measure could be correct answer fill rate and it may determine that over a certain period of time users had a 55 percent correct answer fill rate, that is, 55 percent of the time when they asked a reference question they received a correct answer. A quality standard in this situation might be "90 percent of all quick fact and bibliographic questions will be answered correctly within 6 hours of receipt and be assessed by the user at least at a 4.0 on a scale of satisfaction (1 = not satisfied, 5 = very satisfied)."

In library evaluations, various types of measures and quality standards are important and useful. There is, however, much more use of performance measures than quality standards because many librarians have difficulty in determining what an acceptable quality standard is for a particular service. But if such quality standards are not established, library staff will not know when a library service or program is "good enough" or know what is acceptable quality service at that library.

Those about to embark on library evaluations should review the basic approaches and measures available and (1) draw upon the strategies and approaches developed and validated in these sources, (2) combine and integrate aspects of the existing approaches that are especially useful and appropriate for a particular library setting, and/or (3) expand on the existing approaches and develop an approach to collect data customized for a particular library setting. The third option should only be used by those with significant evaluation experience and knowledge.

MANAGE THE DATA COLLECTED

Before the actual data collection begins, attention needs to be given to managing and integrating the resulting library data.

The evaluator will need to:

- Maintain data in a systematic management information system or decision support system;
- Collect data longitudinally with standard definitions;
- Collect data other than those required by an external governing or national reporting agency;
- Integrate data into other descriptive data from the library's OPAC, ILS, or from community information and community demographics, etc.;
- Establish a formal organizational mechanism with a regular budget for evaluation and assign specific responsibilities for the evaluation effort; and
- Produce regular and timely reports on evaluation results that are targeted at specific audiences, i.e., governing boards, users, trustees, policymakers, etc.

These are but a few of the factors that need to be considered in the management of data. Sadly, evaluation of any type is often a one-shot effort done to meet a pressing need and then the data are misplaced or otherwise not available for the next effort. Development of internal manuals to assist libraries in the evaluation process may be as important as the sources on approaches for how to collect and analyze the evaluation data (see Figure 1, p. 192).

A key issue during the process is to recognize that data collection should be considered as an *on-going process*. That is, the library should be able to proceduralize the activities and learn from each data collection effort such that succeeding efforts can be easier and less time consuming. In addition, maintaining the data that is collected in such a way that the library can use them for a range of decision-making and planning activities is also essential, thus, the need for a statistics database that incorporates and links all the various types of library and demographic statistics that are available.

Quality of Data

The evaluator should be aware of the quality and limitations of the data being collected and analyzed. There are a number of criteria to consider when developing the data collection plan and deciding on measures. First, are the data valid? Validity in terms of data collection means are we measuring what we think we are measuring? For example, asking users about the degree to which they are "satisfied" with a particular library service, e.g., reference services, is likely to raise validity questions. Without a more precise definition of "satisfaction" users could be assessing the courtesy of the librarian in answering the question, whether they were forced to wait a long time in line to obtain an answer, or if they received an answer that was accurate. Thus, in this example, it is not clear what, exactly, is being measured because of a poorly constructed question.

A second criterion used to determine the quality of the data is reliability. Simply stated, reliability is the degree to which the data are consistent or result in the same response or measure every time the evaluator collects that information. For example, if an evaluation question asks for the frequency with which a person visits the library results in different answers every time the question is asked, the data are not reliable. Poor reliability of data can result because much evaluation data are self-reported, that is, they depend on the accuracy of the individual responding to a question. Reliability of data can be improved by making certain that, in this case, the respondent actually has the information and the ability to provide reliable data.

Finally, data that are being collected should be useful and pertinent for decision making. Collecting and analyzing data that have little to do with the evaluation objectives or provide little insight/knowledge regarding possible recommendations and actions that could be taken to improve the situation are not useful. Thus, the evaluator needs to ensure that data collected are specifically related to the evaluation objectives and will produce information that will provide an understanding of the evaluation topic and offer ideas for recommendations to improve that situation.

All data have limitations. This brief discussion of quality of data is only an overview of the various threats to obtaining quality data that can occur. One good strategy to employ prior to conducting the data collection effort is to pretest the data collection instruments (surveys, focus groups, data in the logfile of a Web site, etc.). A second strategy is to ask what are the specific threats that might limit the validity, reliability, and usefulness of the data, and then take steps to minimize those threats. A good evaluation, however, incorporates strategies to ensure that quality data are collected and analyzed. Data describing library services, as with other types of descriptive data, will not be always 100 percent valid, reliable, and useful—but efforts can be taken to ensure that the data are "as good as possible." Indeed, the general advice is: "Better to have poor data and use it wisely for library decision making than to have no data at all."

Analyze and Report the Data

There are numerous approaches to analyzing the data that have been collected. Because of the multiple options available, some planning and thought should go into how best to analyze the data given the time and resource constraints affecting the evaluation. Quantitative data might be coded and entered into a spreadsheet, a database, or a more sophisticated statistical analysis software program such as SPSS (Statistical Package for the Social Sciences). The statistical analyses, however, have to be appropriate for the type of data collected. Qualitative data resulting from interviews and focus groups, for example, may be analyzed by a formal content analysis approach or may be organized by topics and issues by the evaluator. Regardless of the analysis approach to be used, the quality of the data, as discussed above, should be maximized as much as possible.

The analysis of data should result in recommendations that address the evaluation goals and objectives—and assist the library staff in making decisions that can improve library services, resources, use, and programs.

Before collection of data occurs, staff need to consider to whom findings and recommendations will be targeted:

- Library administrators and staff;
- Library users;
- Governing board and institutional administrators;
- Government policymakers;
- Vendors;
- Others.

Depending on the target audience, different types of evaluation reports can be developed with different presentation styles and content to ensure the greatest impact.

In developing evaluation reports the following general guidelines should be considered:

- Include a one–two page executive summary of objectives, key findings, and recommendations;
- Keep the reports short, concise, and to the point;
- Use high-quality graphics, tables, and summary charts—avoid lengthy and detailed descriptions of data in paragraph form;
- Put detailed data, example data collection instruments, etc. in the Appendices;
- Make recommendations explicit and offer specific and practical strategies for how the recommendations can be implemented;
- Determine how the report will be disseminated and to whom—mail-out of actual copies to key stakeholder groups, posting to a Web site, announcement of availability in print or on discussion lists, presentations at conferences, etc.;

- Decide if the library wants feedback and comments on the report and its recommendations; if yes, provide a means for such to occur as input into the next evaluation cycle.

Generally it is a good idea to have at least one and possibly two or three external reviewers or experts edit/review the report for readability and content prior to releasing the report.

THE POLITICS OF EVALUATION

The evaluation process typically occurs in a politically charged environment. That political environment needs to be understood as part of conducting an evaluation and implementing the evaluation results. The political environment includes the views, values, and power of various individuals such as the officials in the larger organization, the users, the library staff, opinion leaders on the faculty or in the local community, and local, state, and national leaders, among others. Politics can have a significant impact on how the evaluation is developed, the type of data that are collected, how they are interpreted, and which recommendations result from the evaluation.

When considering the political environment and the participants in that environment it is useful to consider the type of power that the various individuals may have *viz a viz* the evaluation. Basic types of power come from:

- **Governance**: does the person have direct governing authority over the evaluator or members of the evaluation team?
- **Knowledge**: does the person have better access to and understanding of information related to the evaluation than the people conducting the evaluation?
- **Finances and other resources**: does the person have the authority to control the finances or other resources of the people conducting the evaluation?
- **Personality and relationships**: does the person have excellent interpersonal and personality traits and contacts and associations with others who are affected by the evaluation that the evaluator does not have?
- **Technology**: does the person control the degree to which the people conducting the evaluation can obtain or have access to various types of technology?

Clearly, there are other sources of power than those listed. These, however, provide a sense of how an evaluation can be *influenced* as it is conducted.

A number of librarians who become involved in conducting evaluations are ill-prepared for dealing with the politics of the evaluation. Generally, librarians were never taught how to "work the political environment"; some librarians simply do not like having to deal with politics; nor do some librarians understand the importance and impact of politics on evaluations. The decision to use performance measure *x* as opposed to performance measure *y*, for example, may have serious political implications for the evaluation. Ignoring the political context in which the library conducts evaluations is likely to limit the usefulness and impact of that evaluation.

While every effort should be made to reduce the impact of the political environment on the evaluation, such is often difficult. Value judgments of what to evaluate, how to conduct the evaluation, what data to collect, from what source, and how to report the data with what recommendations, all influence the evaluation. The evaluator should make every effort to recognize when political and other types of value judgments are being made that affect the evaluation and recognize that these may limit the usefulness of the evaluation.

Some strategies for the evaluator to consider to work the political environment better are to understand clearly who are the stakeholders and what are their interests and objectives related to the evaluation. During the evaluation, make certain to stay in touch with the various stakeholders and continue to understand their interests in the evaluation. When meeting with stakeholder groups regarding the evaluation be strategic—know what you will say, how you will say it, and what it is that *you* want to have accomplished at the end of the meeting. And when developing recommendations, consider the impacts of those recommendations and who will gain or lose power. Ultimately, however, the evaluator must minimally understand the political environment affecting the evaluation, and better, be able to work that political environment to conduct an open and objective evaluation.

MAKING A DIFFERENCE WITH EVALUATION

Evaluation of library services, resources, programs, and activities is done best on an ongoing basis. Thus, the library staff should think of evaluation as an ongoing, iterative process in which constant learning and change occurs. What is learned from the first evaluation effort should inform the next effort, and so forth. The more experience with collecting data describing library services the better the results are likely to be. Also, with experience comes the likelihood of completing more complex evaluations that address multiple factors.

The risk to libraries that do not engage in evaluation is to become marginalized. Marginalized means that other services and organizations provide the same services but do it better, with less cost, and with greater impact. Why, for example, do most Web users go directly to a search engine like Google rather than to the homepage of their local academic or public library? Addressing questions such as this one will be critical to the long-term success of libraries. Ongoing assessment of how well libraries provide existing services as a basis for improving them and for developing new and innovative services that compete with other providers will be essential.

The challenges to the library community are to continue evaluation and research in assessing library services and resources, to continue to demonstrate the importance of assessing library services—regardless of library type—and to use the assessment process as a means to a greater end of improving the quality and usefulness of library services to members in the library's community. As libraries rely more on the provision of services and resources in the networked environment, these challenges will only take on increased importance and complexity. Evaluation skills and knowledge—and practicing those skills and knowledge—may be the library's best hope for continuing to play a key role in our society.

SUGGESTIONS FOR FURTHER READING

General

Evaluation Process

Davidson, E. Jane. *Evaluation Methodology Basics: The Nuts and Bolts of Sound Evaluation*. Thousand Oaks, CA: Sage Publications, 2005.

McDavid, James C. and Laura R. L Hawthorn. *Program Evaluation & Performance Measurement: An Introduction to Practice*. Thousand Oaks, CA: Sage Publications, 2006.

Rossi, Peter H., Marke W. Lipsey, and Howard E. Freeman. *Evaluation: A Systematic Approach*. 7th ed. Thousand Oaks, CA: Sage Publications, 2004.

General Introductions to Library Evaluation

Association for Research Libraries (ARL). *New Measures & Assessment Initiatives*. Retrieved January 02, 2008 from http://www.arl.org/stats/initiatives/index.shtml.

Markless, Sharon and David Streatfield. *Evaluating the Impact of your Library*. London: Facet Publishing, 2006.

Matthews, Joseph R. *The Evaluation and Measurement of Library Service*. Westport, CT: Libraries Unlimited, 2007.

———. *Measuring for Results: The Dimensions of Public Library Effectiveness*. Westport, CT: Libraries Unlimited, 2004.

Rubin, Rhea Joyce. *Demonstrating Results: Using Outcome Measurement in your Library*. Chicago: ALA, 2006.

The Association for Research Libraries (ARL) New Measures & Initiatives, http://www.arl.org/stats/initiatives/index.shtml.

The eValued evaluation tool kit for eLibrary development, http://www.evalued.bcu.ac.uk/.

The LibQual project for assessing services quality, http://www.libqual.org/.

Inputs–Outputs evaluation approach with manuals.

Equinox Library Performance Indicators, http://equinox.dcu.ie/.

Statistics, Measures and Quality Standards for Assessing Digital Reference Library Services: Guidelines and Procedures, by Charles R. McClure et al., Syracuse, NY: Syracuse University, the Information Institute, 2001, http://quartz.syr.edu/quality/.

Measuring Academic Library Performance, by Nancy A. Van House, Beth T. Weil, and Charles R. McClure, Chicago: ALA, 1990.

Statistics and Performance Measures for Public Library Networked Services, by John Carlo Bertot, Charles R. McClure, and Joe Ryan, Chicago: ALA, 2001.

Outcomes assessment, http://www.imls.gov/applicants/learning.shtm.

Online instructional modules such as those developed at the Information Institute, Florida State University for the Florida State Library for outcomes assessment (see http://www.lstatoolkit.com) and for e-metrics instruction (see http://www.ii.fsu.edu/emis).

Other Standards and Guidelines

Standards and Assessment for Academic Libraries: A Workbook, by William Neal Nelson and Robert W. Fernekes, Chicago: American Library Association, 2002. This is an especially useful tool.

National Information Standards Organization (NISO). This site contains numerous standards and reference material for Library statistics such as Z39.7 "Library Statistics," http://www.niso.org/.

The Counter Initiative, Code of Practice Governing the Recording and Exchange of Online Usage Data http://www.projectcounter.org/index.html.

Note: Each Uniform Resource Locator (URL) was verified as an active link to the appropriate Web page on January 02, 2008.

Figure 1 Evaluation Methods and Measures.

Moving Beyond Boundaries

LIS Professionals in a Global Society

Barbara J. Ford

Today, the core competencies of library and information professionals must be demonstrated in a global context. The increasing effects of globalization on societies and institutions everywhere and the increasingly interconnected and interdependent world mean that library and information science (LIS) professionals have a responsibility to their clients to provide services with a global perspective.

Library and information professionals can educate, transform, and empower to enhance positive change and development in communities around the world. Information overload makes it increasingly difficult to separate what is important to know in order to make good decisions and be successful in a global society. Libraries can help develop people's capabilities by using technologies that accelerate learning potential and access to information and knowledge.

GLOBALIZATION AND INFORMATION

Globalization is at the forefront of public attention because a rising share of transactions and dissemination of knowledge and information takes place at the international level. The globe is shrinking and bandwidth is increasing, with cyberspace becoming a medium for many interactions and much education and learning.

Ubiquitous, open, free access to information is a key prerequisite for a peaceful, equitable world in the twenty-first century. As we continue to develop and disperse technology, the possibilities for information to flow with total freedom and for everyone on the planet to have free access to human knowledge presents an opportunity unprecedented in global history and unimagined even at the mid-twentieth century. Free access to information around the earth, more than any other development foreseeable, has the possibility of making the future much better than the past, but it also, if mismanaged, could delay that bright future just as easily.

The United Nations Universal Declaration of Human Rights states that all human beings have the fundamental right to have access to all expressions of knowledge, creativity, and intellectual activity and to express their thoughts publicly. Freedom of expression is one aspect of the right to know and to be informed. It is inevitably linked to the freedom of thought and conscience, which is the basis of human advancement and a precondition to democratic process. For example, in Colombia, as literacy increased during the twentieth century, public libraries were instruments to transform the traditional structure of the country. In 1954, UNESCO established the Biblioteca Piloto of Medellin as part of the agency's effort to create model public libraries around the world. A library, where readers could browse and touch the books in open stacks and borrow books and take them home, was very well received by a rapidly expanding school population and a population with rising levels of literacy. With the advent and adoption of new technologies, the number and types of Columbia's public libraries have continued to expand, giving credence to the idea that democracy is based on the development of well-informed citizens. Today, public libraries in Colombia are vibrant, active community centers that encourage literacy and reading.

Paradoxically, at the same time that information and knowledge sets are being liberated from earlier constraints on accessibility or governmental controls or even their language-base, thus becoming a global free commodity, information will become increasingly valuable. Those who can create it and analyze it and manage change on the basis of it will largely control global resources and our global future. They will certainly lead better lives than the information "have-nots." Information technology and advantage in the global marketplace will work hand-in-hand.

Today, the privileged, with access to digital resources and up-to-date information, enjoy the same lucrative future as did the privileged with access to electricity and fossil fuels or new chemical-industrial processes 100 years ago. The key difference between the situation today and that of a century ago is the fact that every region, country, and continent contains such privileged communities. Tomorrow's future prosperity, as well as its tensions and conflicts, will be partially determined by the distribution of information access across "haves" and "have-nots." One hopeful reality about today's information economies is that the future can change as rapidly as new technology and information providers emerge. In places like Kosovo we have seen the impact of a strengthened national and university library as they adopt contemporary technology and enhance access to information.

How this commodity that we are calling "information" is packaged lies at the heart of its value. It will have very limited value, if current information, for instance, is simply recycled into new formats that are selected and censored to reflect only selective visions of what is important. On the other hand, a global public sphere with collective ownership of information, freedom of access and use, and recognition of authors and inventors will bring value to the knowledge sets. This has been most dramatically demonstrated, of late, by the success of projects like Wikipedia. This free, multilingual, Web-based encyclopedia uses software that integrates work on a project by several users at separate workstations, resulting in a collaboratively written, diverse reference source. Global citizenship, with information access as a fundamental right, alongside free communication, will trigger change across the planet as dramatic as was the coming of mass culture to pockets of privilege a century ago. Expanding people's access to relevant information about their global futures, so that they can act upon social and environmental issues, is one likely result, once information is a totally free good. Another result is the challenge to intellectual property rights and international litigation. Building partnerships across global producers and consumers will need to take precedence over attempts to contain, much less to control, the free flow of information in tomorrow's world.

Global mass media and new information technologies have the potential for playing a positive role in linking local causes with larger, global imperatives. New interactive information technologies provide the foundation for a global civic culture that will lead to a shift in power balances as information and knowledge become more readily available to all people everywhere. Virtual learning will be everywhere in a world where knowledge sets are outdated practically overnight and then replaced by more current approaches to particular subjects. "Lifelong learning" will pass from being a catch phrase used to encourage higher education enrollments to a concept describing a critical survival element in a rapidly changing technological world. A good deal of educational information now is available online, and education and training or updating will continue to be core activities at every social level. When we look at topics like HIV/AIDS and how information can be made available, libraries in countries like South Africa provide models that can be used around the world. From distributing condoms in the library to providing free printed and online information and programs, libraries are helping societies address key health and social issues.

There is a need to strengthen education in places where education is crucial to prospects for world peace and democratic societies. The concept of education as a right is growing as individuals recognize that their opportunities depend on education and training, and countries realize that solid education is essential for participation in the global society. Education and the services that LIS professionals provide are essential for positive change in societies. In Africa, foundations are investing in programs to revitalize African universities. As part of this, ten universities in Ghana, Nigeria, Tanzania, and Uganda are receiving professional development guidance from the Mortenson Center for International Library Programs at the University of Illinois at Urbana-Champaign, with assistance from the MacArthur Foundation and Carnegie Corporation, to improve access to information resources through strengthening the technology and online resources available in their libraries and providing continuing education for library staff.

Already, the downside of this new world is apparent: information overload. To counter overload, everyone will need to learn medium-appropriate skills. These skills will include the ability to effectively scan and evaluate electronic information sources; critically assess the validity of data access arrangements designed by myriad, unknown programmers; and understand unknown specialists' decisions about what to include and what to exclude from any particular digitized record. Web sites change quickly, and it is often difficult to evaluate the accuracy of the information presented. The use of this same technology to communicate will be essential, and it will create connections with people around the world as it allows new and different levels of collaboration. Technology and communication will drive much that we do, and virtual reality and artificial intelligence will provide services and products not yet imagined. There are excellent models including Zayed University, a new university for women in the United Arab Emirates, which has been recognized for its model information literacy programs.

What Libraries Can Do

Educating people to effectively and efficiently use information by teaching information management skills at all learning levels will be critical, if tomorrow's world, sketched above, is to be realized. Information is one of the most powerful tools available to people for solving problems, but only when linked to education and a fundamental literacy level across a broad range of subjects. The importance of an educated populace, literate in reading, math, and science, lies at the center of this vision. Without education, including access to information and the knowledge of how to use it, people will become second-class global citizens. Fortunately, one of the great inventions of the nineteenth century will serve us well as a mechanism for leveling the playing field and disseminating information: the public library. In Haiti, we see the effects of investments by the Soros Foundation in forty community libraries that, despite the turmoil, provide good services to library users.

Libraries are natural organizations to encourage global collaboration because they can serve as repositories for larger quantities of reliable information than will be accessible to most information technology providers. Many of us have used digitized resources and know that they are sometimes incomplete and may contextualize information inaccurately. Libraries will be home to the complete and unabridged material that has otherwise been put on the Internet in an incomplete and abridged, digitized form. They will help individuals, businesses, and countries to be smarter and faster about adopting new technologies. The more information that people have about the information they are drowning in, the quicker they can swim to the surface and confront changing demands and expectations.

In a globally networked environment, information resources can be made available worldwide, and this networked environment lends itself to cooperation and sharing of ideas and solutions worldwide. However, the key to this cooperation rests upon the public information clearing house—what we used to call the local library—existing as both a physical and a virtual site. In Vietnam, Atlantic Philanthropies has invested in building learning resource centers (new buildings with up-to-date technology) for a number of universities, and Simmons College (MA) and the Mortenson Center for International Library Programs are now educating librarians to work in these centers.

Library providers have long recognized the importance of adopting standards for organizing and providing access to global information and for allowing work to be broken apart, reassembled, and allowed to flow between various producers. Together, with free access to newly digitized information in libraries and other collections around the world, these standards will spur a new kind of collaboration. New, because it will help level the playing field and empower individuals to produce intellectual work anywhere, and new, because it will encourage a unique kind of volunteerism and an expanded concept of global citizenship.

One model for the future lies in the open source movement, where online volunteers share insights and offer them free to people everywhere to use. These volunteers are building tools and infrastructures so anyone, anywhere can collaborate. This is analogous to the historic role of libraries, which provided free access to information and assistance to anyone. Still, trained intermediaries—librarians—will be necessary to assist readers/users to know how to evaluate and use electronic tools and infrastructures. Without this, not everyone is able to make effective use of all of the varied information sources. Institutional repositories, where university libraries provide easy, well-organized access to the research of their faculty and students, are enhancing access to information and to sharing research.

This concept of open access to all information, a global library movement, will be an abrupt challenge to quarters on this globe where there still exists the desire to control information in order to control political power. Censorship and human rights violations are incompatible with individuals' and countries' ability to take advantage of new technologies and access to information. Both the International Federation of Library Associations and Institutions (IFLA) and the Internet Manifesto clearly state the interrelations between unhindered access to information, freedom, equity, global understanding, and peace. Political reform may be a prerequisite in those areas that do not hold, as part of their traditional values, an obligation to an informed society and a commitment to information access.

With the changes in Eastern Europe, we have seen how access to good information can help change a country's political situation without violence. In addition, positive economic change is evident in places like India, where access to good education and technology has allowed new industries to blossom and grow and parts of society to be transformed dramatically. As the potential to do intellectual work anywhere increases and it is possible to collaborate on a more equal footing, political entities that encourage individual empowerment and horizontal and collaborative structures will flourish. What is less clear is the cost of leaving places like the poorer parts of Africa, Latin America, China, and India out of the information technology loop. But it is likely that, given the previous examples, these regions will continue to advance and join those who are able to take advantage of all the information and telecommunications technologies have to offer.

FLUENCIES FOR A GLOBAL SOCIETY

The founding of global communities across international and cultural boundaries empowers people, insofar as groups can share and organize information when and how they choose. Individuals are free to adopt new processes and technologies and make contributions wherever they are and however they desire. An increasingly horizontal, collaborative model for interactions, at all levels, has been opened because technology has removed barriers and boundaries of both time and space. Information and communication technologies, including speech-recognition, smart computers, enhanced computing power, virtual environments, and other, yet to be imagined, bold inventions will remove yet more spatial and temporal barriers in the years to come.

With each innovation and refinement will come questions of access: will governments now try to control programs and hardware where once they tried controlling what books people could read? This power would need to be in the hands of some authority greater than mere nation-states. This is where information technology becomes the glue, if not the building blocks, for global civil society. Humans will be required to focus on collaboration to emphasize the positive values offered by "horizontality" that leads to the notion of global citizenship. Inclusion, tolerance for diversity of views, freedom, responsibility, and respect are important values that all people will be required to share in their electronic interdependency, where the Internet can make invisible outmoded tags of race, religion, ethnicity, and even language.

One of the greatest challenges in democratizing access to information in the years ahead will be to not overwhelm or leave behind some populations. Countries with few resources will need to pursue innovations to survive. In parts of Africa, for instance, where the cost of bandwidth is very high and there is lack of adequate access to electrical power, foundations and nongovernmental organizations may need to provide resources to be certain that whole populations are not left out of the knowledge-based economies of tomorrow because developments that leave large segments of the global community behind will simply lay the foundation for tension, division, and possibly worse. In some countries, access to technology is considered a birthright, while in other parts of the world, students typically begin college without having had the opportunity to use and learn about the variety of information available electronically.

Places with indigenous and unique languages and cultures can already use technology to cultivate and protect these examples of human creativity and development, just as we protect gene pools and other unique resources. Today, we see these efforts in places like South Africa, where eleven official languages are in use and government programs are working to assure that heritage materials are digitized and available for use. The changes that have happened in South Africa since the end of Apartheid have been assisted by the Library and Information Association of South Africa, which has brought together the previously racially divided organizations and worked with the Mortenson Center, through a grant from the Carnegie Corporation, to train twenty-six leaders for the new association. In Bangladesh, on the other hand, indigenous boats provide free public access to computers and the Internet to residents of impoverished remote communities. Locally developed Web tutorials, recorded documentaries, and other electronic resources, offered on the boats, are helping girls become literate, contributing members of their community. The future surely holds other similar ingenious solutions for addressing the technology divide worldwide.

Global, free access to information is a dramatic new thing and a force for positive change. Education, in general, and libraries, in particular, will be important conduits for global free access to information technology and the information and knowledge it makes available. Even trivial technologies can be used in new ways to provide new services and improve lives. For instance, mobile phones are used in some parts of the world to deliver library and other services such as weather reports and crop prices to farmers. Clearly, technology is not the issue. Rather, the politics of how to use new technologies in positive ways for the benefit of all will be one of the difficult challenges for the future. User-focused services that people can easily access without much instruction will offer expanded opportunities in many parts of the world. Information and communication technologies will continue to evolve and develop, ideally helping eliminate problems like poverty. Resources that leverage existing infrastructure to connect potential entrepreneurs around the world to the resources they need to generate inventions and income to improve their lives can change global power balances. Ideally, the technologically unconnected will soon be connected, making them part of the global educational and creative network. This vision of an information technology future as part of a vision of a global informed civil society is the key to our collective free and open future.

Globalization should allow local, unique cultures to thrive and be protected. The right balance between global and local needs to be found. Global activities will continue to expand, hopefully, while benefiting everyone rather than bypassing some regions or groups. LIS professionals have a set of common values about what is good and what is bad. We must have a set of values on the international level to safeguard ethnic, religious, and other identities irrespective of nationality as the criterion of international rights and obligations. Tolerance means the right to think and act differently from other people but within a mutually agreed framework.

Cultural fluency includes the ability to listen, learn, exchange ideas, and understand local needs in the global context. Communicating and networking with those who speak different languages and come from different cultural backgrounds are important today. We must develop a deeper understanding of values, traditions, and cultures and ensure that society fosters the exchange of ideas, information, and knowledge. With a shrinking planet, it means that aggression and confrontation will not work as we must interact with people we do not know and whose traditional modes of politeness and interactions may not be familiar to us.

LIBRARIES: GLOBAL REACH—LOCAL TOUCH

It is an exciting time to be in the field of library and information science, as we use new tools to work in the global society. Every LIS professional can work toward making their library more global by using some of the ideas below.

Celebrate diversity. Reach out to community or campus groups reflecting other cultures and countries and celebrate that diversity with speakers, exhibits, films, and special performances. Plan programs, displays, and fairs around international holidays, United Nations, and world commemorative days. Sponsor a series of lectures or presentations on different countries or world regions. Invite returned Peace Corps Volunteers, Fulbright Scholars, or others with international experience to speak.

Expand and diversify the library's collection of multicultural and multilingual materials. Add United Nations materials and publications to your collection. Include materials on language learning. Host reading groups with an international focus.

Develop an international dimension to library services. Hold staff seminars on understanding students and library users from other cultures. Make a list of staff who speak other languages and are available to assist in translation. Provide multilingual tours of libraries. Hold workshops for staff on how to incorporate stories and music from various cultures in programming.

Use the Internet to connect to other cultures. Provide lists of international libraries, United Nations, and other Web sites that promote learning about other countries, cultures, international travel, and global cooperation. Bookmark Internet sites of newspapers from various countries that will help promote libraries to immigrants and businesses hoping to expand overseas. Design interactive Web-based materials and training courses to encourage and foster diversity.

Promote public awareness of global resources at your library during National Library Week and every week. Provide monthly suggestions of multicultural celebrations and programs. Look for opportunities to partner with other nonprofit organizations to increase global awareness between libraries and expand the knowledge of the role libraries play in the global settings.

Learn more about global information issues, such as copyright, and how they affect libraries around the world. Become a member of the American Library Association's (ALA) International Relations Round Table and other association divisions and sections with a special focus on international issues, such as preservation. Take advantage of the membership and newsletters of UNESCO's Network of Associated Libraries.

Connect with libraries in other countries. If a city has a Sister City program, seek sponsorship for an exchange of library staff. Work with international library colleagues to organize a conference or training program or focus your state library conference on international issues. Plan to attend the annual conference of the International Federation of Library Associations and Institutions. Seek opportunities to share best practices and learn from others.

Leave home. Join one of the ALA-organized delegations to international book fairs where you can purchase books, enjoy cultural events, network with publishers, visit libraries, and learn from colleagues. Apply for a Fulbright grant or other grants from organizations that support international librarianship. Join the Peace Corps, United Nations Volunteers, or other international volunteer organizations. Join a study tour abroad.

Support libraries overseas by donating funds to purchase materials. Adopt an international library partner of your own or through ALA or IFLA. Become a resource person or correspondent with librarians or library school students abroad.

Increase your global awareness. Learn another language. Take a course in the literature, history, or culture of another country or region. Become a literacy volunteer to teach English as a second language to refugees and immigrants. Read more about the social, economic, political, health, and environmental issues affecting the world. Use your information skills to assist international human rights groups and promote intellectual freedom worldwide.

When you are traveling internationally, think of yourself as an ambassador for libraries. Contact ALA or other associations for material to distribute before you travel, in anticipation of speaking about ALA programs with colleagues abroad. Offer to write an article about an aspect of international librarianship for ALA publications or offer to write about ALA for an international library association publication.

Library and information professionals can use their skills to educate, transform, and empower and to enhance positive change and development in communities around the world. Libraries can help develop people's capabilities by using technologies that accelerate learning potential and access to information and knowledge. Information overload makes it increasingly difficult to separate what is important to know in order to make good decisions and be successful in a global world, and libraries can help with this.

Take advantage of every opportunity to expand your professional global reach and that of the libraries where you work. Today, every library and information professional can and should have a global impact and focus.

SUGGESTIONS FOR FURTHER READING

International Leads. Chicago: American Library Association. This is the publication of the International Relations Round Table of the American Library Association and disseminates information about international librarianship.

Kesselman, Martin Alan and Irwin Weintraub (eds.). *Global Librarianship*. New York: Marcel Dekker, 2004.

McCook, Kathleen de la Peña, Barbara J. Ford, and Kate Lippincott (eds.). *Libraries: Global Reach—Local Touch*. Chicago: ALA, 1998.

Stueart, Robert D. *International Librarianship: A Basic Guide to Global Knowledge Access*. Lanham, MD: Scarecrow Press, 2007.

18

Issues and Trends

Ken Haycock

No matter whom one talks with in this field, there are decipherable trends and issues both in the profession as a whole and in each individual and smaller part of it. As a consequence, any listing cannot help but reflect the interests and concerns of the individual speaker or writer and the particular part of the library and information science world he or she inhabits.

These trends and issues, then, reflect broader issues facing the field overall. They are not trends of interest and concern to those in particular corners, as important as they might be.

These are defined from a management and leadership perspective, looking at the entire enterprise, and of course from one person's vantage point.

THE LIBRARY IS A BUSINESS

There is considerable reluctance among librarians to view their operations as a "business" yet whenever money is given and invested, whether in a "bottom-line" company or not-for-profit service, all of the elements of business activity are involved, from strategic planning to human resources management to financial management (sometimes seemingly the "F-word" in librarianship) to marketing to evaluation of programs and services, among others. The all-too-common refrain "we are not a business, we are a service!" is a bit silly when many retail operations also offer superb customer service.

Increasingly, library leaders do view the library as a business. In the corporate setting, the library or information agency may indeed be a profit center, or at least contributing to the bottom line of the company, whether by saving time and thus money or generating revenue through library-developed or delivered products; examples include legal reports for communities of lawyers, charged to the lawyers and thus the clients, company products for which the ideas are derived from librarians working in special collections, or the sale of photographs by news libraries; public libraries too are developing local information products for sale.

There seems to be less issue with the activities and functions of a business than with labeling the operation as a business. It is increasingly common, however, for librarians to make strategic decisions based on organizational goals and to align resources to achieve those goals and assess results, as any business would do. There is similarly a move, almost completed, to change semantics from patrons or users to customers or clients; some suggest that this has resulted in better service while others decry the use of business language (interestingly, nevertheless, librarians talk about "problem patrons" and "customer service," but not the reverse).

Like any business the library also has competitors. Traditionally (at least for the past 10 years) these have been viewed as big-box bookstores and the Internet. Indeed, bookstores do typically offer longer hours, author programs, study areas, storytelling, and coffee shops, among other services and amenities, and the Internet (specifically the Web) does offer convenient sources of information (setting aside here issues of currency, relevance, and accuracy). But the list goes on ... retail stores of all types are offering traditional library services (e.g., maternity shops offering story times) and community centers provide Internet terminals and training classes as well as book club discussion groups. The greater issue now is the competition for visitors and disposable time and that encompasses a wide range of recreational and educational service providers.

The close connection between effective library leadership and business leadership has also been studied, with strong similarities.[1] What we need in this profession is more entrepreneurs, social entrepreneurs, who understand how to leverage library resources for the greatest possible effect, consistent with the library's mission.

Funding is always an issue, a business issue in the sense of securing the resources necessary to fulfill our community-approved strategic goals and objectives.

There are ancillary trends related to the library as business. First, *the business is community development*. The library is no longer in the isolated "library business." Rather, the public library is in the business of its city or municipality, improving the quality of life for all residents in demonstrable ways; similarly, the academic library advances the mission of the college or university by contributing to the research enterprise and teaching and learning; the school library impacts student achievement through teacher/teacher-librarian collaboration. This means that there has been a notable shift in assessment measures from inputs (e.g., dollars per capita compared to other libraries) through output measures (e.g., circulation, even per hour open and per resident, reference transactions) to outcome measures (e.g., impact on literacy or small business development).

This results in part from the fact that, secondly, *the "public good" is being replaced by public value*. We can decry this turn of events; we can admonish and scorn but it will not change a decided shift in public policy. Public agencies can no longer count on public support solely because they are public goods—schools, hospitals, libraries, and other agencies are under increased scrutiny to demonstrate value. Funders want to see impact on quality of life, on the cultural, economic, educational, social life of the community. In business this is straight return on investment—show us how we received value for the dollars we invested in this service. This is not difficult to do but requires a "sea change" in approach and measures.

Some would suggest that this third related trend is not new but components decidedly are: *the customer is the focus—and the customer wants choices.* Customers have options. They want comfort and convenience or will go elsewhere. They want not only service (beyond access to assistance with deciphering bewildering codes and tools) but also opportunities to participate in programs and socialize in ways different from what has normally been provided to them. At the operational level this not only has expense implications but also causes revenue concerns. One obvious example is notification of late or overdue materials—as libraries become more flexible and adept at informing customers through e-mail notification and voice mail, returned materials should be more current and available to others; conversely, revenue from "fines" (or extended use) at many libraries is in the hundreds of thousands of dollars and would decline precipitously with improved returns. Decreased revenue means decreased service. Similarly, more and more, our users view themselves as consumers and customers, demanding high quality facilities and services.

In some ways libraries suffer from the "curse" of high public satisfaction. We pride ourselves in public libraries on being continually ranked with police and fire (usually above parks and recreation services) in community surveys. But unlike other agencies, we do not have customers calling and complaining to councilors and others about service. There is no "negative" push for more money for more service, only more of the same. The result of high support paradoxically is often: "why do you need more money? no one is complaining."

THE PHYSICAL SPACE IS INCREASINGLY IMPORTANT BUT THEN THE VIRTUAL SPACE IS ALSO INCREASINGLY IMPORTANT

As public space generally declines the library as place takes on greater importance. Communities have reinvested in physical spaces for their libraries both as anchors for downtown economic redevelopment and as neighborhood centers. Libraries now work to attract customers not only to serve their information needs but also as destinations, to provide experiences for discovery and imagination. In colleges and universities, libraries can form a space between academic places (classrooms, content management systems) and social places (dorms, social networking software), responding with more study rooms and cafes and tools for online collaboration and messaging.

The total customer experience is becoming more of a focus. Indeed, some libraries have engaged retail consultants to study and advise on customer movement, signage, and marketing.

As students and young people have changed their information seeking and use behaviors libraries have begun to study market groups more assiduously. It is not sufficient to follow the curve, such as studying virtual reference services when most young people under 35 use instant messaging. Young people are more nomadic in their information use and integrate more forms and formats than before. Gaming in libraries, as an intellectual and imaginative activity, is more common as a result.

Similarly, as virtual use begins to exceed physical use, Web sites are evolving to e-branches with an e-branch manager rather than simply managing the Web site. The challenge is to integrate appropriate and useful Web 2.0 tools and technologies into the new Library 2.0, for "in-house" users, whether present physically or virtually.

Online public access computers (OPACs) are providing greater integration of electronic sources of information whether through library subscription or specified links to Web sources. Some question the continuing utility of the catalogue at all, using instead something like WorldCat as their catalog or open source software like Evergreen rather than a traditional vendor.

E-books, e-journals, and other media are also growing in use and importance.

Information interfaces are featuring tiers for different needs, easier visual displays, opportunities for personalization and recommendation, mapping displays, and information literacy tutorials. Federated searching allowing simultaneous searching of several databases, both free and licensed, is also increasingly popular, and increasingly sophisticated.

There is further recognition of improved methods of storage and access and the growing importance of digital preservation. This is an issue at all levels of use, including government and individual user. Massive digitization means both opportunities and challenges as thousands of digitized books become available on the Internet.

At the same time knowledge production is evolving as a trend. Libraries are looking to capitalize on the physical space, networking, and participation through knowledge production or creation stations, whether resume writing and portfolio development, or planning neighborhood presentations or a family completing a genealogy study and scrapbook together. The concept of the library as neighborhood center means providing opportunities for mock interviews for citizenship and ESL classes and services as well.

In this environment, *the "cult of the amateur" is a reality.*[2] Convenience seems to trump quality every time. There is a growing blur between fact and fiction, between news and infomercials. There is a loss of accuracy from experts. Libraries are struggling to find their place in two venues: [1] the change in role from selecting and organizing sources of information reviewed for accuracy and presentation to assisting users individually and in groups to evaluate the quality of electronic sources and [2] the assessment and place of user-produced content in the "collection." Blended collections, organizing and representing new user-produced content through tagging and folksonomies, all combine to create new issues for traditional roles.

Even the smallest library, through consortia and cooperative arrangements can enjoy access to digital resources previously beyond its capability to afford. While print publication is still most common and accepted in scholarly works more resources are appearing first and only in electronic form. Information available digitally provides for greater accessibility and the possibility of greater interaction.

Partnerships leveraging community assets, including library resources, to address community needs and issues is becoming more apparent.

Technological trends, and available emerging technologies for library use, are well documented on popular blogs.[3]

There is also a growing conflict between customer needs and librarian values. One simple example is around notions of privacy. It is difficult to explain why the library is still investigating and sorting through issues related to privacy in an information-rich environment while a coffee shop has opened across the street providing wireless access right away. As a core value, confidentiality of the record and of the user is challenging to maintain even when there is less and less privacy and stability on the Internet: the public fails to see the issue. Certainly when young adults want to establish social networking opportunities at the library and voluntarily give up their privacy, the library is hard pressed to draw lines around privacy and legal responsibilities. There are other critical conflicts between the interests of users and the values of librarians such as intellectual freedom and intellectual property rights.

ROLES AND RELATIONSHIPS ARE BEING REDEFINED

Library service has been too much about transactions. That is changing in dramatic ways. A redefinition of programs and services in response to client needs is placing a much greater emphasis on collaboration, training, and relationships.

Here are but two examples:

Reference and information services. As users locate more and more of their required information on their own (again setting aside issues of currency and accuracy), there are fewer individuals standing at a reference desk for service. Further, the majority of their questions do not require the abilities of a professional librarian. Three shifts are occurring. First, more trained library technicians are being used for reference services, whether on their own or in a team setting. Second, librarians are working more in communities identifying community needs and addressing information needs onsite such as through a wireless laptop at a neighborhood group meeting or a chamber of commerce meeting. Needs are also being met through information-based programs such as addressing medical issues through a health professional speaker or community development issues through a debate. Third, some libraries are providing opportunities for individual appointments with a reference librarian for highly specialized assistance.

Youth services. Children's librarians have traditionally provided high-quality service to young people who frequent the physical library (and of course there is also a presence for young people on the library Web site); these services include individual reading guidance, book talks, storytelling and story reading programs, and related activities to develop imagination and literacy. Given limited resources, which of these has the biggest impact on literacy development—professional services in the library or training and supporting other service providers? (There is not necessarily a right answer here.) Many libraries are redesigning youth services so librarians manage and train staff to deliver in-library programs while they connect with teachers, preschool supervisors, day-care workers, and others and support and train them to exploit the library's resources and offer onsite programs themselves. Librarians are training others in new materials, book promotion, and storytelling. Their reach is extended; the number of children reached is extended; the library impact is extended. However, many children's librarians did not enter their specialty to work primarily with adults.

These are but two of many examples of changing roles and responsibilities. The more obvious ones of course are in technology but many "changes" there are in process, not fundamental roles. A continuing trend is in the teaching role in information literacy, enabling each individual to access and make effective use of society's recorded information and ideas. This has moved beyond access to sources, to evaluation of information, and analysis and synthesis, all well beyond the simple but critical decoding of text. Guided by their values, librarians have moved more into group as well as individual instruction as they recognize that the "digital divide" is becoming less about equipment, the "physical access" to resources, and more about "intellectual access" to information and ideas.

Librarians are also performing complex roles as publishers, educators, researchers, and policy advocates.

THERE IS CONTINUAL AND PERHAPS INEVITABLE TENSION BETWEEN AND AMONG EDUCATORS OF LIBRARIANS AND MEMBERS OF THE PROFESSION

With the trends and issues noted above, it will be of little surprise that there will be issues surrounding the education of professional librarians. There are several issues:

The LIS program as gatekeeper to the profession. This is one of the oldest and most destructive shibboleths in the profession. The LIS program is not a gatekeeper; if anything, it is a gateway. Students are entering a graduate academic program albeit a professional program. For every personal trait that is touted as essential there is someone for whom an exception should be made. There is also no consensus about who should select just the "right" people. The field has so many different positions and opportunities it falls to the employer to make the right choice for a particular position and institution. A public library director may be looking for exuberance, passion, and retail experience for a public services position while the academic library director wants independence and quiet efficiency for a cataloguing position. The LIS program educates professionals who may or may not have developed the knowledge, skills, and abilities for a particular position but may be well-suited to another, or not. Graduation is no guarantee of employment in a particular environment or in a particular city.

The tension between theory and practice. Graduate education necessitates a grounding in theory and research—why we do what we do. Theory is an essential underpinning. At the same time, graduates need to be able to do something other than theorize. There will always be a tension between the need for thinkers and for "plug and play," not that the two need be mutually exclusive. Indeed, most programs offer internships and practica for students to apply what they have learned under the direct supervision of a professional.

The role of other staff. While disciplinary and organizational knowledge are useful for all positions in libraries more senior specialized positions in human resources, marketing, and information technology are moving from librarians to professionals from those particular disciplines. This is hardly a failing of graduate education but simply a recognition that organizations are becoming more complex, and sophistication in related areas will be increasingly necessary.

Similarly, the number of professional librarians as a percentage of all staff is declining. More trained paraprofessionals are undertaking work traditionally done by professional librarians.

Three characteristics separate professional librarians from other trained staff in libraries. First, professionals understand deeply the theories and principles underlying the collection, organization, and use of resources in order to enable ease of both physical and intellectual access. Second, professionals manage and market information agencies and libraries. The branch head and the academic department head will be a professional librarian who oversees the management of the operation and markets the library and its services, in the sense of understanding the needs and interests of the client groups and adjusting resources and services to meet those changing needs. Third, professional librarians train and develop other staff. Typically there will be one professional librarian in small operations. Technicians, clerks, student assistants, volunteers—all need to be trained for their particular role and position: this is a critical new role for professional staff.

Buyer beware. Be very clear about what you expect someone to achieve in their position, what barriers they will need to overcome, and by what criteria you will determine success. Only then can you define the professional knowledge, skills, abilities, and personal qualities necessary for selecting the right person for your particular position in your particular institution. The specific skill set for professionals in family literacy programs will no doubt have some differences from those in information systems and technology.

While the core values and principles of librarianship remain constant, the tools and techniques necessary to accomplish professional goals continue to change. Similarly, the political and economic landscape continues to change and evolve. Libraries and librarians have always sought to understand deeply their environments, their organizations, and their contributions, and to move forward by navigating trends and issues appropriately and critically to ensure the best service and value for their users.

SUGGESTIONS FOR FURTHER READING

Horrocks, Norman (ed.). *Perspectives, Insights & Priorities; 17 Leaders Speak Freely of Librarianship.* Lanham, MD: Scarecrow Press, 2005.

See, for example, *The LISNews* 10 Blogs to Read in 2008. The descriptions are taken directly from the Web site as posted January 14, 2008, at http://www.lisnews.org/node/28830.

The Annoyed Librarian
David Rothman

iLibrarian
Judge a Book by its Cover
Law Librarian Blog
Library Stuff
Marylaine Block
Off The Mark
ResearchBuzz
Stephen's Lighthouse

The Annoyed Librarian was this year's most popular blogger, by a wide margin. It seems everyone is reading The Annoyed Librarian. I found it difficult to summarize the exact theme @The Annoyed Librarian, other than to say "she's" no fan of the ALA. "The Annoyed Librarian is possibly the most successful, respected, and desirable librarian of her generation. She has no other interest than to bring her wit and wisdom to the huddled librarian masses yearning to breathe free. The Annoyed Librarian is a free spirit and you are lucky to have her."

David Rothman explores "Medical Librarianship and Web Geekery" on his blog. David Rothman now works as the Information Services Specialist at the Community General Hospital Medical Library, managing the day-to-day operation of the CGH Medical Library under the supervision of Wendy Tarby (MLS, AHIP). He writes about issues that influence medical librarians, with a healthy dose of librarian geekery thrown in for good measure.

Picking a blog that focuses on "2.0" techie stuff wasn't easy (There's a million of them), but I quickly saw a standout at iLibrarian for a few months because Ellyssa Kroski points to some good stuff. She tags her blog as "News and resources on Library 2.0 and the information revolution." If you are looking for a techie focus, iLibrarian is one of the best blogs to follow.

We all need to read something that makes us laugh occasionally. Something that is just useless and fun. Judge a Book by its Cover should do the job. Just what, exactly, is Judge a Book by its Cover? For those of you who don't know, Maughta works in a public library. She sees literally thousands of books every week; the good, the bad, and the truly hideous. These are the covers from the latter category.

We had a hard time picking a law librarian blog. Our "final cut" list included three choices, and each seemed worthy to be our single final choice. In the end Law Librarian Blog edged out the others for several reasons. For me the biggest reason was collaboration; Law Librarian Blog has two editors and several contributors. They cover a wide range of topics in the law library niche and point the way to good tools and resources.

Before Steven M. Cohen started Library Stuff and sold out to "The Man," he was blogging at LISNews. Library Stuff was the second most popular blog in voting this year. Most people that nominated him pointed to his frequent posting and his style. Steven tends to post quick takes and short links to interesting stories that range from Law Libraries (He's a law librarian) to Flickr Follies. I like The Stuff because he tends to be somewhat less focused on a single topic, so you'll see funny pictures, stuff about libraries, stuff about his life, and stuff about other blogs. It's all . . . Library Stuff.

Marylaine Block has been online since, well, since there's been an online. She started "Best Information on the Net" way back in 1995! Marylaine.com is full of her writing and speeches and is a worthy weekly stop in your Internet travels. Ex Libris: an E-Zine for Librarians and Other Information Junkies and Marylaine's Neat New Stuff are the two best reasons to make her site a weekly visit or subscribe, but you'll also find other writing and text of her many conference presentations. You may not consider this site a blog, but it should be required reading for anyone interested in staying current. It was a "blog" before there were blogs, and it continues to be a wonderful resource to our profession.

Mark Linder calls himself a "habitually probing generalist" and Off The Mark shows that to be true. He writes and reads ALOT! I've been especially interested in reading his "Some things I read this week" posts because he'll actually point to print resources, a rarity, it seems, in the blogosphere. His links and analysis are standouts in our crowded blogosphere niche. Our list is full of specialists; it's good to have at least a couple generalists.

Tara has been posting "News about search engines, databases, and other information collections." at ResearchBuzz since 1998. ResearchBuzz is simply the best site for the topics she posts. As librarians all of our primary tools are all backed by databases of some type now, and following ResearchBuzz means knowing what's changing in that world.

Stephen's Lighthouse. You might think a man that's on the road nonstop wouldn't have the time to write much. Mr. Abram must have some long lay overs, because he's proven to be a dedicated blogger. As VP Of Innovation At SirsiDynix he's able to add some interesting insights to his posts.

Appendices

Core Values of Librarianship

American Library Association (2004)

The foundation of modern librarianship rests on an essential set of core values that define, inform, and guide our professional practice. These values reflect the history and ongoing development of the profession and have been advanced, expanded, and refined by numerous policy statements of the American Library Association. Among these are:

1. Access
2. Confidentiality/Privacy
3. Democracy
4. Diversity
5. Education and Lifelong Learning
6. Intellectual Freedom
7. Preservation
8. The Public Good
9. Professionalism
10. Service
11. Social Responsibility

It would be difficult, if not impossible, to express our values more eloquently than ALA already has in the Freedom to Read statement, the Library Bill of Rights, the ALA Mission Statement, Libraries: An American Value, and other documents. These policies have been carefully thought out, articulated, debated, and approved by the ALA Council. They are interpreted, revised, or expanded when necessary. Over time, the values embodied in these policies have been embraced by the majority of librarians as the foundations of their practice.

EXCERPTS FROM ALA POLICY

Following are some representative excerpts from ALA policy expressing the values listed above. These selections are direct quotes from the ALA Policy Manual. Please note that many of these statements express the interrelationship of these values.

A more extensive index of ALA policies is available on the ALA Web site.

ACCESS

All information resources that are provided directly or indirectly by the library, regardless of technology, format, or methods of delivery, should be readily, equally, and equitably accessible to all library users. ALA Policy Manual 53.1.14 (Free Access to Information)

CONFIDENTIALITY/PRIVACY

Protecting user privacy and confidentiality is necessary for intellectual freedom and fundamental to the ethics and practice of librarianship. ALA Policy Manual 53.1.16 (Library Bill of Rights)

DEMOCRACY

A democracy presupposes an informed citizenry. The First Amendment mandates the right of all persons to free expression, and the corollary right to receive the constitutionally protected expression of others. The publicly supported library provides free and equal access to information for all people of the community the library serves. Interpretations of the Library Bill of Rights, Economic Barriers to Information Access

DIVERSITY

We value our nation's diversity and strive to reflect that diversity by providing a full spectrum of resources and services to the communities we serve. ALA Policy Manual 53.8 (Libraries: An American Value)

EDUCATION AND LIFELONG LEARNING

ALA promotes the creation, maintenance, and enhancement of a learning society, encouraging its members to work with educators, government officials, and organizations in coalitions to initiate and support comprehensive efforts to ensure that school, public, academic, and special libraries in every community cooperate to provide lifelong learning services to all. ALA Policy Manual 1.1 (Mission, Priority Areas, Goals)

INTELLECTUAL FREEDOM

We uphold the principles of intellectual freedom and resist all efforts to censor library resources. ALA Policy Manual, 54.16 (ALA Code of Ethics, Article II)

THE PUBLIC GOOD

ALA reaffirms the following fundamental values of libraries in the context of discussing outsourcing and privatization of library services. These values include that libraries are an essential public good and are fundamental institutions in democratic societies. 1998–99 CD#24.1, Motion #1

PRESERVATION

The Association supports the preservation of information published in all media and formats. The association affirms that the preservation of information resources is central to libraries and librarianship. ALA Policy Manual 52.2.1 (Preservation Policy)

PROFESSIONALISM

The American Library Association supports the provision of library services by professionally qualified personnel who have been educated in graduate programs within institutions of higher education. It is of vital importance that there be professional education available to meet the social needs and goals of library services. ALA Policy Manual 56.1 (Graduate Programs in Library Education)

SERVICE

We provide the highest level of service to all library users . . . We strive for excellence in the profession by maintaining and enhancing our own knowledge and skills, by encouraging the professional development of co-workers, and by fostering the aspirations of potential members of the profession. ALA Policy Manual 54.16 (Statement of Professional Ethics)

SOCIAL RESPONSIBILITY

ALA recognizes its broad social responsibilities. The broad social responsibilities of the American Library Association are defined in terms of the contribution that librarianship can make in ameliorating or solving the critical problems of society; support for efforts to help inform and educate the people of the United States on these problems and to encourage them to examine the many views on and the facts regarding each problem; and the willingness of ALA to take a position on current critical issues with the relationship to libraries and library service set forth in the position statement. ALA Policy Manual, 1.1 (Mission, Priority Areas, Goals)

B

Code of Ethics

American Library Association (1995)

As members of the American Library Association, we recognize the importance of codifying and making known to the profession and to the general public the ethical principles that guide the work of librarians, other professionals providing information services, library trustees, and library staff.

Ethical dilemmas occur when values are in conflict. The American Library Association Code of Ethics states the values to which we are committed and embodies the ethical responsibilities of the profession in this changing information environment.

We significantly influence or control the selection, organization, preservation, and dissemination of information. In a political system grounded in an informed citizenry, we are members of a profession explicitly committed to intellectual freedom and the freedom of access to information. We have a special obligation to ensure the free flow of information and ideas to present and future generations.

The principles of this Code are expressed in broad statements to guide ethical decision making. These statements provide a framework; they cannot and do not dictate conduct to cover particular situations.

  I. We provide the highest level of service to all library users through appropriate and usefully organized resources; equitable service policies; equitable access; and accurate, unbiased, and courteous responses to all requests.

 II. We uphold the principles of intellectual freedom and resist all efforts to censor library resources.

III. We protect each library user's right to privacy and confidentiality with respect to information sought or received and resources consulted, borrowed, acquired, or transmitted.

IV. We recognize and respect intellectual property rights.

V. We treat co-workers and other colleagues with respect, fairness, and good faith, and advocate conditions of employment that safeguard the rights and welfare of all employees of our institutions.

VI. We do not advance private interests at the expense of library users, colleagues, or our employing institutions.

VII. We distinguish between our personal convictions and professional duties and do not allow our personal beliefs to interfere with fair representation of the aims of our institutions or the provision of access to their information resources.

VIII. We strive for excellence in the profession by maintaining and enhancing our own knowledge and skills, by encouraging the professional development of co-workers, and by fostering the aspirations of potential members of the profession.

Library Bill of Rights

American Library Association (adopted 1948,
most recently revised 1980)

The American Library Association affirms that all libraries are forums for information and ideas, and that the following basic policies should guide their services.

    I. Books and other library resources should be provided for the interest, information, and enlightenment of all people of the community the library serves. Materials should not be excluded because of the origin, background, or views of those contributing to their creation.

    II. Libraries should provide materials and information presenting all points of view on current and historical issues. Materials should not be proscribed or removed because of partisan or doctrinal disapproval.

    III. Libraries should challenge censorship in the fulfillment of their responsibility to provide information and enlightenment.

    IV. Libraries should cooperate with all persons and groups concerned with resisting abridgment of free expression and free access to ideas.

    V. A person's right to use a library should not be denied or abridged because of origin, age, background, or views.

    VI. Libraries which make exhibit spaces and meeting rooms available to the public they serve should make such facilities available on an equitable basis, regardless of the beliefs or affiliations of individuals or groups requesting their use.

Adopted 1948; amended 1961, amended 1967, amended, 1980, inclusion of "age" reaffirmed 1996. A history of the Library Bill of Rights is found in the latest edition of the Association's *Intellectual Freedom Manual.*

INTERPRETATIONS OF THE LIBRARY BILL OF RIGHTS

Although the Articles of the Library Bill of Rights are unambiguous statements of basic principles that should govern the service of all libraries, questions do arise concerning application of these principles to specific library practices.

Following are those documents designated by the American Library Association's Intellectual Freedom Committee as Interpretations of the Library Bill of Rights and background statements detailing the philosophy and history of each.

For convenience and easy reference, the documents are presented in alphabetical order. These documents are policies of the American Library Association, having been adopted by the ALA Council.

Access for Children and Young Adults to Nonprint Materials

Library collections of nonprint materials raise a number of intellectual freedom issues, especially regarding minors. Article V of the Library Bill of Rights states, "A person's right to use a library should not be denied or abridged because of origin, age, background, or views."

Access to Electronic Information, Services, and Networks

Freedom of expression is an inalienable human right and the foundation for self-government. Freedom of expression encompasses the freedom of speech and the corollary right to receive information. Libraries and librarians protect and promote these rights by selecting, producing, providing access to, identifying, retrieving, organizing, providing instruction in the use of, and preserving recorded expression regardless of the format or technology. (Note: Following the initial adoption by the ALA Council of Access to Electronic Information, Services and Networks: An Interpretation of the Library Bill of Rights in January, 1996, the ALA Intellectual Freedom Committee produced a sample set of questions and answers to clarify the this Interpretation's implications and applications.)

Access to Library Resources and Services Regardless of Sex, Gender Identity, or Sexual Orientation

The American Library Association stringently and unequivocally maintains that libraries and librarians have an obligation to resist efforts that systematically exclude materials dealing with any subject matter, including sex, gender identity, or sexual orientation.

Access to Resources and Services in the School Library Media Program

The school library media program plays a unique role in promoting intellectual freedom. It serves as a point of voluntary access to information and ideas and as a learning laboratory for students as they acquire critical thinking and problem-solving skills needed in a pluralistic society. Although the educational level and program of the school necessarily shapes the resources and services of a school library media program, the principles of the Library Bill of Rights apply equally to all libraries, including school library media programs.

Challenged Materials

The American Library Association declares as a matter of firm principle that it is the responsibility of every library to have a clearly defined materials selection policy in written form that reflects the Library Bill of Rights, and that is approved by the appropriate governing authority.

Diversity in Collection Development

Intellectual freedom, the essence of equitable library services, provides for free access to all expressions of ideas through which any and all sides of a question, cause, or movement may be explored. Toleration is meaningless without tolerance for what some may consider detestable. Librarians cannot justly permit their own preferences to limit their degree of tolerance in collection development, because freedom is indivisible.

Economic Barriers to Information Access

A democracy presupposes an informed citizenry. The First Amendment mandates the right of all persons to free expression, and the corollary right to receive the constitutionally protected expression of others. The publicly supported library provides free, equal, and equitable access to information for all people of the community the library serves. While the roles, goals, and objectives of publicly supported libraries may differ, they share this common mission.

Evaluating Library Collections

The continuous review of library materials is necessary as a means of maintaining an active library collection of current interest to users. In the process, materials may be added and physically deteriorated or obsolete materials may be replaced or removed in accordance with the collection maintenance policy of a given library and the needs of the community it serves. Continued evaluation is closely related to the goals and responsibilities of all libraries and is a valuable tool of collection development. This procedure is not to be used as a convenient means to remove materials presumed to be controversial or disapproved of by segments of the community.

Exhibit Spaces and Bulletin Boards

Libraries often provide exhibit spaces and bulletin boards. The uses made of these spaces should conform to the Library Bill of Rights: Article I states, "Materials should not be excluded because of the origin, background, or views of those contributing to their creation." Article II states, "Materials should not be proscribed or removed because of partisan or doctrinal disapproval." Article VI maintains that exhibit space should be made available "on an equitable basis, regardless of the beliefs or affiliations of individuals or groups requesting their use."

Expurgation of Library Materials

Expurgating library materials is a violation of the Library Bill of Rights. Expurgation as defined by this interpretation includes any deletion, excision, alteration, editing, or obliteration of any part(s) of books or other library resources by the library, its agent, or its parent institution (if any).

Free Access to Libraries for Minors

Library policies and procedures that effectively deny minors equal and equitable access to all library resources available to other users violate the Library Bill of Rights. The American Library Association opposes all attempts to restrict access to library services, materials, and facilities based on the age of library users.

Intellectual Freedom Principles for Academic Libraries

A strong intellectual freedom perspective is critical to the development of academic library collections and services that dispassionately meet the education and research needs of a college or university community. The purpose of this statement is to outline how and where intellectual freedom principles fit into an academic library setting, thereby raising consciousness of the intellectual freedom context within which academic librarians work.

Labels and Rating Systems

Libraries do not advocate the ideas found in their collections or in resources accessible through the library. The presence of books and other resources in a library does not indicate endorsement of their contents by the library. Likewise, the ability for library users to access electronic information using library computers does not indicate endorsement or approval of that information by the library. (Note: The ALA Intellectual Freedom Committee developed a Q&A to work in conjunction with Labels and Rating Systems, adopted July 13, 1951, by the ALA Council; amended June 25, 1971; July 1, 1981; June 26, 1990; January 19, 2005. Like Questions and Answers on Privacy and Confidentiality and Questions and Answers: Access to Electronic Information, Services, and Networks, this document will be revised as appropriate.)

Library-Initiated Programs as a Resource

Library-initiated programs support the mission of the library by providing users with additional opportunities for information, education, and recreation.

Meeting Rooms

Many libraries provide meeting rooms for individuals and groups as part of a program of service. Article VI of the Library Bill of Rights states that such facilities should be made available to the public served by the given library "on an equitable basis, regardless of the beliefs or affiliations of individuals or groups requesting their use."

Privacy

Privacy is essential to the exercise of free speech, free thought, and free association. (Note: There is also a Q&A to complement Privacy: An Interpretation of the Library Bill of Rights.)

Restricted Access to Library Materials

Libraries are a traditional forum for the open exchange of information. Attempts to restrict access to library materials violate the basic tenets of the Library Bill of Rights.

The Universal Right to Free Expression

Freedom of expression is an inalienable human right and the foundation for self-government. Freedom of expression encompasses the freedoms of speech, press, religion, assembly, and association, and the corollary right to receive information.

Freedom to Read Statement

American Library Association and the Association of American Publishers (adopted 1953, most recently revised 2004)

The freedom to read is essential to our democracy. It is continuously under attack. Private groups and public authorities in various parts of the country are working to remove or limit access to reading materials, to censor content in schools, to label "controversial" views, to distribute lists of "objectionable" books or authors, and to purge libraries. These actions apparently rise from a view that our national tradition of free expression is no longer valid; that censorship and suppression are needed to counter threats to safety or national security, as well as to avoid the subversion of politics and the corruption of morals. We, as individuals devoted to reading and as librarians and publishers responsible for disseminating ideas, wish to assert the public interest in the preservation of the freedom to read.

Most attempts at suppression rest on a denial of the fundamental premise of democracy: that the ordinary individual, by exercising critical judgment, will select the good and reject the bad. We trust Americans to recognize propaganda and misinformation, and to make their own decisions about what they read and believe. We do not believe they are prepared to sacrifice their heritage of a free press in order to be "protected" against what others think may be bad for them. We believe they still favor free enterprise in ideas and expression.

These efforts at suppression are related to a larger pattern of pressures being brought against education, the press, art and images, films, broadcast media, and the Internet. The problem is not only one of actual censorship. The shadow of fear cast by these pressures leads, we suspect, to an even larger voluntary curtailment of expression by those who seek to avoid controversy or unwelcome scrutiny by government officials.

Such pressure toward conformity is perhaps natural in a time of accelerated change. And yet suppression is never more dangerous than in such a time of social tension. Freedom has given the United States the elasticity to endure strain. Freedom keeps open the path of novel and creative solutions and enables change to come by choice. Every silencing of a heresy, every enforcement of an orthodoxy, diminishes the toughness and resilience of our society and leaves it the less able to deal with controversy and difference.

Now as always in our history, reading is among our greatest freedoms. The freedom to read and write is almost the only means for making generally available ideas or manners of expression that can initially command only a small audience. The written word is the natural medium for the new idea and the untried voice from which come the original contributions to social growth. It is essential to the extended discussion that serious thought requires, and to the accumulation of knowledge and ideas into organized collections.

We believe that free communication is essential to the preservation of a free society and a creative culture. We believe that these pressures toward conformity present the danger of limiting the range and variety of inquiry and expression on which our democracy and our culture depend. We believe that every American community must jealously guard the freedom to publish and to circulate, in order to preserve its own freedom to read. We believe that publishers and librarians have a profound responsibility to give validity to that freedom to read by making it possible for the readers to choose freely from a variety of offerings.

The freedom to read is guaranteed by the Constitution. Those with faith in free people will stand firm on these constitutional guarantees of essential rights and will exercise the responsibilities that accompany these rights.

We therefore affirm these propositions:

1. It is in the public interest for publishers and librarians to make available the widest diversity of views and expressions, including those that are unorthodox, unpopular, or considered dangerous by the majority.

Creative thought is by definition new, and what is new is different. The bearer of every new thought is a rebel until that idea is refined and tested. Totalitarian systems attempt to maintain themselves in power by the ruthless suppression of any concept that challenges the established orthodoxy. The power of a democratic system to adapt to change is vastly strengthened by the freedom of its citizens to choose widely from among conflicting opinions offered freely to them. To stifle every nonconformist idea at birth would mark the end of the democratic process. Furthermore, only through the constant activity of weighing and selecting can the democratic mind attain the strength demanded by times like these. We need to know not only what we believe but why we believe it.

2. Publishers, librarians, and booksellers do not need to endorse every idea or presentation they make available. It would conflict with the public interest for them to establish their own political, moral, or aesthetic views as a standard for determining what should be published or circulated.

Publishers and librarians serve the educational process by helping to make available knowledge and ideas required for the growth of the mind and the increase of learning. They do not foster education by imposing as mentors the patterns of their own thought. The people should have the freedom to read and consider a broader range of ideas than those that may be held by any single librarian or publisher or government or church. It is wrong that what one can read should be confined to what another thinks proper.

3. It is contrary to the public interest for publishers or librarians to bar access to writings on the basis of the personal history or political affiliations of the author. No art or literature can flourish if it is to be measured by the political views or private lives of its creators. No society of free people can flourish that draws up lists of writers to whom it will not listen, whatever they may have to say.

4. There is no place in our society for efforts to coerce the taste of others, to confine adults to the reading matter deemed suitable for adolescents, or to inhibit the efforts of writers to achieve artistic expression.

To some, much of modern expression is shocking. But is not much of life itself shocking? We cut off literature at the source if we prevent writers from dealing with the stuff of life. Parents and teachers have a responsibility to prepare the young to meet the diversity of experiences in life to which they will be exposed, as they have a responsibility to help them learn to think critically for themselves. These are affirmative responsibilities, not to be discharged simply by preventing them from reading works for which they are not yet prepared. In these matters values differ, and values cannot be legislated; nor can machinery be devised that will suit the demands of one group without limiting the freedom of others.

5. It is not in the public interest to force a reader to accept the prejudgment of a label characterizing any expression or its author as subversive or dangerous.

The ideal of labeling presupposes the existence of individuals or groups with wisdom to determine by authority what is good or bad for others. It presupposes that individuals must be directed in making up their minds about the ideas they examine. But Americans do not need others to do their thinking for them.

6. It is the responsibility of publishers and librarians, as guardians of the people's freedom to read, to contest encroachments upon that freedom by individuals or groups seeking to impose their own standards or tastes upon the community at large; and by the government whenever it seeks to reduce or deny public access to public information.

It is inevitable in the give and take of the democratic process that the political, the moral, or the aesthetic concepts of an individual or group will occasionally collide with those of another individual or group. In a free society individuals are free to determine for themselves what they wish to read, and each group is free to determine what it will recommend to its freely associated members. But no group has the right to take the law into its own hands, and to impose its own concept of politics or morality upon other members of a democratic society. Freedom is no freedom if it is accorded only to the accepted and the inoffensive. Further, democratic societies are more safe, free, and creative when the free flow of public information is not restricted by governmental prerogative or self-censorship.

7. It is the responsibility of publishers and librarians to give full meaning to the freedom to read by providing books that enrich the quality and diversity of thought and expression. By the exercise of this affirmative responsibility, they can demonstrate that the answer to a "bad" book is a good one, the answer to a "bad" idea is a good one.

8. The freedom to read is of little consequence when the reader cannot obtain matter fit for that reader's purpose. What is needed is not only the absence of restraint, but the positive provision of opportunity for the people to read the best that has been thought and said. Books are the major channel by which the intellectual inheritance is handed down, and the principal means of its testing and growth. The defense of the freedom to read requires of all publishers and librarians the utmost of their faculties, and deserves of all Americans the fullest of their support.

We state these propositions neither lightly nor as easy generalizations. We here stake out a lofty claim for the value of the written word. We do so because we believe that it is possessed of enormous variety and usefulness, worthy of cherishing and keeping free. We realize that the application of these propositions may mean the dissemination of ideas and manners of expression that are repugnant to many persons. We do not state these propositions in the comfortable belief that what people read is unimportant. We believe rather that what people read is deeply important; that ideas can be dangerous; but that the suppression of ideas is fatal to a democratic society. Freedom itself is a dangerous way of life, but it is ours.

This statement was originally issued in May of 1953 by the Westchester Conference of the American Library Association and the American Book Publishers Council, which in 1970 consolidated with the American Educational Publishers Institute to become the Association of American Publishers.

Adopted 1953 by the ALA and the AAP Freedom to Read Committee; amended 1972, 1991, 2000, and 2004.

A joint statement by:
American Library Association
Association of American Publishers

Subsequently endorsed by:
American Booksellers Foundation for Free Expression
The Association of American University Presses, Inc.
The Children's Book Council
Freedom to Read Foundation
National Association of College Stores
National Coalition Against Censorship
National Council of Teachers of English
The Thomas Jefferson Center for the Protection of Free Expression

Student's Bill of Information Rights

Association for Teacher-Librarianship in Canada (1995)

Our students face an information-rich future in which change will be one of the few constants of their life experience. Their ability to adapt and fulfill their individual potentials will require them to be life-long learners and independent decision-makers.

We believe that all students should have the opportunity to:

- ✓ master the skills needed to access information in print, non-print and electronic sources;
- ✓ understand and master effective research and reporting skills;
- ✓ develop the ability to evaluate, extract, synthesize and utilize information from a variety of sources and media;
- ✓ utilize data and information to expand their own knowledge base;
- ✓ explore the creative use of information;
- ✓ develop an understanding of our Canadian cultural heritage and history, as well as cultures and histories of other societies;
- ✓ enhance their own self knowledge through developing a love of reading;
- ✓ explore the values and beliefs of others by reading world literature;
- ✓ think critically, and make decisions based on personal needs and values as well as upon factual evidence; and
- ✓ actively participate in decisions about their own learning.

Information is a vital component in the development of critical thought and independent decision-making and, consequently, access to the ever-increasing body of available information is vital to the development of students' potentials.

We believe that all students should have the right to:

✓ access a wide range of print, non-print and electronic learning
resources at an appropriate level;

✓ explore materials expressing a variety of opinions and perspectives;
and

✓ freely choose reading, viewing and listening materials for recreational
and study purposes.

F

Libraries: An American Value

American Library Association (1999)

Libraries in America are cornerstones of the communities they serve. Free access to the books, ideas, resources, and information in America's libraries is imperative for education, employment, enjoyment, and self-government.

Libraries are a legacy to each generation, offering the heritage of the past and the promise of the future. To ensure that libraries flourish and have the freedom to promote and protect the public good in the 21st century, we believe certain principles must be guaranteed.

To that end, we affirm this contract with the people we serve:

- We defend the constitutional rights of all individuals, including children and teenagers, to use the library's resources and services;
- We value our nation's diversity and strive to reflect that diversity by providing a full spectrum of resources and services to the communities we serve;
- We affirm the responsibility and the right of all parents and guardians to guide their own children's use of the library and its resources and services;
- We connect people and ideas by helping each person select from and effectively use the library's resources;
- We protect each individual's privacy and confidentiality in the use of library resources and services;
- We protect the rights of individuals to express their opinions about library resources and services;
- We celebrate and preserve our democratic society by making available the widest possible range of viewpoints, opinions and ideas, so that all individuals have the opportunity to become lifelong learners—informed, literate, educated, and culturally enriched.

Change is constant, but these principles transcend change and endure in a dynamic technological, social, and political environment.

By embracing these principles, libraries in the United States can contribute to a future that values and protects freedom of speech in a world that celebrates both our similarities and our differences, respects individuals and their beliefs, and holds all persons truly equal and free.

Appendix G

Sample Policies: National Information Services and Responsibilities

American Library Association

Policy Manual Excerpt

50. NATIONAL INFORMATION SERVICES AND RESPONSIBILITIES

50.1 Support for "Goals for Action" of the National Commission on Libraries and Information Science
The American Library Association concurs in concepts and recommendations contained in "Goals for Action," a report of the National Commission on Libraries and Information Science, and commits the Association and its units to maximum cooperation with the National Commission in implementation and further development of "Goals for Action."

50.2 Equal Rights Amendment Legislation
The American Library Association supports the equality of women both in the profession and in society at large. To this end the Association (a) supports implementation of the national plan of action as amended at the National Women's Conference in Houston in November 1977; (b) supports through employment practices policy the equal treatment of women in the work place; (c) supports the Equal Rights Amendment legislation; (d) supports the elimination of sex-stereotyping terminology through avoiding the use of such terminology in ALA publications and (e) supports adherence to affirmative action policies through its support of the enforcement of such policies in its library school accreditation standards and guidelines.

50.3 Free Access to Information

The American Library Association asserts that the charging of fees and levies for information services, including those services utilizing the latest information technology, is discriminatory in publicly supported institutions providing library and information services.

The American Library Association shall seek to make it possible for library and information service agencies which receive their major support from public funds to provide service to all people without additional fees and to utilize the latest technological developments to insure the best possible access to information, and ALA will actively promote its position on equal access to information.

50.4 Bibliographic Data Bases

The American Library Association supports open access to information, including the information contained in online data bases, and encourages data base providers and other organizations to minimize restrictions placed on their members' use of bibliographic records maintained in their online data bases.

50.5 Funding for Community Access Cable Programming

Libraries should work cooperatively with other groups in promoting the widest possible access to communications and information, including community access cablecasting. The American Library Association, in order to support stable sources of funding for community access channels, endorses the following principles articulated by Open Channel and Publicable, two organizations with knowledge and experience in community access cablecasting:

1. That a portion of cable revenues be designated to provide financial and technical assistance for community access programming.
2. That this support be sufficient to promote genuine access.
3. That this assistance increase as the cable operator's revenue increases.
4. That the specific structures, funding formulas, and monitoring arrangements be left to the local community.

50.6 Literacy

50.6.1 Literacy and State Library Agencies

The American Library Association supports the achievement of national literacy through educational activities utilizing the historical and cultural experience of libraries and librarians.

The American Library Association urges state library agencies to address the problems of illiteracy and give high priority to solutions in their short- and long-range plans for library development and the use of federal and state funds.

50.6.2 Literacy and the Role of Libraries

The American Library Association reaffirms and supports the principle that lifelong literacy is a basic right for all individuals in our society and is essential to the welfare of the nation. ALA advocates the achievement of national literacy through educational activities utilizing the historical and cultural experiences of libraries and librarians. ALA confirms that libraries of all types, as appropriate to their mission, have the responsibility to make literacy a high priority in planning and budgeting for library services. As pioneer and equal partners in the national literacy movement, libraries will continue to take a strong leadership role and must join with other literacy providers to urge local, state, federal, and private agencies to promote active development of literacy on a policy level and to support funding of the literacy services in libraries.

50.7 Nominations to the Posts of Librarian of Congress and of Archivist of the United States

The privilege of reviewing nominations made by the President of the United States to the highest government posts in their respective professions is one accorded the major national professional organizations. The American Library Association strongly supports the extension of a similar privilege to ALA, enabling it to review the recommendations and nominations for the positions of Librarian of Congress and of Archivist of the United States whenever new appointments to those posts are under consideration.

50.8 Financing of Libraries

In order to assist libraries facing severe economic problems resulting from inflation, the American Library Association will engage in a broad media information program to make the public aware of the benefits to be gained through tax support of libraries, and will simultaneously explore public financing alternatives for libraries facing financial problems.

50.9 NCLIS Membership

The American Library Association supports the appointment of members to the National Commission on Libraries and Information Science in an expeditious manner with appointees who fully meet the requirements of the statute.

50.10 Disarmament and Conflict Solving Information in Libraries

Libraries should make available and readily accessible information on possibilities for disarmament and alternative ways of solving conflicts.

50.11 Nuclear Freeze, the Arms Race and National Security

The American Library Association supports the concept of a nuclear freeze on the development and deployment of nuclear weapons. It urges libraries to establish balanced up-to-date collections of library materials on national security in the nuclear age, on nuclear arms, and the movements for disarmament and a nuclear moratorium. The Association furthermore urges libraries to stimulate public interest in these issues and make information available about various courses of action concerned individuals may take.

50.12 Environmental Issues

The American Library Association urges librarians and library governing boards to collect and provide information on the condition of our Earth, its air, ground, water, and living organisms from all available sources.

50.13 National Library Symbol
The American Library Association endorses the symbol recommended by the ALA President's Task Force and promotes its use.

50.14 Trade Publishers Discounts
The American Library Association supports the concept of equal discounts on equal volume orders for all buyers.

Retention of Library Usage Records

American Library Association (2006)

WHEREAS, "Protecting user privacy and confidentiality is necessary for intellectual freedom and fundamental to the ethics and practice of librarianship" (ALA Policy Manual, 53.1.16; Privacy: An Interpretation of the Library Bill of Rights); and

WHEREAS, Library usage records containing personally identifiable information (PII) are maintained for the sole purpose of effectively managing library resources; and

WHEREAS, The confidentiality of library usage records is protected by law in all fifty states and in the District of Columbia (see http://www.ala.org/oif/stateprivacylaws); and

WHEREAS, "The government's interest in library use represents a dangerous and fallacious equation of what a person reads with what that person believes or how that person is likely to behave" (ALA Policy Manual, 52.4.2; Confidentiality of Personally Identifiable Information About Library Users); and

WHEREAS, The American Library Association strongly recommends the adoption of policies recognizing "circulation records and other records identifying the names of library users with specific materials to be confidential" (ALA Policy Manual, 52.4; Confidentiality of Library Records); now, therefore, be it

RESOLVED, That the American Library Association urges all libraries to:

- Limit the degree to which personally identifiable information is collected, monitored, disclosed, and distributed; and
- Avoid creating unnecessary records; and
- Limit access to personally identifiable information to staff performing authorized functions; and
- Dispose of library usage records containing personally identifiable information unless they are needed for the efficient and lawful

operation of the library, including, but not limited to data-related logs, digital records, vendor-collected data, and system backups; and

- Ensure that the library work with its organization's information technology unit to ensure that library usage records processed or held by the IT unit are treated in accordance with library records policies; and

- Ensure that those records that must be retained are secure; and

- Avoid library practices and procedures that place personally identifiable information on public view; and

- Assure that vendor agreements guarantee library control of all data and records; and

- Conduct an annual privacy audit to ensure that information processing procedures meet privacy requirements by examining how information about library users and employees is collected, stored, shared, used, and destroyed; and, be it further

RESOLVED, That the American Library Association urges all libraries to adopt or update a privacy policy protecting users' personally identifiable information, communicating to library users how their information is used, and explaining the limited circumstances under which personally identifiable information could be disclosed; and, be it further

RESOLVED, That the American Library Association urges members of the library community to advocate that records retention laws and regulations limit retention of library usage records containing personally identifiable information to the time needed for efficient operation of the library.

School Library Position Statements

American Association of School Librarians

Different library environments (academic, public, school, special) will require specific documents to advance the role of the library or information agency in that particular setting. These position statement titles are illustrative only of the policies developed by one association for the K–12 sector. Policy statements are generally available on the Web site of the sponsoring association (see Appendix L for a directory of the primary associations.)

- On the Strengthening Kids' Interest in Learning and Libraries (SKILLs) Act
- On Instructional Classification
- Support for National Board of Professional Teaching Standards Certification
- Access to Resources and Services in the School Library Media Program: An Interpretation of the Library Bill of Rights
- Appropriate Staffing for School Library Media Centers
- Confidentiality of Library Records
- Flexible Scheduling
- Preparation of School Library Media Specialist
- Resource Based Instruction: Role of the School Library Media Specialist in Reading Development
- Role of the School Library Media Program
- Role of the Library Media Specialist in Outcomes-Based Education
- Role of the School Library Media Specialist in Site-Based Management
- School Library Media Supervisor
- Value of Independent Reading in the School Library Media Program
- Value of Library Media Programs in Education

Each policy statement is available in full text on the ALA/American Association of School Librarians Web site.

Competencies for Information Professionals of the Twenty-first Century

Special Libraries Association (1997, revised 2003)

Prepared for the Special Libraries Association Board of Directors by the Special Committee on Competencies for Special Librarians: Eileen Abels, Rebecca Jones, John Latham, Dee Magnoni, Joanne Gard Marshall

What Is an *Information Professional*?

An Information Professional ("IP") strategically uses information in his/her job to advance the mission of the organization. The IP accomplishes this through the development, deployment, and management of information resources and services. The IP harnesses technology as a critical tool to accomplish goals. IPs include, but are not limited to librarians, knowledge managers, chief information officers, web developers, information brokers, and consultants.

What Are *Information Organizations*?

Information organizations are defined as those entities that deliver information-based solutions to a given market. Some commonly used names for these organizations include libraries, information centers, competitive intelligence units, intranet departments, knowledge resource centers, content management organizations, and others.

Background

The Special Libraries Association (SLA), an organization of dynamic and change-oriented IPs, has long been interested in the knowledge requirements of the field. The Association's members have explored and shared their vision of the competencies and skills required for specialized information management in many forums over the years. The first edition of the competencies document published in 1997 attempted to synthesize and build on earlier work in the light of ongoing social, technological and workplace change. This document has been widely used by IPs, as well as educators, employers, and current and prospective students. The 1997 edition may be found at: http://www.sla.org/content/learn/comp2003/97comp.cfm.

In preparation for the 2003 revision, the committee discussed the latest trends and reviewed other competency documents in peer industries. SLA's revised research statement, Putting OUR Knowledge to Work, with its emphasis on evidence-based practice, was also found to be highly relevant. Evidence-based practice involves consciously and consistently making professional-level decisions that are based on the strongest evidence from research and best practice about what would work best for our clients. The research statement is recommended as a companion document to the competencies. The SLA research statement may be found at www.sla.org/researchstatement/

In the information and knowledge age, specialists in information management are essential—they provide the competitive edge for the knowledge-based organization by responding with a sense of urgency to critical information needs. Information, both internally and externally produced, is the lifeblood of the knowledge-based organization and essential for innovation and continuing learning. Information sharing is also essential for any organization that is attempting to understand and manage its intellectual capital, often in a global context. IPs play a unique role in gathering, organizing and coordinating access to the best available information sources for the organization as a whole. They are also leaders in devising and implementing standards for the ethical and appropriate use of information.

If IPs did not exist they would be reinvented as organizations struggle to gain control over ever-increasing amounts of information in multiple storage formats. The astounding growth of the Internet and the rise of electronic communications and storage media generally have transformed our work and personal lives. Information overload is a growing problem and IPs are needed more than ever to quality filter and provide needed information in an actionable form. In order to fulfil their purpose, IPs require two types of competencies:

Professional Competencies relate to the practitioner's knowledge of information resources, access, technology and management, and the ability to use this knowledge as a basis for providing the highest quality information services. There are four major competencies, each augmented with specific skills:

   A. Managing Information Organizations
   B. Managing Information Resources
   C. Managing Information Services
   D. Applying Information Tools and Technologies

Applied scenarios illustrate many of the myriad roles and responsibilities that IPs perform in organizations of all types.

Personal Competencies represent a set of attitudes, skills and values that enable practitioners to work effectively and contribute positively to their organizations, clients and profession. These competencies range from being strong communicators, to demonstrating the value-add of their contributions, to remaining flexible and positive in an ever-changing environment.

Core Competencies anchor the professional and personal competencies. These two core competencies are absolutely essential for every information professional. As educated professionals, IPs understand the value of developing and sharing their knowledge; this is accomplished through association networks and by conducting and sharing research at conferences, in publications and in collaborative arrangements of all kinds. IPs also acknowledge and adhere to the ethics of the profession. The importance of these two cardinal core competencies cannot be emphasized enough; these are paramount to the value and viability of the profession.

The competencies outlined in this document are a set of tools for professional growth, recruitment, and assessment. Specific jobs will require specific sets of competencies at various skill levels. We encourage you to use these competencies to create roadmaps of growth and development for yourself, your colleagues and your organizations.

Core Competencies

    I. Information professionals contribute to the knowledge base of the profession by sharing best practices and experiences, and continue to learn about information products, services, and management practices throughout the life of his/her career.

   II. Information professionals commit to professional excellence and ethics, and to the values and principles of the profession.

Professional Competencies

A. Managing Information Organizations

Information professionals manage information organizations ranging in size from one employee to several hundred employees. These organizations may be in any environment from corporate, education, public, government, to nonprofit. Information professionals excel at managing these organizations whose offerings are intangible, whose markets are constantly changing and in which both high-tech and high-touch are vitally important in achieving organizational success.

A.1 Aligns the information organization with, and is supportive of, the strategic directions of the parent organization or of key client groups through partnerships with key stakeholders and suppliers.

A.2 Assesses and communicates the value of the information organization, including information services, products and policies to senior management, key stakeholders and client groups.

A.3 Establishes effective management, operational and financial management processes and exercises sound business and financial judgments in making decisions that balance operational and strategic considerations.
A.4 Contributes effectively to senior management strategies and decisions regarding information applications, tools and technologies, and policies for the organization.
A.5 Builds and leads an effective information services team and champions the professional and personal development of people working within the information organization.
A.6 Markets information services and products, both formally and informally, through web and physical communication collateral, presentations, publications and conversations.
A.7 Gathers the best available evidence to support decisions about the development of new service and products, the modification of current services or the elimination of services to continually improve the array of information services offered.
A.8 Advises the organization on copyright and intellectual property issues and compliance.

Applied Scenarios

- Develops strategic and business plans that support the host organization's goals and that establish long-term stretch targets and near-term priorities for the information organization.

- Inspires a shared vision and creates a compelling mission for the organization that energizes people to work towards achieving its strategies and delighting its clients and key stakeholders.

- Conducts market research of the information behaviors and problems of current and potential client groups to identify concepts for new or enhanced information solutions for these groups. Transforms these concepts into specialized information products and services.

- Sets clear performance expectations linked to organizational strategies and priorities.

- Provides professional development opportunities for staff members.

- Calculates a return on investment for information services and products or develops other measurable contributions of the information organization.

- Clearly demonstrates the value-add of the information organization to clients and key stakeholders through communications with top management.

B. *Managing Information Resources*
Information professionals have expertise in total management of information resources, including identifying, selecting, evaluating, securing and providing access to pertinent information resources. These resources may be in any media or format. Information professionals recognize the importance of people as a key information resource.

B.1 Manages the full life cycle of information from its creation or acquisition through its destruction. This includes organizing, categorizing, cataloguing, classifying, disseminating; creating and managing taxonomies, intranet and extranet content, thesauri etc.
B.2 Builds a dynamic collection of information resources based on a deep understanding of clients' information needs and their learning, work and/or business processes.
B.3 Demonstrates expert knowledge of the content and format of information resources, including the ability to critically evaluate, select and filter them.
B.4 Provides access to the best available externally published and internally created information resources and deploys content throughout the organization using a suite of information access tools.
B.5 Negotiates the purchase and licensing of needed information products and services.
B.6 Develops information policies for the organization regarding externally published and internally created information resources and advises on the implementation of these policies.

Applied Scenarios

- IPs are experts in identifying the best information resources, comparing free versus fee resources to determine if value-added features warrant the cost, examining features of resources available from multiple vendors, and providing access to those resources for the organization by negotiating cost-effective contracts with vendors.

- IPs select and secure information resources that are appropriate in terms of format, language, content, coverage and that provide special features that tailor the content and retrieval capabilities to specific needs of the user group;

- IPs may work together to provide group pricing or other cooperative arrangements both inside and outside the organization that provide the maximum value for the investment made.

- IPs integrate externally published and internally created information resources as well as knowledge resources to create new client-specific information collections and sources.

- IPs may use off-the-shelf information products recognizing that these products could require modifications to meet the needs of specific user groups; IPs then select or design and implement the required modifications.

- IPs select, preserve and make accessible technical reports, standards, best practices guidelines and other internal documents for ongoing use.

- IPs establish document retention schedules and access procedures to meet regulatory requirements.

C. Managing Information Services

Information professionals manage the entire life cycle of information services, from the concept stage through the design, development, testing, marketing, packaging, delivery and divestment of these offerings. Information professionals may oversee this entire process or may concentrate on specific stages, but their expertise is unquestionable in providing offerings that enable clients to immediately integrate and apply information in their work or learning processes.

C.1 Develops and maintains a portfolio of cost-effective, client-valued information services that are aligned with the strategic directions of the organization and client groups.

C.2 Conducts market research of the information behaviors and problems of current and potential client groups to identify concepts for new or enhanced information solutions for these groups. Transforms these concepts into customized information products and services.

C.3 Researches, analyzes and synthesizes information into accurate answers or actionable information for clients, and ensures that clients have the tools or capabilities to immediately apply these.

C.4 Develops and applies appropriate metrics to continually measure the quality and value of information offerings, and to take appropriate action to ensure each offering's relevancy within the portfolio.

C.5 Employs evidence-based management to demonstrate the value of and continually improve information sources and services.

Applied Scenarios

- Seeks opportunities to work with clients on projects or within their environments or operations to fully understand their processes, information behaviors and how information services can most effectively be utilized.

- Analyzes and synthesizes information into accurate answers or actionable information for clients, and ensures that clients have the tools or capabilities to immediately apply these.

- Customizes information services to better meet the specific needs and usage patterns of clients.

- Develops and delivers specific information packages or alerting services for clients such as competitive intelligence, business intelligence, industry monitors, topic or issue indicators.

- Develops, delivers and manages curricula educating clients in information literacy, Internet usage, and locating and interpreting information sources.

- Uses evidence-based management to present reasoned evidence of a service's value and an organization's abilities. Develops and applies measures of service/product usage, client satisfaction and the organizational or client impact of services and products. Regularly assesses clients' information wants and gaps using market research tools including questionnaires, surveys, interviews, focus groups and observation.

D. Applying Information Tools & Technologies

Information professionals harness the current and appropriate technology tools to deliver the best services, provide the most relevant and accessible resources, develop and deliver teaching tools to maximize clients' use of information, and capitalize on the library and information environment of the 21st century.

D.1 Assesses, selects and applies current and emerging information tools and creates information access and delivery solutions

D.2 Applies expertise in databases, indexing, metadata, and information analysis and synthesis to improve information retrieval and use in the organization

D.3 Protects the information privacy of clients and maintains awareness of, and responses to, new challenges to privacy

D.4 Maintains current awareness of emerging technologies that may not be currently relevant but may become relevant tools of future information resources, services or applications

Applied Scenarios

- IPs are active partners with technology vendors, providing feedback, suggesting improvements, and keeping the needs of the clients in the forefront.

- IPs maintain awareness of emerging technologies through reading professional and popular documents, participating in peer dialogs, and attending courses, workshops, and conferences. IPs are prepared to advise all levels of the organization on how technology trends will affect the organization and the clients.

- IPs lead technology initiatives in their organizations by forming partnerships, obtaining buy-in of upper management, overseeing the project management life-cycle, and communicating to all critical levels of the organization.

- IPs test, select and use new technology tools as they are developed.

- IPs maintain awareness of the latest policy and legislative initiatives that will impact privacy, accessibility, and openness of information use and transfer, and of technology deployment.

- IPs educate others in the use of information tools and technologies in a variety of ways, from training people in finding the information they want on the Internet or in proprietary databases to integrating information tools into their clients' workflow or curriculum.

Personal Competencies

Every information professional:

- *Seeks out challenges and capitalizes on new opportunities*
- *Sees the big picture*
- *Communicates effectively*
- *Presents ideas clearly; negotiates confidently and persuasively*
- *Creates partnerships and alliances*

- *Builds an environment of mutual respect and trust; respects and values diversity*
- *Employs a team approach; recognizes the balance of collaborating, leading and following*
- *Takes calculated risks; shows courage and tenacity when faced with opposition*
- *Plans, prioritises and focuses on what is critical*
- *Demonstrates personal career planning*
- *Thinks creatively and innovatively; seeks new or 'reinventing' opportunities*
- *Recognizes the value of professional networking and personal career planning*
- *Balances work, family and community obligations*
- *Remains flexible and positive in a time of continuing change*
- *Celebrates achievements for self and others*

Applied Scenarios
as prepared by the Competencies Development Committee, January 2004:

Seeks out challenges and capitalizes on new opportunities

- Actively pursues new roles in the organization that require an information leader.
- Demonstrates that their professional knowledge and skills solve a variety of information problems in a wide range of settings.
- Foresees changes impacting clients or patrons and aggressively explores services and programs options and offerings.
- Helps others develop their new ideas.
- Views and uses technology as an enabler of new information ideas, products and services.

Sees the big picture

- Understands the environment in which her/his parent organization is operating and how the library or information services contribute towards those operations.
- Views the library and its information services as part of the bigger process of making informed decisions; gives the highest priority to demands and projects critical to the organization's competitive advantage.
- Monitors major trends and world events that may impact the parent organization and/or the library profession; considers the impacts of these trends and pro-actively realigns library and information services to take advantage of them.

Communicates effectively

- Presents ideas clearly, succinctly and enthusiastically, either verbally or in writing, always in the 'language' of the audience, and with an understanding of their perceptions and perspectives.
- Demonstrates a professional, approachable presentation style with all audiences.
- Actively listens, considers and then responds.
- Requests feedback on communications skills and uses it for self-improvement.

Presents ideas clearly; negotiates confidently and persuasively

- Conveys effective, clear and assertive messages and coaches others to do the same.
- Believes in his/her ability to provide the best possible information service and relays that message to staff, management and clients alike.
- Demonstrates well-honed negotiation skills and the ability to secure the terms most beneficial for all concerned.

Creates partnerships and alliances

- Seeks alliances with other functions in the organization, such as information technology or human resources, to optimize complementary knowledge and skills.
- Forms partnerships with other libraries or information services inside or outside the organization to optimize resource sharing.
- Seeks alliances with content and technology suppliers and other information providers to improve products, services and operations.
- Seeks alliances with researchers in faculties of library and information studies to conduct relevant and practical studies.

Builds an environment of mutual respect and trust; respects and values diversity

- Treats others with respect and values diversity.
- Knows own strengths and the complementary strengths of others.
- Delivers on time and on target and expects others to do the same.
- Creates a problem-solving environment in which everyone's contribution is valued and acknowledged, and helps others optimize their contribution.
- Advocates for a work environment that encourages and supports ongoing knowledge development and that values the contribution of people.

Employs a team approach; recognizes the balance of collaborating, leading and following

- Works as part of the team regardless of his/her position or level.
- Develops and uses leadership and collaboration skills.
- Keeps abreast of trends in leadership skills and styles, using this knowledge to help self and others develop the most effective and appropriate approaches in different contexts. Willing to share leadership or to follow when this is in the best interests of all involved.
- Mentors other team members and asks for mentoring from others when it is needed.

Takes calculated risks; shows courage and tenacity when faced with opposition

- Shows courage when faced with opposition.
- Works closely with those in power who may say 'no' to clearly understand what's required to arrive at 'yes.'
- Asks "what's the worst that can happen?" and, if they can live with the answer, goes for it.

Plans, prioritizes and focuses on what is critical

- Recognizes that in order to use resources (including human resources, content and financial resources) most effectively, ongoing, careful planning is required.
- Refuses to let the 'cry of the urgent' drown out the 'drone of the critical' if the urgent is not aligned with where the library or service organization is strategically headed.
- Incorporates strategic imperatives into the individual goals and objectives of self and others to ensure long-term plans drive daily decisions and operations.
- Regularly reviews plans to ensure the organization is still on track or is responsive to unforeseen developments.

Demonstrates personal career planning

- Is committed to a career that involves ongoing learning and personal growth. Takes personal responsibility for finding these opportunities for learning and enrichment as well as for long-term career planning. Maintains a strong sense of self-worth based on the achievement of a balanced set of evolving personal and professional goals.
- Seeks out performance feedback from management, clients and/or mentors and uses it for continuous improvement.
- Envisions his/her individual 'preferred' future and maps a path to arrive there successfully.

Thinks creatively and innovatively; seeks new or 'reinventing' opportunities

- Pursues positions or projects outside the information service department or library to gain a better understanding of how other functions apply information in their work; uses this understanding to create inventive services and programs that are indispensable to patrons and clients.
- Regularly scans for new ideas both within and beyond the library field to anticipate the future, "guesstimate" the implications and carve out new opportunities.
- Looks at existing operations, processes and services and asks "why?" Examines changes to these operations, processes and services and asks "why not?"

Recognizes the value of professional networking

- Actively contributes to and participates in SLA and other professional associations, sharing insight, knowledge and skills; bench marks against other information service providers and to form partnerships and alliances.
- Recognizes the need for a forum where information professionals can communicate with each other and speak with one voice on important information policy issues, such as copyright and the global information infrastructure.
- Contributes towards the building and maintenance of a strong profession, thereby enhancing its value in the eyes of colleagues, clients and the broader community.

Balances work, family and community obligations

- Supports self and others in the continual search for a balanced lifestyle. Optimises opportunities for all those involved to lead healthy and satisfying professional and personal lives.

Remains flexible and positive in a time of continuing change

- Willingly assumes different responsibilities at different points in time that respond to changing needs.
- Maintains a positive attitude and helps others to do the same.
- Seeks solutions and initiates problem-solving processes.

Celebrates achievements for self and others

- Nominates employees and colleagues for awards in the organization, association or community.

- Creates and contributes towards an environment where achievements, large and small, are acknowledged, celebrated and rewarded.
- Knows that "little things count" and encourages mutual support and sharing in the organization and within the profession.
- Celebrates own success and that of others; takes pride in a job well done.

CONCLUSION

These are the competencies of Information Professionals for the 21st century. They have their roots in the past and reach far into the future. These competencies form the basis for growth in the information age. IPs recognize and embrace the expanding nature of the field and the challenges facing them.

Although the core of the profession remains the same, the methods and tools for information delivery and the scope of the enterprise continue to grow and change dramatically. While maintaining their client and content-centered approach, practitioners increasingly require advanced knowledge of information technology to realize their full potential. Continually emerging opportunities will propel the prepared professional into as yet unseen realms of advanced information retrieval, interpretation, synthesis, product development and virtual services on a global scale.

The Special Committee on Competencies hopes that this document will evolve and grow through continuing discussion of our expanding knowledge and practice base. We encourage SLA members to provide examples of their activities in relation to these competencies. Mutual support in the form of building a shared culture of evidence-based practice will be a key to meeting the challenges ahead. The Committee recommends that members consult the association's research statement Putting OUR Knowledge to Work cited earlier for additional information on this concept.

A regularly updated Career Planning and Competencies Portal can be found at www.sla.org/competenciesportal.

Reproduced with permission of SLA, www.sla.org.

Appendix

K

Students' Information Literacy Needs in the Twenty-first Century: Competencies for Teacher-librarians

Association for Teacher-librarianship in Canada (ATLC) and the Canadian School Library Association (CSLA) (1997)

OUTLINE

Introduction

Professional Competencies

The Teacher-librarian:

1.1 places a priority on staff relationships and leadership in the implementation of change;

1.2 provides leadership in collaborative program planning and teaching to ensure both physical and intellectual access to information and commitment to voluntary reading;

1.3 knows curriculum programs mandated by the province, district and school;

1.4 understands students and their social, emotional, and intellectual needs;

1.5 has expert knowledge in evaluating learning resources in different formats and media, both on-site and remote, to support the instructional program;

1.6 develops and promotes the effective use of informational and imaginative resources in all formats through cooperative professional activities;

1.7 provides appropriate information, resources or instruction to satisfy the needs of individuals and groups;

1.8 uses appropriate information technology to acquire, organize and disseminate information;

1.9 manages library programs, services and staff to support the stated educational goals of the school;

1.10 evaluates program and services.

Personal Competencies

The Teacher-librarian:

2.1 is committed to program excellence;

2.2 seeks out challenges and sees new opportunities both inside and outside the library;

2.3 sees the big picture;

2.4 looks for partnerships and alliances;

2.5 creates an environment of mutual respect and trust;

2.6 has effective communications skills;

2.7 works well with others in a team;

2.8 provides leadership;

2.9 plans, prioritizes and focuses on what is critical;

2.10 is committed to lifelong learning;

2.11 is flexible and positive in a time of continuing change.

Glossary of Terms

Acknowledgements

Provincial Guidelines

INTRODUCTION

Students in Canada today need to be able to think rationally and logically. With more and more sources of information, both print and electronic, and the increasing difficulty of ensuring that students can derive meaning from this information, the role of the teacher-librarian becomes central. Teacher-librarians are skilled in accessing and evaluating information regardless of delivery system, book or computer, and providing leadership in the appropriate use of newer information technologies.

There is a significant body of research that demonstrates that a qualified teacher-librarian has a positive impact on school culture and student achievement. Indeed, several studies have established that teachers collaborate more in schools with a teacher-librarian and students read more, enjoy reading more, write better, access and use information more effectively, and excel in academic content areas. This does not happen by chance, however.

In these schools information literacy is incorporated into school and classroom programs because:

✓ the program is recognized as a partnership of the principal, teacher and teacher-librarian, supported by the school district and community;

✓ the district insists on flexible scheduling [the teacher-librarian is not the preparation time or "relief" for classroom colleagues];

✓ the principal encourages collaboration and team teaching through this flexible schedule;

✓ teachers acknowledge that the processing and use of information is a school-wide concern, for integration with classroom content instruction; the teacher-librarian takes the initiative, places a priority on cooperative program planning with colleagues and encourages team planning.

✓ The teacher-librarian is a highly skilled teacher, with competencies provided by a combination of teacher education, classroom experience and courses in teacher-librarianship and information studies. The teacher-librarian should be in the forefront of curriculum and staff development, familiar with the full range of instructional strategies and learning styles, able to organize time and resources, and active in professional concerns within the school and the district.

In approving this document, school boards, agencies and professional associations affirm the research evidence that indicates that integrated library programs impact positively on collaboration, leadership and student achievement when the teacher-librarian has experience as a classroom teacher, qualifications in teacher-librarianship, information studies and learning resources management, preferably at the graduate level, and works collaboratively with teachers in flexibly scheduled programs to integrate information problem-solving skills and strategies in the ongoing instructional program.

The competent teacher-librarian is committed to:

• the principles outlined in the Students' Bill of Information Rights;
• implementing curriculum with colleagues;
• initiating collaboratively planned and taught programs to integrate information literacy in the context of the curriculum; and
• the effective use of information technologies.

Professional Competencies relate to the teacher-librarians' knowledge and skill in the areas of collaboration and leadership, curriculum and instruction, cooperative program planning and teaching, information resources, information access, technology, management and research, and the ability to apply these abilities as a basis for providing library and information services.

Personal Competencies represent a set of skills, attitudes and values that enable teacher-librarians to work efficiently and effectively, be good communicators, focus on continuing learning throughout their careers, demonstrate the value-added nature of their contributions and thrive in the new world of education.

The following sections highlight the major professional and personal competencies of teacher-librarians and provide practical examples of the multitude of roles and tasks that teacher-librarians can perform. The examples are illustrative and are tempered by critical factors such as the nature of school leadership and culture, the climate for collaboration and innovation in the work environment, flexible scheduling, the time allocation of professional and support staff and the specific education and training of the teacher-librarian to do the job.

PROFESSIONAL COMPETENCIES

The Teacher-librarian:
1.1 places a priority on staff relationships and leadership in the implementation of change.

Examples: Establishes rapport with school staff, students and the community. Develops a collaborative approach with the principal, teachers and other staff. Provides an environment conducive to learning. Keeps abreast of and communicates developments in curriculum, instructional strategies, and newer information technologies. Participates in the school's governance by serving on advisory and decision-making bodies.

1.2 provides leadership in collaborative program planning and teaching to ensure both physical and intellectual access to information and commitment to voluntary reading.

Examples: Advocates the integration of information skills and strategies in classroom programs through collaborative program planning and team teaching with colleagues. Develops with teachers a coordinated approach to information literacy, including decision-making, problem-solving and research strategies, integrated with classroom instruction. Understands and distinguishes between physical and intellectual access to information. Provides leadership for reading and research programs, incorporating both informational and imaginative literature and technologies. Plans and teaches with teachers from establishing objectives through to student assessment and unit evaluation.

1.3 knows curriculum programs mandated by the province, district and school.

Examples: Is aware of new curricula and implications for implementation. Provides support for teachers through training and implementation. Understands the appropriate integration of resources and technologies with specific curriculum areas. Promotes congruence of stated learning outcomes, delivered curriculum, assessment and supporting resources and technologies.

1.4 understands students and their social, emotional, and intellectual needs.

Examples: Understands child and adolescent growth and development for the age levels of the school. Can respond to student needs and interests. Works with teachers and others to match resources to a variety of learning styles and requirements and to adapt the curriculum and program for students with special needs.

1.5 has expert knowledge in evaluating learning resources in different formats and media, both on-site and remote, to support the instructional program.

Examples: Works within written school and district policies on the selection of learning resources and their appropriate use. Works within a written school policy on the purchase and management of all school resources and their access. Evaluates print, CD-ROM and on-line versions of databases. Selects the best books, journals, nonprint and electronic resources for specific curriculum areas and specific learning outcomes using authoritative evaluation sources and selection "tools". Organizes teacher involvement in evaluation. Compiles guides to resources both on and off site. Develops and manages a collection of quality materials that reflect resource-based units of study.

1.6 develops and promotes the effective use of informational and imaginative resources in all formats through cooperative professional activities.

Examples: Promotes voluntary reading throughout the school. Develops themes and celebrations that reflect the school's curriculum and unique community. Designs and produces materials for specific instructional purposes, where commercial materials are not available. Assists students and teachers in the effective use of resources and technologies.

1.7 provides appropriate information, resources or instruction to satisfy the needs of individuals and groups.

Examples: Recommends learning resources for specific learning outcomes. Works with individuals and groups to identify problems, frame questions, check authority, evaluate information and develop critical thinking. Provides guidance on accessing information appropriate to the specific need. Understands the design and structure of bibliographic and other databases. Conducts searches from complex or difficult sources. Answers questions using on-site and remote resources. Assists students and teachers with using authoring tools in print, electronic and multimedia formats. Supports colleagues who are accessing information services from the classroom.

1.8 uses appropriate information technology to acquire, organize and disseminate information.

Examples: Establishes, maintains and teaches the use of an on-line catalogue of the library collection. Works on information management teams to select appropriate software, hardware and security for desktop access. Contributes to a home page for the World Wide Web for the school. Links the library page to other relevant curriculum sites. Informs school community of copyright issues. Keeps up-to-date with new products and modes of information delivery. Plans and participates in the development and provision of information networks.

1.9 manages library programs, services and staff to support the stated educational goals of the school.

Examples: Develops an integrated library program linked to the curricular goals of the school. Develops procedures for the cost-effective selection, acquisition, organization, management and use of resources. Manages professional and support staff. Recruits, selects, trains and motivates volunteers. Manages space and equipment. Maintains an inventory of materials and equipment. Plans and manages a budget which reflects the instructional program. Develops a marketing plan for specific audiences. Plans strategies for securing support for learning resource services in the school and community.

1.10 evaluates program and services.

Examples: Actively seeks opportunities for improvement and strives for excellent programs and services. Involves school staff in program evaluation. Conducts regular needs assessments using research tools such as questionnaires, focus groups and interviews. Prepares oral and written reports on program development. Reports regularly and confers with the principal and staff on program implementation. Conducts research related to the solution of information management problems. Demonstrates how library and information services add value to the school. Refocuses programs and services on new needs.

PERSONAL COMPETENCIES

The Teacher-librarian:
2.1 is committed to program excellence.

Examples: Seeks feedback and uses it for continuous improvement. Celebrates own success and that of others. Takes pride in a job well done. Shares new knowledge with others at conferences and in the professional literature. Uses the research base of education and teacher-librarianship as a resource for improving services.

2.2 seeks out challenges and sees new opportunities both inside and outside the library

Examples: Takes on new roles in the school community that require an information leader. Uses library-based knowledge and skills to solve a variety of information problems. Expands the library collection beyond traditional media such as books and journals. Creates the "library without walls".

2.3 sees the big picture.

Examples: Recognizes that information seeking and use are part of the creative process for individuals. Sees the library and its information services as part of the bigger process of making informed decisions. Anticipates trends and proactively realigns library and information services to take advantage of them.

2.4 looks for partnerships and alliances.

Examples: Provides leadership in information management. Forms partnerships with other libraries for resource sharing. Seeks alliances with vendors to improve products and services. Seeks alliances with researchers in education and library and information studies to conduct relevant studies.

2.5 creates an environment of mutual respect and trust.

Examples: Knows own strengths and the complementary strengths of others. Is dependable. Values and acknowledges the contributions of others in a problem solving environment.

2.6 has effective communications skills.

Examples: Runs meetings effectively. Presents ideas clearly and enthusiastically both orally and in writing. Requests feedback on communication skills and uses it for self improvement.

2.7 works well with others in a team.

Examples: Seeks out opportunities for team participation. Asks for mentoring from others when needed. Looks for ways to enhance personal performance.

2.8 provides leadership.

Examples: Exercises leadership as a member of teams within the school and community. Seeks opportunities for leadership.

2.9 plans, prioritizes and focuses on what is critical.

Examples: Recognizes that ongoing planning and time management are required. Reviews goals with administrators and colleagues on a regular basis.

2.10 is committed to lifelong learning.

Examples: Advocates for a learning environment to encourage the contributions of staff members. Participates in professional associations.

2.11 is flexible and positive in a time of continuing change.

Examples: Willing to take on different responsibilities and respond to changing needs. Maintains a positive attitude and helps others to do the same. Looks for solutions. Uses technology as an enabler.

GLOSSARY OF TERMS

Teacher-librarian: A professional teacher with a minimum of two years of successful classroom experience and additional qualifications in the selection, management and utilization of learning resources, who manages the school library and works with other teachers to design and implement resource-based instructional programs.

School library: The instructional centre in the school that coordinates and provides on site and offsite access to information, resources, services and programs that integrate information literacy, the intellectual access to information, with teachers, to develop independent learners who are effective users of information and ideas and committed to informed decision-making.

School library program: The collaboratively planned and taught units of study developed through the shared expertise and equal partnership of classroom teachers and teacher-librarians based on the principles of resource based learning and designed to achieve the educational goals of the school.

Support staff: Under the direction of a teacher-librarian, may include graduates of a post-secondary library technician program who organize and maintain the resources and equipment and provide reference and technical support services to teachers and students; clerical staff who provide support services in areas such as acquisition, circulation, and processing of resources, shelving and filing of materials, and typing or word processing; adult and student volunteers.

Information literacy: The ability to: recognize the need for information to solve problems and develop ideas; pose important questions; use a variety of information gathering strategies; locate relevant and appropriate information; assess information for quality, authority, accuracy and authenticity. Includes the abilities to use the practical and conceptual tools of information technology to understand form, format, location and access methods, how information is situated and produced, research processes, and to format and publish in textual and multimedia formats and to adapt to emerging technologies.

ACKNOWLEDGMENTS

This document is based on prior work by the Association for Teacher-librarianship in Canada and the Canadian School Library Association.

The format has been adapted with permission from one developed by the Special Libraries Association (Washington, DC).

Prepared by a joint committee of the Association for Teacher-librarianship in Canada and the Canadian School Library Association—Joan Harper (CSLA); Ken Haycock (ATLC/CSLA Chair), Judith Kootte (CSLA); Pat Parungao (ATLC); Liz Austrom (ATLC)—in consultation with provincial and national education groups and associations and a national response panel.

Research evidence for these competencies has been reported in scholarly and professional journals and monographs and in Australia, Canada, the United Kingdom and the United States.

PROVINCIAL GUIDELINES

NEWFOUNDLAND AND LABRADOR. Learning to learn: Policies and guidelines for the implementation of resource-based learning in Newfoundland Labrador schools Newfoundland and Labrador Department of Education, 1991.

PRINCE EDWARD ISLAND. School library policy for the province of Prince Edward Island Prince Edward Island Department of Education, 1989.

NOVA SCOTIA. Nova Scotia school libraries: Standards and practices. Nova Scotia Teachers Union, 1987.

NEW BRUNSWICK. Standards and practices for New Brunswick school libraries. New Brunswick Teachers Association Library Council, 1989.

QUEBEC. Direction générale d'évaluation et des ressources didactiques. Also: Library resources in the schools: Pedagogical and organizational aspects [English translation]. Québec Ministère de l'Education, 1987.

ONTARIO. Partners in action: The library resource centre in the school curriculum. Ontario Ministry of Education, 1982. Also: Information literacy and equitable access: A framework for change. Ontario Ministry of Education, 1995.

MANITOBA. Resource-based learning: An educational model. Manitoba Education and Training, 1994.

SASKATCHEWAN. Resource-based learning: Policies, guidelines and responsibilities for Saskatchewan learning resource centers. Saskatchewan Education, 1988.

ALBERTA. Focus on learning: An integrated program model for Alberta school libraries. Alberta Education, 1985. Also: Focus on research: A guide to developing student research skills. Alberta Education, 1990.

BRITISH COLUMBIA. Developing independent learners: The role of the school library resource centre. British Columbia, Ministry of Education, 1991.

NORTHWEST TERRITORIES. Guidelines for the development of school information centres. Northwest Territories Education, 1990.

Appendix

Professional Associations

There are professional associations for every conceivable interest and specialization in Library and Information Science. These entries cover only the major national and international associations open to individual membership; however, each state and many regions have library associations, sometimes further divided by general (typically academic and public), school, and trustee associations. Some national associations (notably the Special Libraries Association) also have regional/state chapters. There are also important associations open only or primarily to institutions, such as the Association of Research Libraries and the Urban Libraries Council.

This list provides a brief introduction to the major associations and an overview of some of the more popular areas of affiliation. Associations exist by type of environment (academic, public, special, school), by even greater specialization (e.g., church, law, medical, theater), by function (e.g., advocacy, cataloguing, reference), by background of the individual (e.g., ethnicity, orientation) or service population interest (e.g., rural areas, youth), and by state and national boundaries. Consult the current edition of the Bowker Annual (Information Today) for a full and current listing of related associations.

GENERAL

American Library Association (ALA)
50 East Huron Street, Chicago, IL 60611. Telephone: (800) 545-2433.
Web site: http://www.ala.org/.

The American Library Association (ALA) was founded in 1876 in Philadelphia and subsequently chartered in the Commonwealth of Massachusetts. Its mission is to provide leadership for the development, promotion, and improvement of library and information services and the profession of librarianship in order to enhance learning and ensure access to information for all. Its membership is open to any person, library, or other organization interested in library service and librarianship. ALA is home to eleven membership divisions, each focused on a type of library or type of library function. It also includes round tables, groups of members interested in the same field of librarianship not within the scope of any division. A network of affiliates, chapters, and other organizations enables ALA to reach a broad audience.

Primary Journal: *American Libraries*.

EXAMPLES BY ENVIRONMENT

American Association of School Librarians (AASL)

A division of the American Library Association, 50 East Huron Street, Chicago, IL 60611. Telephone: (312) 280-4382.
Web site: www.ala.org/ala/aasl/.

AASL advocates excellence, facilitates change, and develops leaders in the school library media field. AASL works to ensure that all members of the school library media field collaborate to:

- provide leadership in the total education program
- participate as active partners in the teaching/learning process
- connect learners with ideas and information, and
- prepare students for life-long learning, informed decision-making, a love of reading, and the use of information technologies.

Primary Journal: *Knowledge Quest*.

Association of College and Research Libraries (ACRL)

A division of the American Library Association. 50 East Huron Street, Chicago, IL 60611. Telephone: (312) 280-2523.
Web site: http://www.ala.org/ala/acrl/.

ACRL is a professional association of academic librarians and other interested individuals. It is dedicated to enhancing the ability of academic library and information professionals to serve the information needs of the higher education community and to improve learning, teaching, and research.

Primary Journal: *College & Research Libraries*.

Public Library Association (PLA)

A division of the American Library Association. 50 East Huron Street, Chicago, IL 60611. Telephone: (800) 545-2433 ext. 5028.
Web site: www.pla.org.

The Public Library Association's core purpose is to strengthen public libraries and their contribution to the communities they serve. PLA is a member-driven organization that exists to provide a diverse program of communication, publication, advocacy, continuing education, and programming for its members and others interested in the advancement of public library service. PLA provides visionary leadership, is focused on and responsive to member needs, respects diversity of opinion and community needs, and is committed to excellence and innovation.

Primary Journal: *Public Libraries*.

See also:

Association for Library Service to Children (ALSC)

A division of the American Library Association. 50 East Huron Street, Chicago, IL 60611. Telephone: (800) 545-2433 ext. 2163.
Web site: http://www.ala.org/ala/alsc/.

The Association for Library Service to Children (ALSC) is the world's largest organization dedicated to the support and enhancement of service to children in all types of libraries. Its core purpose is to create a better future for children through libraries. Its primary goal is to lead the way in forging excellent library service for all children.

Primary Journal: *Children and Libraries.*

Young Adult Library Services Association (YALSA)

A division of the American Library Association. 50 East Huron Street, Chicago, IL 60611.
Telephone: (800) 545-2433 ext. 4390.
Web site: www.ala.org/ala/yalsa/.

The Association's goal is to advocate, promote, and strengthen service to young adults (teens) as part of the continuum of total library services.

Primary Journal: *Young Adult Library Services.*

Special Libraries Association (SLA)

331 South Patrick Street, Alexandria, VA 22314-3501. Telephone: (703) 647-4900.
Web site: http://www.sla.org/.

The Special Libraries Association (SLA) is the international association representing the interests of thousands of information professionals in over eighty countries worldwide. The Special Libraries Association is the global organization for innovative information professionals and their strategic partners. It promotes and strengthens its members through learning, advocacy, and networking initiatives.

Primary Journal: *Information Outlook.*

See also:

American Association of Law Librarians

53 W. Jackson, Suite 940, Chicago, IL 60604. Telephone: (312) 939-4764.
Web site: http://www.aallnet.org/index.asp.

The American Association of Law Libraries was founded in 1906 to promote and enhance the value of law libraries to the legal and public communities, to foster the profession of law librarianship, and to provide leadership in the field of legal information. The Association represents law librarians and related professionals who are affiliated with a wide range of institutions: law firms; law schools; corporate legal departments; courts; and local, state, and federal government agencies.

Primary Journal: *Law Library Journal.*

American Theological Library Association

300 South Wacker Drive, Suite 2100, Chicago, IL 60606-6701. Telephone: (888) 665- 2852.

Web site: http://www.atla.com/atlahome.html.

The American Theological Library Association (ATLA) is a professional association providing programs, products, and services in support of theological and religious studies libraries and librarians. ATLA's ecumenical membership represents many religious traditions and denominations.

Primary Journal: Theological Librarian.

Art Libraries Society of North America (ARLIS/NA)

232-329 March Road, Box 11, Ottawa, ON K2K 2E1. Telephone: (800) 817-0621.

Web site: http://www.arlisna.org/.

The mission of ARLIS/NA is to foster excellence in art and design librarianship and image management. The membership includes architecture and art librarians, visual resources professionals, artists, curators, educators, publishers, and others interested in visual arts information. To serve this diverse constituency, the Society provides a wide range of programs and services within an organizational structure that promotes participation at all levels.

Primary Journal: *Art Documentation.*

Church and Synagogue Library Association

2920 SW Dolph Ct., Ste. 3A, Portland, OR 97219-3962. Telephone: (503) 244-6919 or (800) 542-2752. Web site: http://cslainfo.org/.

The CSLA serves librarians, many of whom are nonprofessional volunteers, through publications, a network of religious libraries, and training sessions offered at regional and national workshops. It also provides counseling and guidance for individual libraries through its Library Services Committee, composed of experienced congregational librarians, establishes regional chapters to provide ongoing service and fellowship in local areas and holds an annual three-day conference in various parts of the country, providing the opportunity for continuing education in library practice and sharing experience in the field.

Primary Journal: *Congregational Libraries Today.*

Medical Library Association (MLA)

65 East Wacker Place, Suite 1900, Chicago, IL 60601-7246. Telephone: (312) 419-9094.

Web site: http://www.mlanet.org/.

Founded in 1898 by librarians and physicians, the Medical Library Association is dedicated to improving excellence and leadership of the health information professional to foster the art and science of health information services.

Primary Journal: *Bulletin of the Medical Library Association.*

Music Library Association

8551 Research Way, Suite 180, Middleton, WI 53562. Telephone: (608) 836-5825.

Web site: http://www.musiclibraryassoc.org/.

The Music Library Association provides a forum for issues surrounding music, music in libraries, and music librarianship. Members include music librarians, librarians who work with music as part of their responsibilities, composers and music scholars, and others interested in the program of the association.

Primary Journal: *Music Cataloging Bulletin.*

Society of American Archivists

527 South Wells Street, 5th Floor, Chicago, IL 60607. Telephone: (312) 922-0140.

Web site: http://www.archivists.org/.

The Society of American Archivists serves the educational and informational needs of its members and provides leadership to help ensure the identification, preservation, and use of the nation's historical record.

Primary Journal: *American Archivist.*

Association of Independent Information Professionals (AIIP)

8550 United Plaza Blvd., Suite 1001, Baton Rouge, Louisiana 70809. Telephone: (225) 408-4400.

Web site: http://www.aiip.org/index.html.

AIIP's members are owners of firms providing such information-related services as online and manual research, document delivery, database design, library support, consulting, writing, and publishing.

Primary Journal: *Connections.*

EXAMPLES BY FUNCTION/POSITION

American Society for Information Science and Technology (ASIS&T)

1320 Fenwick Lane, Suite 510, Silver Spring, MD 20910. Telephone: (301) 495-0900.

Web site: www.asis.org

Since 1937, the American Society for Information Science and Technology (ASIS&T) has been the society for information professionals leading the search for new and better theories, techniques, and technologies to improve access to information. ASIS&T has members in over fifty countries worldwide, with fifty-six chapters throughout the United States and abroad and twenty SIGs in a variety of fields, such as Bioinformatics to Visualization, Images, and Sound.

Primary Journal: *Journal of the American Society for Information Science and Technology.*

ARMA International—The Association for
Information Management Professionals
13725 W. 109th Street, Suite 101, Lenexa, KS 66215. Telephone: (800) 422-2762.
Web site: http://www.arma.org/.

ARMA International is a not-for-profit professional association and the authority on managing records and information. Its members include records managers, archivists, corporate librarians, imaging specialists, legal professionals, IT managers, consultants, and educators, all of whom work in a wide variety of industries, including government, legal, healthcare, financial services, and petroleum in the United States, Canada, and thirty-plus other countries.

Primary Journal: *Information Management Journal.*

Association for Library and Information Science Education (ALISE)
65 East Wacker Place, Suite 1900, Chicago, IL 60601-7246. Telephone: (312) 795-0996.
Web site: http://www.alise.org/.

The Association for Library and Information Science Education provides a forum for library educators to share ideas, to discuss issues, and to seek solutions to common problems.

Primary Journal: *Journal of Education for Library and Information Science (JELIS).*

Association for Library Collections & Technical Services (ALCTS)
A division of the American Library Association. 50 East Huron Street, Chicago, IL 60611. Telephone: (800) 545-2433 ext. 5030.
Web site: http://www.ala.org/ala/alcts/.

The Association for Library Collections & Technical Services is responsible for the following activities: acquisition, identification, cataloging, classification, and preservation of library materials; the development and coordination of the country's library resources; and those areas of selection and evaluation involved in the acquisition of library materials and pertinent to the development of library resources.

Primary Journal: *Library Resources & Technical Services.*

Association of Specialized and Cooperative Library Agencies (ASCLA)
A division of the American Library Association. 50 East Huron Street, Chicago, IL 60611.
Telephone: (312) 280-4395.
Web site: http://www.ala.org/ala/ascla/.

The Association of Specialized and Cooperative Library Agencies enhances the effectiveness of library service by providing networking, enrichment, and educational opportunities for its diverse members, who represent state library agencies, libraries serving special populations, multitype library organizations and independent librarians.

Primary Journal: *Interface.*

Library Administration and Management Association (LAMA)
A division of the American Library Association. 50 East Huron Street, Chicago, IL 60611.
Telephone: (800) 545-2433.
Web site: http://www.ala.org/ala/lama/.

The mission of the Library Administration and Management Association is to encourage and nurture current and future library leaders, and to develop and promote outstanding leadership and management practices. Attuned to ever-changing technological, economic, political, and cultural conditions, LAMA equips library professionals with tools for building vibrant library services and successful careers. Highlighting all aspects of library management, LAMA's sections (special interest groups) offer not only opportunities to connect with people of similar interests, but also to exchange ideas, collaborate on projects, publish research, mentor future leaders, and hone leadership and managerial skills.

Primary Journal: *Library Administration & Management.*

Library and Information Technology Association (LITA)
A division of the American Library Association. 50 East Huron Street, Chicago, IL 60611. Telephone: (312) 280-4267.
Web site: http://www.lita.org/ala/lita/litahome.cfm

The Library and Information Technology Association is the leading organization reaching out across types of libraries to provide education and services for a broad membership, including new professionals, systems librarians, library administrators, library schools, vendors, and anyone else interested in leading edge technology and applications for librarians and information providers. Programs are offered for everyone from absolute beginners to hi-tech professionals. Continuing education is provided through workshops, institutes, and an annual National Forum.

Primary Journal: *Information Technology and Libraries.*

Reference and User Services Association
A division of the American Library Association. 50 East Huron Street, Chicago, IL 60611. Telephone: 1-800-545-2433 x4395.
Web site: www.ala.org/ala/rusa/.

The Reference and User Services Association is responsible for stimulating and supporting excellence in the delivery of general library services and materials to adults, and the provision of reference and information services, collection development, and resource sharing for all ages, in every type of library.

Primary Journal: *Reference & User Services Quarterly.*

EXAMPLES BY BACKGROUND

American Indian Library Association (AILA)
Web site: www.ailanet.org/

The American Indian Library Associaction is a membership action group that addresses the library-related needs of American Indians and Alaskan natives. It is an affiliate of the American Library Association and meets twice a year in conjunction with the ALA. Members are individuals and institutions interested in working to improve library services.

Primary Journal: American Indian Libraries Newsletter

Asian/Pacific American Librarians Association (APALA)

P. O. Box 1592, Goleta, CA 93116-1592.

Web site: http://www.apalaweb.org/.

The Asian/Pacific American Librarians Association provides a forum for discussing problems of APA librarians and for the exchange of ideas by APA librarians with other librarians. It also supports and encourages library services to APA communities and recruits and mentors APA librarians in the library/information science professions.

Primary Journal: *APALA Newsletter.*

The Black Caucus of the American Library Association (BCALA)

P.O. Box 1738, Hampton, VA 23669.

Web site: http://www.bcala.org/.

The Black Caucus of the American Library Association serves as an advocate for the development, promotion, and improvement of library services and resources to the nation's African American community and provides leadership for the recruitment and professional development of African American librarians.

Primary Journal: *BCALA Newsletter.*

Chinese American Librarians Association (CALA)

Membership: Hong Wang, Reference Librarian, California State University Sacramento, 2000 State University Drive East, Sacramento, CA 95819-6039.

Web site: http://www.cala-web.org/.

CALA enhances communication among Chinese American librarians, serves as a forum for the discussion of professional concerns and problems, and promotes the understanding and exchanges among librarians in the United States and abroad, with special emphasis in Asia and Pacific Rim countries.

Primary Journal: *Chinese American Librarians Association Newsletter.*

REFORMA (National Association to Promote Library and Information Services to Latinos and the Spanish-Speaking)

c/o Sandra Rios Balderrama, P.O. Box 4386, Fresno, CA 93744. Telephone: (480) 734-4460.

Web site: http://www.reforma.org/.

The goals of REFORMA include development of Spanish-language and Latino-oriented library collections, recruitment of bilingual, multicultural library personnel, promotion of public awareness of libraries and librarianship among Latinos, and advocacy on behalf of the information needs of the Latino community.

Primary Journal: *REFORMA Newsletter.*

ADVOCACY GROUPS

Association for Library Trustees and Advocates (ALTA)

A division of the American Library Association. 50 East Huron Street, Chicago, IL 60611.

Telephone: (800) 545- 2433.

Web site: http://www.ala.org/ala/alta/.

Founded as the American Library Trustee Association, today's Association for Library Trustees and Advocates is the only division of the American Library Association dedicated to providing resources, programs, publications, and services to America's public library trustees and advocates. ALTA represents library trustees, advocates, volunteers, and friends throughout United States and Canada.

Primary Journal: *The Voice.*

Friends of Libraries U.S.A.

1420 Walnut St., Suite 450, Philadelphia, PA 19102-4017. Telephone: (215) 790-1674.

Web site: http://www.folusa.org/.

The mission of FOL is to motivate and support state and local library support groups in their efforts to preserve and strengthen libraries and to create awareness and appreciation of library services.

Primary Journal: *News Update.*

CANADA

Canadian Library Association

328 Frank Street, Ottawa, ON K2P 0X8. Telephone: (613) 232-9625.

Web site: http://www.cla.ca/.

The Canadian Library Association is a nonprofit voluntary organization, governed by an elected Executive Council, which is advised by over thirty interest groups and committees. CLA members work in college, university, public, special (corporate, nonprofit, and government), and school libraries. Others sit on boards of public libraries, work for companies that provide goods and services to libraries, or are students in graduate level or community college programs. The CLA has different divisions for different interests.

Primary Journal: *Feliciter,*

INTERNATIONAL ORGANIZATIONS

International Association of School Librarianship (IASL)

PO Box 83, Zillmere, Queensland 4034, Australia.

Web site: http://www.iasl-online.org/index.htm.

The mission of IASL is to provide an international forum for those people interested in promoting effective school library media programs as viable instruments in the educational process. IASL also provides guidance and advice for the development of school library programs and the school library profession. Membership is worldwide, and includes school librarians, teachers, librarians, library advisers, consultants, educational administrators, and others who are responsible for library and information services in schools.

Primary Journal: *School Libraries Worldwide.*

International Federation of Library Associations and Institutions (IFLA)
P.O. Box 95312, 2509 CH The Hague, The Netherlands.
Web site: http://www.ifla.org/.

IFLA is the leading international body representing the interests of library and information services and their users. It is the global voice of the library and information profession, an independent, international, nongovernmental, not-for-profit organization. Its aims are to promote high standards of provision and delivery of library and information services; encourage widespread understanding of the value of good library and information services, and represent the interests of members throughout the world.

Primary Journal: *IFLA Journal.*

Notes

Each Uniform Resource Locator (URL) in this book was verified as an active link to the appropriate Web page on January 02, 2008.

Introduction

The guiding principles are based on the work of Shiyali Ramamrita Ranganathan, *The Five Laws of Library Science*. Madras, India: Madras Library Association, 1931; Also: London: Blunt and Sons, Ltd. and Edward Goldston. For a scanned copy, see http://dlist.sir.arizona.edu/1220/.

Chapter 1

The ALA Core Values, the ALA Code of Ethics, and the ALA Library Bill of Rights can be found in Appendix A, B, and C, respectively.

1. Elizabeth L. Eisenstein, *The Printing Press as an Agent of Change: Communications and Cultural Transformations in Early Modern Europe.* Cambridge: Cambridge University, 1979.

2. Michael H. Harris, "The Purpose of the American Public Library: A Revisionist Interpretation of History," *Library Journal* 98 (1973), 2509–2514.

3. Dee Garrison, "The Tender Technicians: The Feminization of Public Librarianship," *Journal of Social History* 6 (Winter 1972–1973), 131–159.

4. Carl M. White, *A Historical Introduction to Library Education: Problems and Progress to 1951.* New York: Scarecrow, 1976.

5. Michael Winter, *The Culture and Control of Expertise: Toward a Sociological Understanding of Librarianship.* Westport, CT: Greenwood, 1988.

6. Cathy De Rosa et al., *Perceptions of Libraries and Information Resources: A Report to the OCLC Membership.* Dublin, OH: OCLC, 2005.

Chapter 2

This piece is based on, and in some cases, quotes verbatim from the author's book *Our Enduring Values: Librarianship in the 21st Century*, Chicago: ALA, 2000, and a number of his other writings and speeches in the last few years. Readers will also want to consult the ALA statement on Core Values (Appendix A), Code of Ethics (Appendix B), and the Library Bill of Rights (Appendix C).

Chapter 3

The authors write from the perspective of their life-time professional connection to the American Library Association. They urge the reader to review the documents and policies of sister national associations (e.g., REFORMA, AALL, MLA, AILA) and state chapters for a complete picture. (See Appendix L for a listing of professional associations.)

1. Kathleen McCook, *Introduction to Public Librarianship.* New York: Neal-Schuman, 2004, p. 36.

2. Katharine Phenix, "Dignity and Justice for All of Us: The Universal Declaration of Human Rights 1948–2008," *Progressive Librarian* 30 (Winter 2007–2008), 1–2.

3. Nancy Kranich (ed.), *Libraries and Democracy: The Cornerstones of Liberty.* Chicago: ALA, 2001.

4. Frank Adams and Myles Horton, *Unearthing Seeds of Fire: The Idea of Highlander.* Winston-Salem, NC: John F. Blair, 1975.

5. See Appendix D: American Library Association's *Freedom to Read Statement.*

6. Robert Jensen, "The Myth of the Neutral Professional," *Progressive Librarian* (Winter 2004–2005), 24, 28–35.

7. McCook, *Introduction to Public Librarianship*, p. 51.

8. Joyce M. Latham, *White Collar Read: The American Public Library and the Left Led CIO: A Case Study of the Chicago Public Library, 1929–1952*, Ph.D. dissertation, University of Illinois, 2007.

9. Ibid., p. 149.

10. Louise S. Robbins, *Censorship and the American Public Library: The American Library Association's Response to Threats to Intellectual Freedom: 1939–1969.* Westport, CT: Greenwood, 1996, p. 166.

11. Geoffrey R. Stone, *Perilous Times: Free Speech in Wartime.* New York: W.W. Norton, 2004.

12. Latham, *White Collar Read*, p. 149.

13. Ibid., p. 717.

14. United Nations, *Universal Declaration of Human Rights* (1948). Retrieved January 02, 2008, from the United Nations Web site http://www.un.org/Overview/rights.html.

15. Johannes Morsink, *The Universal Declaration of Human Rights: Origins, Drafting and Intent.* Philadelphia, PA: University of Pennyslvania Press, 1999, p. xii.

16. Mary Ann Glendon, *A World Made New.* New York: Random House, 2002, p. 241.

17. McCook, *Introduction to Public Librarianship,* pp. 74–75.

18. For this paper we honor and commend some of the many librarians who have fought for human rights: Joan Airoldi, Barbara Bailey, Sanford Berman, Joan Bodger, Clara Estelle Breed, Ruth Brown, John Chancellor, Peter Chase, George Christian, Blanche Collins, John Forsman, Barbara Gittings, Daniel Gore, T. Ellis Hodgin, Zoia Horn, Agnes Inglis, E.J. Josey, Abram Boris Korman, Stanley Kunitz, Gordon McShean, Lucy Randolph Mason, Juliette Hampton Morgan, Janet Nocek, Michele Reutty, Mark C. Rosenzweig, Loriene Roy, Toni Samek, Anita Schiller, Ann Sparanese, Yongyi Song, Arnulfo Trejo, Jerilynn Adams Williams, and Deloris Wilson who have all shown by their example a commitment to human rights and democracy in the context of librarianship. We have reviewed their particular contributions while writing this essay and gained inspiration and hope from them. Their contributions are also documented in our paper "A Commitment to Human Rights: Let's Honor the Qualities Required of a Librarian Dedicated to Human Rights," *Information for Social Change* 25. Retrieved January 02, 2008, from http://libr.org/isc/toc.html.

19. George W. Loveland, "The Highlander Library: Educating for a People's Democracy," *Virginia Libraries* 44(1) (January/February/March 1998), 12–14.

20. Michael Gorman, *Our Enduring Values: Librarianship in the 21st Century.* Chicago: ALA, 2000, pp. 144–145.

21. Patterson T. Graham, *A Right to Read: Segregation and Civil Rights in Alabama's Public Libraries, 1900–1965.* Tuscaloosa, AL: Alabama University Press, 2002.

22. Louise S. Robbins, *The Dismissal of Miss Ruth Brown: Civil Rights, Censorship, and the American Library.* Norman, OK: University of Oklahoma Press, 2001.

23. Kathleen McCook, *Rocks in the Whirlpool: Equity of Access and the American Library Association,* 2002, ERIC ED 462981.

24. Joan Airoldi, "Case Study: A Grand Jury Subpoena in the PATRIOT Act Era," *Library Administration and Management* 20 (Winter 2006), 26–29.

25. American Civil Liberties Union. "Supreme Court Unseals Documents in Patriot Act Case," 2006. Retrieved January 02, 2008, from http://www.aclu.org/safefree/nationalsecurityletters/26379prs20060803.html.

26. See the appendices for current policy statements. See also American Library Association, *Privacy Toolkit.* Retrieved January 02, 2008, from http://www.ala.org/ala/oif/iftoolkits/toolkitsprivacy/privacy.htm.

27. Bernadine E. Abbot-Hoduski, *Lobbying for Libraries and the Public's Access to Government Information: An Insider's View.* Totawa, NJ: Rowman and Littlefield, 2004.

28. Kera Bolonik, "Muzzling Moore," *Salon,* January 7, 2002. Retrieved January 02, 2008, from http://archive.salon.com/books/feature/2002/01/07/moore/print.html.

29. Kathleen McCook and Katharine Phenix, "Public Librarians and Human Rights," *Public Library Quarterly* 25(1/2), 57–73.

30. John N. Berry, III, "Toni Samek: The Winner of the First Annual LJ Teaching Award, Sponsored by ProQuest, Is a Light for Human Rights and Core Values." Retrieved January 02, 2008, from http://www.libraryjournal.com/article/CA6497260.html.

31. Toni Samek, *Librarianship and Human Rights: A Twenty-First Century Guide*. Oxford: Chandos, 2007, p. 7.

32. Adama Samassékou, "The Promise of Information and Communication Societies," in Rikke Frank (ed.), *Human Rights in the Global Information Society*. Cambridge: MIT Press, 2006, p. vii.

33. Rikke Frank Jorgenesen (ed.), *Human Rights in the Global Information Society*. Cambridge: MIT Press, 2006.

34. Samek, *Librarianship and Human Rights*, p. 181.

Chapter 4

1. Donald O. Case, *Looking for Information: A Survey of Research on Information Seeking, Needs, and Behavior*, 2nd ed. New York: Academic Press/Elsevier, 2006.

2. Karen E. Fisher, Sandra Erdelez, and Lynne E. F. McKechnie (eds.), *Theories of Information Behavior*. Medford, NJ: Information Today, 2005.

3. Thomas Mann (ed.), "The Principle of Least Effort," in *Library Research Models: A Guide to Classification, Cataloging and Computers*. New York: Oxford University Press, 1993, pp. 91–101.

4. George Kingsley Zipf, *Human Behavior and the Principle of Least Effort: An Introduction to Human Ecology*. Cambridge, MA: Addison-Wesley, 1949.

5. Brenda Dervin, "Strategies for Dealing with Human Information Needs: Information or Communication?" *Journal of Broadcasting* 20(3), 324–351.

6. Tom D. Wilson, "Human Information Behavior," *Informing Science* 3(2), 49–56.

7. Mary K. Chelton and Colleen Cool (eds.), *Youth Information-seeking Behavior: Theories, Models and Issues*. Lanham, MD: Scarecrow Press, 2004.

Chapter 6

1. Warren Bennis, *On Becoming a Leader*. Reading, MA: Addison-Wesley, 1989.

2. Bernard M. Bass, *Bass and Stodgill's Handbook of Leadership*, 3rd ed. New York: The Free Press, 1990.

3. Marcus Buckingham and Daniel O. Clifton, *Now, Discover Your Strengths*. New York: The Free Press, 2001.

4. Ibid.

5. Peter Drucker, "What Executives Should Remember," *Harvard Business Review* 84(2), 144–152.

6. A.J.P. Taylor, Speech given at Stalinist Cultural Congress, Wroclaw, Poland, 1948.

7. Robert S. Kaplan, "What to Ask the Person in the Mirror," *Harvard Business Review* 85(1), 86–95.

8. M.G.E. Evans, "The Effects of Supervisory Behavior on the Path-Goal Relationship," *Organizational Behavior and Human Performance* 5(3), 277–298.

9. R.J. House, "A Path-Goal Theory of Leader Effectiveness," *Administrative Science Quarterly* 16(3), 321–340.

10. Peter G. Northouse, *Leadership Theory and Practice*. Thousand Oaks, CA: Sage, 2004.

11. Cary Cherniss and Daniel Goleman, *The Emotionally Intelligent Workplace*. San Francisco: Jossey-Bass, 2001.

12. Ibid.

13. Brooke E. Sheldon, *Leaders in Libraries: Styles and Strategies for Success*. Chicago: ALA, 1991.

14. John W. Gardner, *On Leadership*. New York: The Free Press, 1993.

15. Bennis, *On Becoming a Leader*.

16. Interview with John Berry by the author, New York, June 1990.

17. Sheldon, *Leaders in Libraries*.

Chapter 7

A portion of this chapter is a revision of material contained in Chapter 1 of Robert D. Stueart and Barbara B. Moran's *Library and Information Center Management*, 7th ed., Westport, CT: Libraries Unlimited, 2007.

1. Mary Follett, *Dynamic Administration*. London: Pitman. 1941.

2. Henry Mintzberg, *The Nature of Managerial Work*. New York: Harper-Collins, 1973.

3. Robert Katz, "Skills of an Effective Administrator," *Harvard Business Review* 52(5) (September–October 1974), 90–102.

4. Edgar H. Schein, *Career Anchors*, 3rd ed. San Francisco: Pfeiffer, 2006.

Chapter 8

1. The author expresses special thanks to Professor Emeritus of Marketing, College of Business, Florida State University, Persis E. Rockwood, who taught me everything I know about marketing and its applications to libraries.

2. Philip Kotler, *Strategic Marketing for Nonprofit Organizations*. New York: Prentice, 1980, p. 6.

3. Ibid.

Chapter 10

The author wishes to thank Daniel N. Joudrey, Simmons College, for reading the manuscript and for making very helpful suggestions. Portions of this chapter are based on Chapters 1 and 5 of Arlene G. Taylor, *The Organization of Information*, 2nd ed., Westport, CT: Libraries Unlimited, 2004.

1. Ronald Hagler, *The Bibliographic Record and Information Technology*, 3rd ed. Chicago: ALA, 1997, p. 13.

2. Christine L. Borgman, *From Gutenberg to the Global Information Infrastructure: Access to Information in the Networked World*. Cambridge, MA: MIT Press, 2000, p. 48.

3. *Digital Library Technology Trends*. Santa Clara, CA: Sun Microsystems, 2002, p. 3. Retrieved January 02, 2008, from http://www.sun.com/products-n-solutions/edu/whitepapers/pdf/digital_library_trends.pdf.

4. Andrew Dillon, "Information Architecture in JASIST: Just Where Did We Come From?" *Journal of the American Society for Information Science and Technology* 53(10) (August 2002), 821.

Chapter 11

1. Herbert A. Simon, *The Sciences of the Artificial*, 3rd ed. Cambridge: MIT Press, 1996.

2. Suzanne Briet, *Qu'est-ce que la Documentation?* Paris: EDIT (Editions Documentaires Industrielles et Techniques), 1953. For a discussion in English, see Michael K. Buckland, "What is a Document?" *Journal of the American Society for Information Science* 48 (1997), 804–809.

3. Horst W. J. Rittel and Melvin M. Webber, "Dilemmas in a General Theory of Planning," *Policy Sciences* 4, 155–169.

4. Ibid., p. 159.

5. Geoffrey Bowker and Susan Leigh Star, *Sorting Things Out: Classification and Its Consequences*. Cambridge: MIT Press, 1999.

6. National Information Standards Organization, *Understanding Metadata*. Bethesda, MD: NISO Press, 2004.

7. www.steve.museum. The Art Museum Social Tagging Project.

8. http://clusty.com/. The Clustering Search Engine.

9. Bill Maron, quote.

10. Jakob Nielsen, useit.com: Jakob Nielsen's Web site, 2007. Retrieved March 19, 2006, from http://www.useit.com/.

11. Peter Morville, *Ambient Findability: What We Find Changes Who We Become*. Sebastopol, CA: O'Reilly Media, 2005.

12. Patrick Wilson, "The Future of Research in our Field," in Johan Olaisen, Erland Much-Petersen, and Patrick Wilson (eds.), *Information Science: From the Development of the Discipline to Social Interaction*. Oslo: Scandinavian University Press, 1996, pp. 319–323.

Chapter 12

1. *ALA Glossary of Library and Information Science*. Chicago, ALA, 1983.

2. Ibid.

3. *Harrod's Librarians' Glossary and Reference Book: A Directory of over 10,200 Terms, Organizations, Projects and Acronyms in the Areas of Information Management, Library Science, Publishing and Archive Management*. London: Ashgate, 2005.

4. Samuel Swett Green, "Personal Relations between Librarians and Readers," *Library Journal* 1 (1876), 74–81.

5. Henry Ephron (Producer), Phoebe and Henry Ephron (Writers), and Henry Ephron (Director), *Desk Set* [Motion Picture], Twentieth Century-Fox, 1957.

6. Morton DaCosta (Producer/Director), Meredith Willson (Writer), *Music Man* [Motion Picture], Warner Brothers, 1962.

7. John Greenfieldt, *Fiction Catalog*. New York: H.W. Wilson Company, 2007.

8. *The NoveList*. EBSCO Database (www.ebsco.com)

9. American Library Association, Reference and User Services Association, *Guidelines for Behavioral Performance of Reference and Information Service Providers*. Retrieved January 02, 2008, from http://www.ala.org/ala/rusa/rusaprotools/referenceguide/guidelinesbehavioral.cfm.

10. Peter Hernon and Charles R. McClure, "Unobtrusive Reference Testing: The 55 Percent Rule," *Library Journal* 111, 37–41.

11. Jerry D. Campbell, "Shaking the Conceptual Foundations of Reference: A Perspective," *Reference Services Review* 20(29), 35.

12. Joan Durrance, "Factors That Influence Reference Success: What Makes Questioners Willing to Return?" *The Reference Librarian* 23(49/50), 243–265.

Chapter 13

1. Tim O'Reilly, The Architecture of Participation, O'Reilly Web site. Retrieved January 02, 2008, from http://www.oreillynet.com/pub/a/oreilly/tim/articles/architecture_of_participation.html.

2. Steven Johnson, *Everything Bad is Good for You: How Today's Popular Culture Is Actually Making Us Smarter*. New York: Riverhead Books, 2006.

3. Retrieved January 02, 2008, from http://www.npr.org/roughcuts/.

4. Retrieved January 02, 2008, from http://www.wikinomics.com.

5. Michael Stephens, Tame the Web: Libraries and Technologies, 2006. Retrieved January 02, 2008, from http://tametheweb.com/2006/11/ten_ways_to_use_flickr_in_your.html.

6. Retrieved January 02, 2008, from http://www.connotea.org.

7. Benjamin Woolley, *Virtual Worlds*. London: Penguin, 1993, p. 235.

8. Lee Rainie, Internet Librarians Own the Future, November 15, 2004. Retrieved January 02, 2008, from http://www.infotoday.com/il2004/presentations/Rainie.pdf.

Chapter 14

1. Louise Rosenblatt, *Literature as Exploration*, 5th ed. New York: Modern Language Association of America, 1995.

2. Herbert J. Gans, *Popular Culture and High Culture: An Analysis and Evaluation of Taste*. New York: Basic Books, 1974.

3. Pierre Bourdieu, *Distinction: A Social Critique of the Judgement of Taste*. Cambridge, MA: Harvard, 1984.

4. Catherine S. Ross, Lynne E. F. McKechnie, and Paulette M. Rothbauer, *Reading Matters: What the Research Reveals about Reading, Libraries, and Community.* Westport, CT: Greenwood, 2006.

5. Elizabeth Long, *Book Clubs: Women and the Uses of Reading in Everyday Life.* Chicago: University of Chicago Press, 2003.

6. NoveList. Retrieved January 02, 2008, from http://www.epnet.com/thisTopic.php?marketID=6=16.

7. Ursula K Le Guin, "Genre: A Word only a Frenchman Could Love," *Public Libraries* 44(1) (January–February 2005), 21–23.

8. Joyce G. Saricks, *Reader's Advisory Service in the Public Library*, 3rd ed. Chicago: ALA, 2005.

9. *NextReads*, an offshoot service of NoveList's e-mail and indexing capability, http://www.nextreads.com/.

10. *BookLetters*, http://www.bookletters.com/.

11. Marion Nestle, *What to Eat.* New York: North Point Press, 2006.

12. Paco Underhill, *Why We Buy: The Science of Shopping.* New York: Simon & Schuster, 1999.

13. DorothyL. www.dorothyl.com/.

14. Romance Readers Anonymous RRA-L. www.toad.net/~dolma/.

15. Fiction_L. www.webrary.org/rs/Flmenu.html.

16. Graphic Novels in Libraries GNLIB-L. www.angelfire.com/comics/gnlib/.

Chapter 15

1. Ronald R. Powell, "Recent Trends in Research: A Methodological Essay," *Library & Information Science Research* 21, 91–119.

2. Ronald R. Powell and Lynn S. Connaway, *Basic Research Methods for Librarians*, 4th ed. Westport, CT: Libraries Unlimited, 2004, p. 278.

3. Thomas W. Shaughnessy, "Library Research in the 70's: Problems and Prospects," *California Librarian* 37, 51.

4. Ronald R. Powell, Lynda M. Baker, and Joseph J. Mika, "Library and Information Science Practitioners and Research," *Library & Information Science Research* 24, 49–72.

5. Ibid.

Chapter 16

Some of the materials in this chapter have been drawn from the author's previous teaching, writing, and research on this topic.

Chapter 17

The section on "Libraries: Global Reach—Local Touch" draws from ideas that were developed during the author's ALA presidency and that have been discussed in a variety of venues.

Chapter 18

This section is based in part on prior writings of the author, for example, "Librarianship: Intersecting Perspectives from the Academy and the Field," in Norman Horrocks (ed.), *Perspectives, Insights & Priorities: 17 Leaders Speak Freely of Librarianship*. Lanham, MD: Scarecrow Press, 2005, pp. 63–71.

1. See for example Brooke E. Sheldon, *Leaders in Libraries: Styles and Strategies for Success*. Chicago: ALA, 1991; Jim Collins, *Good to Great*. New York: HarperCollins, 2001; and *Good to Great and the Social Sectors*. Boulder, CO: Author, 2005.

2. Andrew Keen, *The Cult of the Amateur: How Today's Internet Is Killing Our Culture*. New York: Doubleday, 2007.

3. The *LISNews* 10 Blogs to Read in 2008. Retrieved January 24, 2008, from http://www.lisnews.org/node/28830.

Index

281

About the Editors and Contributors

DONALD O. CASE is a former Director and now Professor of the School of Library and Information Science, University of Kentucky. Previously, Dr. Case taught at UCLA, and was a Research Advisor at the Center for Advanced Study, Stanford University. Currently, he teaches and conducts research on various aspects of information seeking, information policy, and social informatics. In 2008 Dr. Case will become President of the American Association for Information Science and Technology.

MARY K. CHELTON is Professor, Queen's College Graduate School of Library and Information Studies. She characterizes herself as "an advocate for various neglected and stigmatized categories of library services and users such as readers advisory services and YA services, teenagers, adoption searchers, genre fiction readers in general and romance readers in particular . . . " She has published over sixty articles in library literature, and has 20+ years experience as a public librarian. She is a recipient of ALA's Grolier Award for outstanding work with young people and the Romance Writers of America's first "Librarian of the Year."

G. EDWARD EVANS retired from his position as University Librarian at Loyola Marymount University (LMU) but as he found retirement too boring, he is now Librarian of the Harold S. Colton Memorial Library and Archives at the Museum of Northern Arizona. His career has included both practice and teaching, often at the same time. During his tenure at LMU he taught part-time at UCLA's Graduate School of Education and Information Studies. As a Fulbright scholar, he taught management and collection development courses in library schools in Norway, Denmark, Sweden, Finland, and Iceland. He has published several textbooks on those subjects.

293

BARBARA J. FORD is the Director of the Mortenson Center for International Library Programs and Mortenson Distinguished Professor at the Library of the University of Illinois at Urbana-Champaign. She is a past President of the American Library Association and of the Association of College and Research Libraries. She previously worked as Assistant Commissioner at the Chicago Public Library, Director of the Virginia Commonwealth University Libraries, and at the libraries at Trinity University in San Antonio and the University of Illinois at Chicago. She is a member of the governing board of the International Federation of Library Associations and Institutions. She was a Peace Corps volunteer in Panama and Nicaragua.

MICHAEL GORMAN is University Librarian Emeritus, Henry Madden Library, California State University-Fresno and past President of the American Library Association. Other positions held include Head of Technical Services, and Acting Librarian, University of Illinois, Urbana-Champaign. He was Head of the Office of Bibliographic Standards, at the British Library. He is the first editor of the *Anglo-American Cataloging Rules*, 2nd ed., 1977 and on the 1988 revision, and author of *Our Enduring Values* (2000), *Our Own Selves; More Meditations for Librarians* (2005), and many other publications. He is the recipient of the Margaret Mann Citation, the Melvil Dewey Medal, and the Highsmith Award.

KEN HAYCOCK is Professor and Director of the School of Library and Information Science at San Jose State University. He was previously Professor and Director of the School of Library, Archival and Information Studies at the University of British Columbia in Vancouver. The past president of several national and international associations and the recipient of numerous awards for research, teaching and service, Dr. Haycock holds graduate degrees in Education and in Business Administration as well as Library and Information Science.

LAURA KANE is the Assistant Director for Information Services at the School of Medicine Library of the University of South Carolina. She earned her Master's Degree in Library and Information Science from the University of South Carolina. She has a bachelor's degree in Spanish, and is fluent in both Spanish and Italian. She is the author of *Straight from the Stacks; A Firsthand Guide to Careers in Library and Information Science*.

CHRISTIE KOONTZ is the director of GeoLib and member of the faculty, College of Information, Florida State University in Tallahassee. Koontz teaches marketing and management and conducts marketing workshop for colleagues around the globe. She writes a column for *Marketing Library Services*, a publication of Information Today.

LINDA MAIN is Professor and Associate Director, School of Library and Information Science, San Jose State University. She is the author of *Building Websites for a Multinational Audience* and many articles. Her research interests are in designing information products for a global audience, and Web programming languages delivered online. She has been involved in consultancy projects for such agencies as the British Library, the Bibliotheque Nationale,

The State Technical Library, Prague and the Benito Juarez Autonomous University (Oaxaca).

CHARLES R. McCLURE is the Frances Eppes Professor of Information Studies and Director of the Information Use Management and Policy Institute (http://www.ii.fsu.edu/) at Florida State University, College of Information. He has written extensively on topics related to library planning and evaluation, information policy, and digital information services. He has received numerous awards for his research and writings. Currently he is completing projects related to national surveys of public libraries and the Internet funded by the American Library Association and Web-based instructional modules for librarians to better select and use various evaluation methods and approaches, funded by the U.S. Institute of Museum and Library Services.

KATHLEEN DE LA PEÑA McCOOK is Distinguished University Professor at the University of South Florida. She was President of the Association for Library and Information Science Education in 1988 and was the 2002 Latino Librarian of the Year (Trejo Award). She received the Beta Phi Mu Award for distinguished service to education for librarianship in 2003 and is author of *Introduction to Public Librarianship* (2004); *A Place at the Table:Participating in Community Building* (2000); and *Ethnic Diversity in Library and Information Science* (2000). She currently serves on the Coordinating Committee of the Progressive Librarians Guild.

BARBARA B. MORAN is former Dean and now Professor at the University of North Carolina at Chapel Hill, School of Information and Library Science. She teaches primarily in the management area with research interests in new organizational structures in academic libraries and human resources management. Her many articles and books include coauthorship of several editions of *Library and Information Center Management*, a standard text in library schools.

KATHARINE PHENIX is the Adult Services Librarian, Rangeview Library District, Colorado. She has been Academic Collections Manager at Netlibrary in Boulder and Head of Circulation at Westminister Public Library where she put the first bookmobile online in 1986. She was a columnist for *Wilson Library Bulletin*, chair of the ALA Council Standing Committee on the Status of Women in Librarianship, and visiting instructor at LSU. She is the author of *On Account of Sex; An Annotated Bibliography on the Status of men in Librarianship* and *The Subject Guide to Women of the World*.

RON POWELL is Professor in the Library and Information Science Program, Wayne State University, Detroit, Michigan. His teaching and research interests include research methods, academic libraries, education for librarianship, and the measurement and evaluation of library and information resources and services. Among his publications are *Qualitative Research in Information Management* (coedited with Jack Glazier), *Basic Research Methods for Librarians* (with Lynn Connaway), and *The Next Library Leadership* (with Peter Hernon and Arthur Young).

RICHARD E. RUBIN is Director and Professor at the School of Library and Information Science, Kent State University. He is the current chair of the ALA Committee on Accreditation. His research interests include human resources management, library administration, intellectual freedom and censorship, research methods. His many publications include *Foundations of Library and Information Science* (in several editions), *Human Resource Management in Libraries,* and *Critical Issues in Library Personnel Management.*

BROOKE E. SHELDON is Professor and Dean Emerita at Texas Woman's University, the University of Arizona, and the University of Texas at Austin. She is a past president of the American Library Association (ALA) and recipient of the outstanding contributions to education award from the Association for Library and Information Science Education (ALISE).

ARLENE G. TAYLOR is Professor Emerita, School of Information Sciences, University of Pittsburgh. She has held positions in The Library of Congress, Christopher Newport College, and Iowa State University. She is the author of several books and many articles including *The Organization of Information, Introduction to Cataloging and Classification,* and *Understanding FRBR: What it is and how it will affect our retrieval tools.* The recipient of the 1996 Margaret Mann citation, Dr. Taylor consults extensively for such organizations as the Bodleian Library, Oxford University, and libraries in Brazil and Italy.

DAVID A. TYCKOSON is Associate Dean of the Henry Madden Library, California State University, Fresno. He came to Fresno as Head of Reference in 1997 and previously held positions at SUNY-Albany, Iowa State University, and Miami (Ohio) University. He has also served as an adjunct professor at the University of Illinois and SUNY-Albany. Dave has been involved with reference service for 25 years and has written extensively on the subject. He has also developed and taught online continuing education courses on the Reference Interview and was elected the 2007–2008 President of the Reference and User Services Association (RUSA).

JUDITH WEEDMAN is Professor, School of Library and Information Science, San Jose State University. Within the field of Information Science, her specialty is knowledge production. Her research includes the growth of knowledge in the sciences, humanities and professions, invisible colleges, interdisciplinary cooperation in research projects, and the design of vocabularies for information retrieval. She has published in the journals of several disciplines including communication and information science.

vitiated - spoil, impare the quality of